MyMaths
for Key Stage 3

D1363007

2B

powered by MyMaths.co.uk

OXFORD
UNIVERSITY PRESS

OXFORD
UNIVERSITY PRESS

Great Clarendon Street, Oxford, OX2 6DP, United Kingdom

Oxford University Press is a department of the University of Oxford. It furthers the University's objective of excellence in research, scholarship, and education by publishing worldwide. Oxford is a registered trade mark of Oxford University Press in the UK and in certain other countries

© Oxford University Press 2014

British Library Cataloguing in Publication Data
Data available

978-0-19-830457-9

10 9 8 7 6 5 4 3 2 1

Paper used in the production of this book is a natural, recyclable product made from wood grown in sustainable forests. The manufacturing process conforms to the environmental regulations of the country of origin.

Printed in Great Britain

Acknowledgements

Although we have made every effort to trace and contact copyright holders before publication this has not been possible in all cases. If notified, the publisher will rectify any errors or omissions at the earliest opportunity.

p2–1: John Lamb/Digital Vision/Getty Images; **p4:** Natursports/Dreamstime; **p5:** Louis16/iStockphoto; **p10:** OUP; **p17:** mikkelwilliam/iStockphoto; Feng Yu; **p24–25:** Oliviero Olivieri/Robert Harding World Imagery/ Corbis; **p26:** DenisNata/Shutterstock; OUP; 3dfoto/ iStockphoto; Dreamgirl007/Dreamstime; scanrail/iStockphoto; OUP; Paul Fell/Shutterstock; **p26:** Martinmark/Dreamstime; **p27:** Steve Cole/iStockphoto; **p30:** M R/Shutterstock.com; **p33:** OUP; **p35:** Pxhidalgo/Dreamstime; **p40–41:** David A Hardy/Science Photo Library; **p49:** Elina Manninen/ Shutterstock; **p50:** mgkaya/iStockphoto; **p51:** andreiorlov/ iStockphoto; **p60–61:** Martin Siepmann/Glow Images; **p62:** Fergy/Dreamstime; **p65:** Odyssei/Dreamstime; **p66:** Andreykuzmin/Dreamstime; **p69:** Konstantinpetkov/ Dreamstime; **p70:** Emicristea/Dreamstime; **p80–81:** Dennis Hallinan/Alamy; **p85:** Rabbit75/Dreamstime; **p86:** Jlvdream/ Dreamstime; **p90:** Philip Lange/Shutterstock; **p93:** doug4537/ iStockphoto; **p98–99:** Warren Faidley/Corbis/Glow Images; **p101:** Jayne Duncan/Shutterstock; **p109:** Deniskelly/ Dreamstime; **p113:** Kingjon/dreamstime; **p116–117:** sciencephotos/Alamy; **p118:** Phillipgray/Dreamstime; **p119:** Ros Drinkwater/Alamy; **p120:** TT/iStockphoto; **p121:** John Cairns/iStockphoto; **p127:** UmbertoPantalone/ iStockphoto; Maxx-Studio/Shutterstock; razorpix/Alamy; **p128:** Vorminbeeld/Dreamstime; **p129:** Vorminbeeld/ Dreamstime; **p133:** Nivi/Dreamstime; kiboka/Shutterstock; hermi/iStockphoto; shnycel/iStockphoto; OUP; **p134–135:** The Art Archive/Alamy; **p142:** blackred/iStockphoto; **p145:** UmbertoPantalone/iStockphoto; kavram/Shutterstock; **p146:** Phillipgray/Dreamstime; **p147:** sbayram/iStockphoto; hp_photo/iStockphoto; **p154:** UmbertoPantalone/ iStockphoto; KentWeakley/iStockphoto; **p158–159:** Godong/ Universal Images Group/Getty Images; **p164:** Lotophagi/ Dreamstime; **p176–177:** Grant Glendinning/Shutterstock; **p184:** Sergej Razvodovskij/Shutterstock; Winston Link/ Shutterstock; **p190–191:** compuinfoto/Fotolia; **p192:** antb/ Shutterstock; **p203:** Mikelane45/Dreamstime; **p210–211:** Eric Gevaert/Shutterstock;**p220:** Steven Davies/Dreamstime; **p221:** Dvu/Dreamstime; bergamont/Shutterstock; **p222:** mevans/iStockphoto; **p223:** Tommason/Dreamstime; **p234–235:** Denys Rudyi/Fotolia; **p241:** Yeko Photo Studio/ Shutterstock; **p242:** tattywelshie/iStockphoto; **p248–249:** Jonathan Feinstein/Shutterstock; **p250:** Wisconsinart/ Dreamstime; **p251:** SeanPavonePhoto/Shutterstock.com; **p256:** Davidmartyn/Dreamstime; Roel Smart/iStockphoto; Eutoch/Dreamstime; **p266–267:** Photodisc/OUP; **p272:** Sjonja/iStockphoto; **p273:** UmbertoPantalone/iStockphoto; **p276:** Davidwatmough/Dreamstime; **p279:** Raoul Dixon/ Corbis; **p284–285:** Uppercut RF/Glow Images; **p286:** Shime/ Dreamstime; **p287:** Ruslan Semichev/Shutterstock; **p288:** Claudiodivizia/Dreamstime; **p291:** Davebris33/Dreamstime; **p295:** eldirector77/Shutterstock.

Artwork by: Phil Hackett, Erwin Haya, Paul Hostetler, Dusan Pavlic, Giulia Rivolta, Katri Valkamo & QBS.

Contents

Number

Geometry

Algebra

Number

MyMaths.co.uk

MyMaths for Key Stage 3 is an exciting new series designed for schools following the new National Curriculum for mathematics. This book has been written to help you to grow your mathematical knowledge and skills during Key Stage 3.

Each topic starts with an Introduction that shows why it is relevant to real life and includes a short *Check in* exercise to see if you are ready to start the topic.

Inside each chapter, you will find lots of worked examples and questions for you to try along with interesting facts. There's basic practice to build your confidence, as well as problem solving. You might also notice the **4-digit codes** at the bottom of the page, which you can type into the search bar on the *MyMaths* site to take you straight to the relevant *MyMaths* lesson for more help in understanding and extra practice.

At the end of each chapter you will find *My Summary*, which tests what you've learned and suggests what you could try next to improve your skills even further. The *What next?* box details further resources available in the supporting online products.

Maths is a vitally important subject, not just for you while you are at school but also for when you grow up. We hope that this book will lead to a greater enjoyment of the subject and that it will help you to realise how useful maths is to your everyday life.

1 Whole numbers and decimals

Introduction

When people pay using a credit card on the internet they need to know that their financial details are safe. The financial transaction is turned into a secret code, it is encrypted, using the product of two very large prime numbers. The person receiving the message has to know both of these prime numbers so that they can decrypt the message and read it.

The problems involved in writing very large numbers as the product of two prime numbers makes it very difficult for someone intercepting the message to crack the code.

What's the point?

Prime numbers allow people to be confident that their bank accounts will not be hacked into.

Objectives

By the end of this chapter, you will have learned how to ...

 Order and compare decimals.

● Add, subtract, multiply and divide integers.

● Recognise and use multiples and factors.

● Use divisibility tests.

● Find the prime factor decomposition of a number.

● Find the lowest common multiple and highest common factor of two numbers.

● Recognise and use cube and square numbers, cube and square roots.

Check in

1 Put these numbers in order from smallest to largest.

   a   0.5, 0.512, 0.55, 0.47, 0.52   **b**   3, -4, 5, -6, 9, -10

2 Calculate   **a** $4 - 9$ **b** $-8 + 5$ **c** $-6 - 3$

3 Calculate   **a** 7×5 **b** $12 \div 4$ **c** 9×6 **d** $72 \div 8$

4 **a**   Write down the first three *multiples* of 7.

   b   List all the *factors* of 12.

   c   Write down first 5 *prime* numbers.

5 Use your calculator to find   **a** $3.5 \times 3.5 \times 3.5$ **b** 6^3 **c** $(-4)^4$

Starter problem

A million dollar reward awaits the person who can find a rule (function) for generating all the prime numbers.

Here are some of the formulae that have been tried

    $6n + 1$

    $6n - 1$

    $n^2 - n + 41$

    $2^n - 1$

Test out these formulae and see if they really work.

1a Integers and decimals

Being able to order decimal numbers is important. In athletics, runners are given times when they finish a race and it is important to know the order in which they finished.

- To compare the size of **positive** and **negative decimals**, use a number line.

Which is smaller, -0.3 m or -0.29 m?

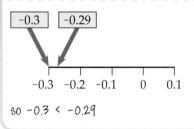

so $-0.3 < -0.29$

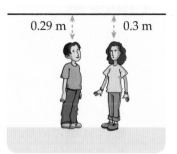

0.29 m   0.3 m

To put decimals in **order**, for example 0.3   -0.1   -0.15   -0.2, sketch their positions on a number line.

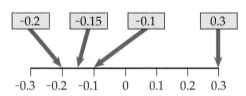

Remember:
< means less than
and
> means greater than.

- Adding a negative **integer** is the same as subtracting a positive integer.

$42 + -51 = 42 - 51$
$\qquad\quad = -9$

Adding -51 is the same as subtracting 51.

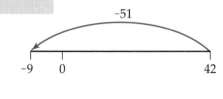

-51

-9   0   42

- Subtracting a negative integer is the same as adding a positive integer.

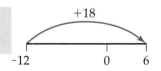

+18

-12   0   6

$-12 - -18 = -12 + 18$
$\qquad\qquad = 6$

Subtracting -18 is the same as adding 18.

Exercise 1a

1. Place < or > between these pairs of numbers to show which number is the larger.
   a. -8 and 6
   b. -7 and -5
   c. -5 and -4.5
   d. -3.2 and -3
   e. -1.5 and -1.49
   f. -2.7 and -2.8
   g. -0.37 and -0.39
   h. -0.0235 and -0.024

2. Put these numbers in order from smallest to largest.
   a. -8   -6   3   5   -12
   b. 0.5   1.4   -3.5   -1.5   -8
   c. 3.2   -1.4   -2.9   4.7   -1.6
   d. -2.5   1.35   -2.9   -2.3   -3

3. Calculate
   a. 3 + 12
   b. 15 − 7
   c. 14 − 18
   d. 12 − 21
   e. 6 − 26
   f. -4 + 3
   g. -5 + 9
   h. -12 + 8
   i. -14 + 20
   j. -15 + 27

4. Calculate
   a. 7 + -7
   b. 4 + -4
   c. 8 + -5
   d. -6 + -5
   e. -9 + -5
   f. 7 − -4
   g. 6 − -8
   h. 3 + -3
   i. -7 − -10
   j. -11 − -15
   k. -13 − -8
   l. -16 + -9
   m. -8 − -13
   n. -8 + -13

Problem solving

5. Solve each of these problems.
   a. Aftab owes £13 to his dad and £8.50 to his mum. How much money does he owe altogether?
   b. Bella and Carson are on holiday. Bella is swimming 3.5m under water. Carson is standing on the diving board directly above Bella. He is 2.5m above the water. How far below Carson is Bella?

6. Complete these number pyramids.
   a. Add the right-hand number and the left-hand number to find the number directly above it.

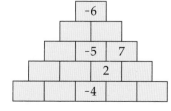

   | 11 |
   | -4 | -2 | -7 | 3 | 8 |

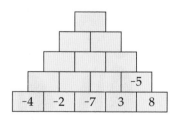

   | -5 |
   | -4 | -2 | -7 | 3 | 8 |

   b. Subtract the right-hand number from the left-hand number to find the number directly above it.

   | -6 |
   | -5 | 7 |
   | 2 |
   | -4 |

   c. Each number is the sum of the two numbers directly below it.

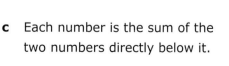

A simple rule to remember when multiplying or dividing a pair of **integers** is
- ▶ if the signs are different the answer will be **negative**
- ▶ if the signs are the same the answer will be **positive**.

Multiply or divide	Positive Integer	Negative Integer
Positive Integer	+Answer	−Answer
Negative Integer	−Answer	+Answer

Example

Calculate

a -2 × 3   **b** -2 × -3

a -2 × 3

Multiply the numbers	2 × 3 = 6
Check the sign	negative × positive = negative
Write the answer	-2 × 3 = -6

A number line shows this is correct.

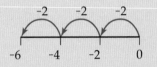

You can think of -2 × 3 as three lots of -2.

b -2 × -3

Multiply the numbers	2 × 3 = 6
Check the sign	negative × negative = positive
Write the answer	-2 × -3 = 6

Example

Calculate

a -6 ÷ -2   **b** -6 ÷ 3   **c** 6 ÷ -2

a -6 ÷ -2

Divide the numbers	6 ÷ 2 = 3
Check the sign	negative ÷ negative = positive
Write the answer	-6 ÷ -2 = 3

b -6 ÷ 3

Divide the numbers	6 ÷ 3 = 2
Check the sign	negative ÷ positive = negative
Write the answer	-6 ÷ 3 = -2

c 6 ÷ -2

Divide the numbers	6 ÷ 2 = 3
Check the sign	positive ÷ negative = negative
Write the answer	6 ÷ -2 = -3

You know from the first example that -2 × 3 = -6 so it follows that -6 ÷ -2 = 3.

This is the **inverse** relationship.

Exercise 1b

1 Ffion is trying to write out the negative times tables. Copy and complete these.

a $7 \times 3 = 21$ **b** $-5 \times 3 = -15$

  $7 \times 2 = 14$ $-5 \times 2 = \square$

  $7 \times 1 = \square$ $-5 \times 1 = \square$

  $7 \times 0 = \square$ $-5 \times 0 = \square$

  $7 \times -1 = \square$ $-5 \times -1 = \square$

  $7 \times -2 = \square$ $-5 \times -2 = \square$

  $7 \times -3 = \square$ $-5 \times -3 = \square$

  $7 \times -4 = \square$ $-5 \times -4 = \square$

2 a Copy and complete the multiplication grid below.

×	-4	-3	-2	-1	0	1	2	3	4
4					0				
3					0				
2					0				
1					0				
0	0	0	0	0	0	0	0	0	0
-1					0				
-2					0				
-3					0				
-4					0				

b Use the multiplication grid to answer these questions.

  i What is two lots of -3?

  ii What is -3×-2

2 b iii How many -4s are there in -12?

  iv What number do you multiply by -4 to make 12?

  v The answer is -12. Give two possible questions.

  vi The answer is 8. Give four possible questions.

3 Calculate

a 3×-4 **b** -2×5

c -4×-3 **d** -5×-7

e -10×4 **f** -3×-8

g 5×-5 **h** -9×-9

i -11×11 **j** -15×-10

k $-20 \div -5$ **l** $-30 \div 10$

m $-26 \div -2$ **n** $-33 \div -3$

o $60 \div -20$ **p** -11×4

q -5×12 **r** -15×-6

s $-42 \div -7$ **t** $-80 \div 5$

4 Copy and complete these calculations.

a $5 \times \square = -20$ **b** $-30 \div \square = -6$

c $-4 \times \square = 28$ **d** $-40 \div \square = 8$

e $\square \times -7 = -49$ **f** $-6 \times \square = -54$

g $\square \div -4 = 9$ **h** $\square \div -9 = -4$

i $\square \div -10 = 10$ **j** $72 \div \square = -9$

k $-3 \times \square = 51$ **l** $\square \times -37 = -111$

Problem solving

5 Eric's classwork has been marked by his teacher. Explain why each of the questions that have been marked with a cross is wrong, and write the correct answer.

a $2 \times -3 = 6$ ✗   **b** $10 \div -2 = 8$ ✗   **c** $-40 \div -8 = -5$ ✗

d $-4 \times 2 = -8$ ✓   **e** $7 \times -4 = -3$ ✗   **f** $-12 \div 3 = 4$ ✗

6 Copy and complete these multiplication grids.

a

×	4		-6	
		-10	12	
3		15		
	-28			-56
				-72

b

×				
		1		4
	-12		18	
	4			-8
5			-15	

1c Multiples and factors

● The **multiples** of a number are those numbers that divide by it exactly, leaving no **remainder**.

The first three multiples of 25 are 25, 50 and 75.

1 × 25 = 25	2 × 25 = 50	3 × 25 = 75

Finding multiples is the same as writing out the times table.

Any whole number can be written as the **product** of **factors**. Most numbers have more than two factors.

● The factors of a number are numbers that divide into it exactly.

The factors of 36 are 1, 2, 3, 4, 6, 9, 12, 18 and 36

1 × 36 = 36	2 × 18 = 36	3 × 12 = 36
4 × 9 = 36	6 × 6 = 36	

You can find the factors by listing all the factor pairs.

You can use simple **divisibility tests** to help you find all the factors of a number.

Divisibility tests	
÷2	number ends in 0, 2, 4, 6 or 8
÷3	sum of digits divisible by 3
÷4	half the number divisible by 2
÷5	number ends in 0 or 5
÷6	number divisible by both 2 and 3

÷7	no easy check
÷8	half the number divisible by 4
÷9	sum of digits divisible by 9
÷10	number ends in 0
÷11	alternate digits add to same sum
÷12	number divisible by both 3 and 4

Example

Is 9 a factor of 189?

Yes, because 1 + 8 + 9 = 18, and 18 is a multiple of 9.

Note 1 + 8 = 9 so 18 is a multiple of 9.

Check 189 ÷ 9 = 21

$$\begin{array}{r} 21 \\ 9{\overline{\smash{\big)}\,189}} \\ \underline{-180} \\ 9 \\ \underline{-9} \\ 0 \end{array}$$

9 × 20 = 180

9 × 1 = 9

9 × 21 = 189

Exercise 1c

1 Write the first three multiples of

    a 5   **b** 14   **c** 21   **d** 35

    e 48   **f** 115   **g** 45   **h** 90

2 Write all the factors of

    a 20   **b** 28   **c** 45   **d** 52

    e 66   **f** 84   **g** 16   **h** 32

3 **a** Write a multiple of 30 between 100 and 140.

    b Write a multiple of 45 between 100 and 140.

    c How many multiples of 10 are there between 100 and 200?

    d How many multiples of 58 are there between 1000 and 1040?

    e How many multiples of 10 are there between 100 and 1000?

4 Use the divisibility tests to answer each of these questions. In each case explain your answer.

    a Is 2 a factor of 74?

    b Is 3 a factor of 72?

    c Is 4 a factor of 102?

    d Is 5 a factor of 135?

    e Is 6 a factor of 156?

    f Is 8 a factor of 200?

    g Is 9 a factor of 178?

    h Is 10 a factor of 520?

    i Is 12 a factor of 168?

    j Is 11 a factor of 264?

5 Find the missing digit * in each of these numbers.

    a 834 *25 is divisible by 9

    b 3*4 582 is divisible by 11

Problem solving

6 For each of these questions show your working out and explain your thinking.

    a The Headteacher wants to divide 248 students into nine equal-size groups. Is it possible?

    b Aunt Hilda wants to divide £540 equally between her 12 nieces and nephews. Can she do it?

    c Mr Ball is a PE teacher. He has a class of 24 students. Sometimes he organises his class into three groups of eight students. In how many different ways can he organise his class into equal size groups?

    d Charlie is absent from Mr Ball's PE class. How many equal size groups are now possible?

7 In these productogons the number in each square is the product of the numbers in the circles on each side of it. Find the missing numbers.

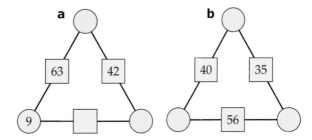

8 Jermaine thinks that if a number is divisible by both 3 and 5 then it will also be divisible by 15.

    a Investigate to see if Jermaine is correct.

    b Invent a divisibility rule of your own for 18.

1d Prime numbers

Prime numbers play an important part in online security, and in codes and codebreaking.

● A **prime number** is a number with exactly two factors: the number itself and 1.

I used the divisibility tests to find all the primes between 1 and 100.

Michael uses **divisibility** tests to check if 65 is a prime number. He works through the prime numbers starting with 2.

Is 65 divisible by...		Reason
2	✗	because 65 does not end in 0, 2, 4, 6 or 8
3	✗	because 6 + 5 = 11, which is not a multiple of 3
5	✓	because 65 ends in a 5

1	2	3	4	5	6	7	8	9	10
11	12	13	14	15	16	17	18	19	20
21	22	23	24	25	26	27	28	29	30
31	32	33	34	35	36	37	38	39	40
41	42	43	44	45	46	47	48	49	50
51	52	53	54	55	56	57	58	59	60
61	62	63	64	65	66	67	68	69	70
71	72	73	74	75	76	77	78	79	80
81	82	83	84	85	86	87	88	89	90
91	92	93	94	95	96	97	98	99	100

65 is not a prime number.

You can use **factor trees** to break a number down into factors until you reach prime numbers.

Example

Write 90 as the **product** of its **prime factors**.

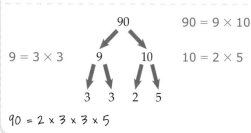

$90 = 9 \times 10$

$9 = 3 \times 3$

$10 = 2 \times 5$

$90 = 2 \times 3 \times 3 \times 5$

2, 3 and 5 are the **prime factors** of 90.

Prime numbers are the building blocks of numbers.

● Every whole number can be written as the product of its prime factors.

For example, $36 = 2 \times 2 \times 3 \times 3$

Exercise 1d

1 Write all the factors of

   a 30   **b** 48   **c** 67

   d 58   **e** 53   **f** 111

   Use your results to identify which are prime numbers.

2 Use divisibility tests to answer each of these questions.

   In each case explain your answer.

   a Is 5 a factor of 135?

   b Is 3 a factor of 186?

   c Is 2 a factor of 458?

   d Is 11 a factor of 143?

   e Is 6 a factor of 486?

3 Letitia has started trying to check if 59 is a prime number.

   a Complete Letitia's working out to see if 59 is a prime number.

   b Use the same method to check if 67 is a prime number.

3

2 is not a factor	because 59 does not end in 0, 2, 4, 6 or 8
3 is not a factor	because 5 + 9 = 14, which is not a multiple of 3
5 is not a factor	because 59 does not end in a 0 or a 5 ...

4 Use the divisibility tests for prime numbers to see which of these numbers are prime.

   In each case explain your answer.

   a 75   **b** 31   **c** 47   **d** 87

   e 54   **f** 79   **g** 85   **h** 89

   i 96   **j** 105   **k** 107   **l** 133

5 Write each of these numbers as the product of its prime factors.

   a 15   **b** 24   **c** 40   **d** 27

   e 64   **f** 56   **g** 48   **h** 72

   i 80   **j** 96   **k** 1000   **l** 210

Problem solving

6 Bob is trying to find the first prime number greater than 200. On the right is his working out so far.

200	✗ Divides by 2
201	✗ Divides by 3
202	✗ Divides by 2
203	✗ Divides by 7
204	✗ Divides by 2
205	✗ Divides by 5
206...	

   a What is the first prime number greater than 200?

   b Is 223 a prime number? Explain your method.

7 It is claimed that every even number (greater than 2) can be written as the sum of two prime numbers, for example, 16 = 5 + 11.

7 Can you do this for

   a 22   **b** 30   **c** 32   **d** 60?

8 The number 20 can be written as $2 \times 2 \times 5$. So you can say that it has three prime factors (2, 2 and 5).

   a Find four different numbers with exactly three prime factors.

   b Find the smallest number larger than 100 with exactly three prime factors.

Did you know?

The largest known prime number (as of 2013) is 17 425 170 digits long.

1e LCM and HCF

p.295 >

● The **highest common factor (HCF)** of two numbers is the largest number that will divide into both of them.

● The **lowest common multiple (LCM)** of two numbers is the smallest number that appears in both times tables.

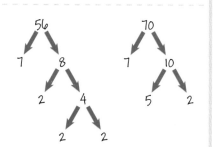

8 is the HCF of 16 and 24.

18 is the LCM of 6 and 9.

You can find the HCF and LCM by using **prime factors**.

Example

Find the HCF and LCM of 56 and 70.

Write both numbers as the product of their prime factors.
56 = ②× 2 × 2 ×⑦
70 = ②× 5 ×⑦
Multiply the prime factors they have in common.
2 × **7** = 14
HCF of 56 and 70 = 14
Now take the remaining prime factors.
56 = 2 × ② × ② × 7
70 = 2 × ⑤ × 7
Multiply by the HCF.
2 × **2** × **5** × 14 = 280
LCM of 56 and 70 = 280

```
      56                    70
   7      8             7       10
        2   4                 5    2
          2   2
```

● A Venn diagram can be useful in arranging numbers into their factors.
  You can then easily find the HCF and LCM.

Alternatively, you can use a **Venn diagram.**

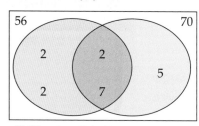

HCF = 2 × 7 = 14
LCM = 2 × 2 × 2 × 7 × 5 = 280

Write the common factors in the shared area and the other factors in the outer areas.

• The HCF is the product of the numbers in the shared area.

• The LCM is the product of the numbers in both the shared and non-shared areas.

Use your own Venn diagram to find the HCF and LCM of 28 and 42.

Exercise 1e

1 Copy and complete this table.

Numbers	Factors	HCF	First five multiples	LCM
4	1, 2, 4		4 8 12 16 20	
6				

2 Use an appropriate method to find the HCF of

   a 8 and 12   **b** 14 and 21

   c 32 and 40   **d** 39 and 52

   e 56 and 32   **f** 35 and 49

3 Use an appropriate method to find the LCM of

   a 8 and 12   **b** 14 and 21

   c 32 and 40   **d** 39 and 52

   e 24 and 30   **f** 28 and 49

4 Use an appropriate method to find the HCF and LCM of

   a 28 and 42   **b** 56 and 91

   c 72 and 108   **d** 120 and 144

   e 225 and 270   **f** 128 and 192

Problem solving

5 In these productogons the number in each square is the product of the numbers in the circles on each side. Find the missing numbers.

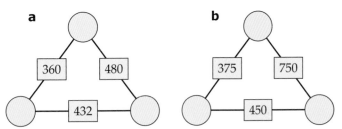

6 Solve these problems.

   a Two cars are on a race track. They start at the same place at the same time. The first car takes 54 seconds to complete a lap, the second car takes 63 seconds to complete a lap. After how many seconds will the cars be back at the starting place at exactly the same time?

   b Lola is planning to tile the floor of her new kitchen with square tiles. The kitchen measures 256 cm by 384 cm. Square tiles come in all sizes from 5 cm by 5 cm up to 20 cm by 20 cm. Lola wants to use tiles of the same size. What is the largest size of square tile that can be used to cover the floor, without needing to break any tiles?

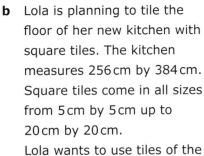

Did you know?

Some species of cicada have 13-year or 17-year life cycles. A prime number life cycle helps to defend them against predators!

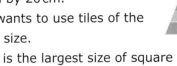

1f Squares and cubes

Here is a sequence of square patterns.

$1 \times 1 = 1$ $2 \times 2 = 4$ $3 \times 3 = 9$ $4 \times 4 = 16$

1, 4, 9 and 16 are the first four **square numbers**.

Here is a sequence of cube patterns.

   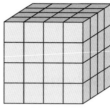

$1 \times 1 \times 1 = 1$ $2 \times 2 \times 2 = 8$ $3 \times 3 \times 3 = 27$ $4 \times 4 \times 4 = 64$

1, 8, 27 and 64 are the first four **cube numbers**.

 p.44 >

● You can use **index notation** to write squares and cubes.

The small number, or **index**, tells you how many times the number appears in a multiplication.

$3^2 = 3 \times 3 = 9$ $4^3 = 4 \times 4 \times 4 = 64$

Example

Work out the value of   **a** 6^3 **b** $(-9)^2$ **c** 3.5^2

a $6^3 = 6 \times 6 \times 6$
      $= 216$

b $(-9)^2 = -9 \times -9$ negative × negative = positive
       $= 81$

c $3.5^2 = 3.5 \times 3.5$
      $= 12.25$

With $(-9)^2$, you should square everything inside the brackets.

Example

Write the square number that is between 750 and 800.

$27^2 = 27 \times 27 = 729$ Guess a number to start.
$28^2 = 28 \times 28 = 784$ If the answer is too small
$29^2 = 29 \times 29 = 841$ try a larger number.
28^2 lies between 750 and 800.

Exercise 1f

1 Find
  a the 6th square number
  b the 9th square number
  c the 12th square number
  d the 15th square number
  e the 6th cube number
  f the 10th cube number.

2 Work out these quantities, using a calculator where appropriate.
  a 14^2 **b** 18^2
  c 24^2 **d** 13^3
  e 17^3 **f** $(-7)^2$
  g 14^3 **h** 2.5^2
  i 10^3 **j** 1.5^3
  k 7.5^3 **l** $(-5)^3$
  m 1.1^2 **n** 1.1^3
  o 0.9^2 **p** 0.9^3

3 **a** Match the amounts in box A with their estimate in box B.
  b Check your answers using your calculator.

> **BOX A**
> **A** 3.5^2 **B** 7.8^2 **C** 11.1^2 **D** 5.3^2
> **E** 13.9^2 **F** 3.5^3 **G** 5.7^3 **H** 2.9^3

> **BOX B**
> **a** 120   **b** 30   **c** 40   **d** 10   **e** 20
> **f** 180   **g** 60   **h** 190

4 **a** Write the cube number nearest to 350.
  b Write the square number which is between 280 and 290.
  c Find three numbers less than 1000 that are both square numbers and cube numbers.

Problem solving

5 **a** A square has an area of $121\,\text{cm}^2$. What is the length of a side of the square?
  b Karim thinks of a number. He multiplies the number by itself. The answer is 3136. What is Karim's number?
  c Billy wants to build a square house. An architect designs the ground floor of his house in the shape of a square with an area of $1000\,\text{m}^2$. What is the length of a side of the ground floor? (Give your answer to the nearest metre.)

6 Find two consecutive numbers with a product of 2070. Explain your method for solving the problem.

7 Tim thinks that every square number can be written as the sum of two prime numbers.
For example $9^2 = 81 = 2 + 79$
Investigate whether Tim is correct by seeing which square numbers up to 12^2 can be written as the sum of two prime numbers.

8 Some square numbers can be written as the sum of two other square numbers.
For example $25 = 16 + 9$ ($5^2 = 4^2 + 3^2$).
Find three similar results.

The area of this **square** is

$6 \times 6 = 36 \, cm^2$

6 cm

6 cm

6 squared is 36 and the square root of 36 is 6.

$6^2 = 36$
$\sqrt{36} = 6$

The sign $\sqrt{\ }$ comes from the letter r which is the initial of the Latin word 'radix' meaning 'root'.

Finding a **square root** is the **inverse** of squaring.
This number line shows the **integer** square roots up to 100.

The number line also shows that, for example, $\sqrt{30}$ lies between 5 and 6.

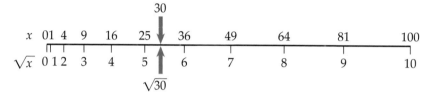

The square root of most numbers is not a whole number.

⬤ You can find square roots by using
 ▶ a calculator
 ▶ a **trial-and-improvement** method.

Example

Find $\sqrt{30}$ correct to 1 decimal place

a by using a trial-and-improvement method   **b** by using a calculator.

a

x	x^2	Comment
5	25	too low
6	36	too high
5.5	30.25	too high
5.4	29.16	too low
5.45	29.7025	too low

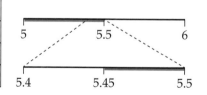

$\sqrt{30}$ lies between 5.45 and 5.5 so must be 5.5 to 1 dp.

From the table and number line.

$\sqrt{30} = 5.5$ correct to 1 decimal place.

b

$\sqrt{30}$
    5.477225575

$\sqrt{30} = 5.5$ to 1 dp

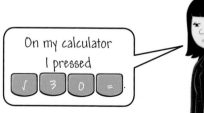

On my calculator I pressed
[√] [3] [0] [=].

Exercise 1g

1 Find the length of the sides of these squares.

a

16 cm²

b
25 cm²

2 Write the values of these square roots.

a $\sqrt{16}$ **b** $\sqrt{49}$ **c** $\sqrt{81}$

d $\sqrt{100}$ **e** $\sqrt{144}$ **f** $\sqrt{169}$

3 The square roots of these numbers are not integers. Between which two consecutive integers do each of these square roots lie? Use the number line on the opposite page to help you.

3 **a** $\sqrt{20}$ **b** $\sqrt{50}$ **c** $\sqrt{28}$

d $\sqrt{95}$ **e** $\sqrt{105}$ **f** $\sqrt{156}$

4 Use a trial-and-improvement method to find the square roots of these numbers to 1 decimal place. The first one is started for you in the table.

x	x^2	
8	64	too low
9	81	just too high

a $\sqrt{80}$ **b** $\sqrt{55}$ **c** $\sqrt{38}$

d $\sqrt{70}$ **e** $\sqrt{95}$ **f** $\sqrt{20}$

g $\sqrt{10}$ **h** $\sqrt{105}$ **i** $\sqrt{140}$

j $\sqrt{2}$ **k** $\sqrt{50}$ **l** $\sqrt{7.5}$

Problem solving

5 A window is a square of area 1.5 m². Find the length of its sides to the nearest whole cm.

6 When you stand h metres above sea-level, the horizon is x km away from you, where $x = \dfrac{7\sqrt{h}}{2}$

For example, when you are two metres above sea level

$$h = 2, \quad x = \frac{7 \times \sqrt{2}}{2}$$
$$= 4.95 \ (2\,dp)$$

so you can see 4.95 km to the horizon.

a Find x when $h = 10$.

b Find x when $h = 200$.

c Find h when $x = 30$ km.

Did you know?

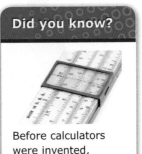

Before calculators were invented, people used slide rules or mathematical tables to calculate square roots.

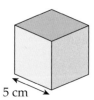

1h Cube roots

The volume of this **cube** is
$5\,cm \times 5\,cm \times 5\,cm = 125\,cm^3$.

5 cubed is 125 and the cube root of 125 is 5.

$5^3 = 125$

$\sqrt[3]{125} = 5$

5 cm

Finding a **cube root** is the **inverse** of finding a cube.

The $\sqrt{}$ sign by itself means square root. With a small^3, the sign $\sqrt[3]{}$ means cube root.

⬤ You can find cube roots by using
  ▶ **trial-and-improvement**
  ▶ a calculator if it has a $\boxed{\sqrt[3]{}}$ key.

Example

Find $\sqrt[3]{40}$ correct to 1 decimal place
a using trial-and-improvement
b using a calculator.

a

x	x^3	Comment
3	27	too low
4	64	too high
3.5	42.875	still too high
3.4	39.304	too low
3.45	41.063	too high

40 is between 27 and 64, so $\sqrt[3]{40}$ lies between 3 and 4.

$\sqrt[3]{40}$ lies between 3.4 and 3.45

$\sqrt[3]{40} = 3.4$ to 1 dp

b

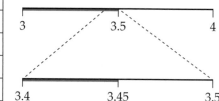

$\sqrt[3]{40}$

3.419951893

$\sqrt[3]{40} = 3.4$ to 1 dp

On my calculator I pressed
$\boxed{SHIFT}$ $\boxed{x^3}$ $\boxed{4}$ $\boxed{0}$ $\boxed{=}$
What do you have to press on your calculator?

1 8 27 64 125 216 343
512 729 1000 1331 1728

Here are the first twelve cube numbers.

Rough check
$3 \times 3 \times 3 = 27 \rightarrow$ too small
$4 \times 4 \times 4 = 64 \rightarrow$ too big
so 3.42 is probably okay

Exercise 1h

1 Calculate these cubes and cube roots.

  a 4^3 and $\sqrt[3]{64}$ **b** 2^3 and $\sqrt[3]{8}$

  c 5^3 and $\sqrt[3]{125}$ **d** 3^3 and $\sqrt[3]{27}$

  e 6^3 and $\sqrt[3]{216}$ **f** 10^3 and $\sqrt[3]{1000}$

2 **a** Find the volumes of these cubes.

  i   **ii**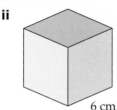

    4 cm   6 cm

  b Find the side lengths of these cubes.

  i   **ii**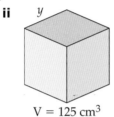

    x y

    $V = 8\ \text{cm}^3$ $V = 125\ \text{cm}^3$

3 If your calculator has a $\sqrt[3]{\ }$ key, find these cube roots, correct to 2 decimal places.

  a $\sqrt[3]{50}$ **b** $\sqrt[3]{60}$ **c** $\sqrt[3]{63}$

  d $\sqrt[3]{65}$ **e** $\sqrt[3]{124}$ **f** $\sqrt[3]{126}$

  g $\sqrt[3]{26}$ **h** $\sqrt[3]{100}$ **i** $\sqrt[3]{-64}$

4 Use a trial-and-improvement method to find the cube roots of these numbers to 2 decimal places. The first one is started for you in the table. Check your answers.

x	x^3	
3	27	too low
4	64	too high

  a $\sqrt[3]{38}$ **b** $\sqrt[3]{80}$ **c** $\sqrt[3]{67}$

  d $\sqrt[3]{70}$ **e** $\sqrt[3]{95}$ **f** $\sqrt[3]{131}$

  g $\sqrt[3]{10}$ **h** $\sqrt[3]{105}$ **i** $\sqrt[3]{140}$

Problem solving

5 A child's set of building blocks has cubes of volume of 27 cm³ each. How long are the edges of these cubes?

6 The central heating oil for a house is stored in a cubical tank which can hold 9 m³. To find the length x of the edges of the tank, use a trial-and-improvement method. Give your answer to 1 dp.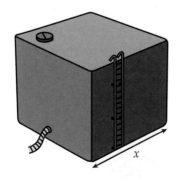

    x

7 **a** Find two numbers x for which the cube of the number equals the number itself. In other words, find x so that $x^3 = x$.

  b Find another number for which the cube of the number is 10 times the number itself. In other words, find x so that $x^3 = 10x$.

8 Find

  a $\sqrt[3]{8^2}$ and $(\sqrt[3]{8})^2$

  b $\sqrt[3]{5^2}$ and $(\sqrt[3]{5})^2$

  c Can you spot a general rule?

9 Cube A has 8 times the volume of cube B. How many times longer is the side of cube A than cube B?

Check out

You should now be able to ...

Test it ➡

Questions

✓ Order and compare decimals.	⑤	1, 2
✓ Add, subtract, multiply and divide integers.	⑤	3, 4
✓ Recognise and use multiples and factors.	④	5
✓ Use divisibility tests.	⑤	6
✓ Find the prime factor decomposition of a number.	⑤	7, 8
✓ Find the lowest common multiple and highest common factor of two numbers.	⑤	9, 10
✓ Recognise and use cube and square numbers, cube and square roots.	⑥	11–13

Language	Meaning	Example
Decimal	A number which has digits after the decimal point	3.25 and 4.13 are decimal numbers
Multiple	A number which is part of a number's times table	12 and 18 are both multiples of 6
Factor	A number which exactly divides another number	4 and 6 are both factors of 12
Product	Another word for multiplication	The product of 3 and 4 is 12
Factor tree	A method for finding the prime factor decomposition of a number	See page 10
Highest common factor (HCF)	The biggest number which divides both of two other numbers	6 is the highest common factor of 12 and 18
Lowest common multiple (LCM)	The smallest number which is in the times tables of two other numbers	30 is the lowest common multiple of 5 and 6
Square number Cube number	A number which is found by multiplying an integer by itself twice or three times	$9 = 3 \times 3 = 3^2$ is the square of 3 and $27 = 3 \times 3 \times 3 = 3^3$ is the cube of 3
Square root Cube root	The opposite of a square number or a cube number	$3 = \sqrt{9}$ is the square root of 9 $3 = \sqrt[3]{27}$ is the cube root of 27

1 Write < or > between these pairs of numbers to show which number is the larger.
 a -16 and -16.5 **b** 0.457 and 0.52
 c 0.043 and 0.34 **d** -0.56 and -0.055

2 Put these numbers in order from smallest to largest.
 a 6   - 3   0   -5
 b 1.3   - 2.4   -2.6   -0.9

3 Calculate
 a -8 + -7   **b** -9 − 5
 c 5 − -4   **d** -11 − -19

4 Calculate
 a 5 × -3   **b** -7 × -4
 c 30 ÷ -6   **d** -50 ÷ -5

5 Which of these numbers are
 a factors of 6
 b multiples of 6?

  1 3 4 6 12 14 15 18

6 Use divisibility tests to say if these statements are true or false and explain your answer.
 a 3 is a factor of 965
 b 9515 is divisible by 11
 c 770 is a multiple of 8
 d 143 is a prime number

7 Which of the following numbers are prime numbers?

  1 2 3 4 5

8 Write each of these numbers as a product of its prime factors.
 a 63   **b** 385

9 Find the highest common factor of each pair of numbers.
 a 25 and 75   **b** 11 and 17

10 Find the lowest common multiple of each pair of numbers.
 a 28 and 84   **b** 16 and 24

11 Which of the following numbers are square numbers?

  1 2 4 6 8

12 Write down the value of these square roots.
 a $\sqrt{64}$ **b** $\sqrt{25}$
 c $\sqrt{121}$ **d** $\sqrt{1}$

13 Calculate
 a 2^3 **b** $\sqrt[3]{64}$
 c 4^3 **d** $\sqrt[3]{216}$

What next?

Score		
	0 – 4	Your knowledge of this topic is still developing. To improve look at Formative test: 2B-1; MyMaths: 1032, 1034, 1035, 1044, 1053, 1068 and 1072
	5 – 11	You are gaining a secure knowledge of this topic. To improve look at InvisiPen: 111, 113, 122, 123, 171, 172, 173, 174 and 181
	12 – 13	You have mastered this topic. Well done, you are ready to progress!

1 MyPractice

1a

1 Put these numbers in order from smallest to largest.

a	-5	4	-3	2	-1
b	1.5	-2.4	-3.1	-0.9	-2
c	3.2	-1.4	-2.6	2.7	-1.1
d	-1.5	0.15	-2.1	-1.6	-0.5

2 Calculate

a 8 + -4	**b** 6 + -9	**c** 4 + -8	**d** -3 + -7	**e** -11 + -2
f 9 − -2	**g** 3 − -12	**h** 1 − -5	**i** -8 − -4	**j** -6 − -11
k -9 − -3	**l** -6 − -12	**m** -13 + -21	**n** 12 + -15	**o** 17 − -12
p 11 + -21	**q** 13 − -24	**r** 28 + -23	**s** 35 − -21	**t** -17 + -31

1b

3 Calculate

a 2 × -5	**b** -4 × 3	**c** -6 × -4	**d** -8 × -5	**e** -9 × 6
f -7 × -9	**g** 9 × -9	**h** -12 × -3	**i** -14 × 5	**j** -15 × -6
k -40 ÷ -8	**l** -35 ÷ 7	**m** -36 ÷ -9	**n** -56 ÷ -8	**o** 45 ÷ -9
p -13 × 5	**q** -25 × 4	**r** -11 × -15	**s** -84 ÷ -7	**t** -96 ÷ 8

4 Copy and complete these calculations.

a $8 \times \square = -72$ **b** $-54 \div \square = -6$ **c** $-7 \times \square = 49$

d $-104 \div \square = 8$ **e** $\square \times -12 = -48$ **f** $-6 \times \square = -72$

g $\square \div -4 = 64$ **h** $\square \div -9 = -14$ **i** $128 \div \square = -16$

1c

5 Write all the factors of

a 30	**b** 48	**c** 65	**d** 72	**e** 96	**f** 100
g 130	**h** 108	**i** 120	**j** 132	**k** 144	**l** 150

6 Use the divisibility tests to answer each of these questions.
In each case explain your answer.

a Is 2 a factor of 98?   **b** Is 3 a factor of 93?

c Is 4 a factor of 112?   **d** Is 5 a factor of 157?

e Is 6 a factor of 184?   **f** Is 8 a factor of 196?

g Is 9 a factor of 289?   **h** Is 10 a factor 362?

i Is 12 a factor of 200?   **j** Is 11 a factor of 385?

1d

7 Use the divisibility tests for prime numbers to see which of these numbers are prime. In each case explain your answer.

a 35	**b** 38	**c** 37	**d** 47	**e** 51	**f** 53
g 75	**h** 79	**i** 76	**j** 85	**k** 93	**l** 91

8 Write each of these numbers as the product of its prime factors.

    a 18   **b** 28   **c** 45   **d** 57   **e** 63   **f** 76

    g 88   **h** 92   **i** 108   **j** 115   **k** 130   **l** 132

    m 144   **n** 160   **o** 170   **p** 175   **q** 188   **r** 240

9 Use an appropriate method to find the HCF (highest common factor) of

    a 6 and 10   **b** 12 and 16   **c** 18 and 27

    d 15 and 20   **e** 24 and 32   **f** 25 and 30

    g 28 and 40   **h** 56 and 80   **i** 54 and 90

10 Use an appropriate method to find the LCM (lowest common multiple) of

    a 6 and 10   **b** 12 and 16   **c** 18 and 27

    d 15 and 20   **e** 16 and 24   **f** 24 and 30

    g 28 and 32   **h** 50 and 56   **i** 7 and 13

11 In these productogons the number in each square is the product of the numbers in the circles on each side of it. Find the missing numbers in each of these productogons.

> Write each number as the product of its prime factors.

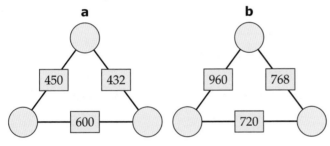

12 Work out these using a calculator where appropriate.

    a 7^3 **b** 13^2 **c** 21^2 **d** 9^3 **e** 15^3 **f** $(-3)^2$

    g 24^3 **h** 0.5^2 **i** 0.1^2 **j** 0.1^3 **k** $(-2)^2$ **l** $(-2)^3$

13 Write the values of these square roots.

    a $\sqrt{36}$ **b** $\sqrt{169}$ **c** $\sqrt{40}$ **d** $\sqrt{30}$ **e** $\sqrt{77}$

14 Find two consecutive numbers with the product 2162.

15 Use trial and improvement to find these cube roots to 1 decimal place.

    a $\sqrt[3]{27}$ **b** $\sqrt[3]{125}$ **c** $\sqrt[3]{89}$ **d** $\sqrt[3]{56}$ **e** $\sqrt[3]{90}$

16 Find three consecutive numbers with the product 10626.

MyMaths.co.uk

2 Measures, perimeter and area

Introduction

Geometry evolved because of the need to measure shapes. The ancient Egyptians are often said to be the first people who used geometry as a major feature of their society. Besides building pyramids for pharaohs, geometry was used to solve practical problems such as measuring the area of a farmer's land so that he could be taxed appropriately. This often proved difficult due to the annual flooding of the river Nile.

What's the point?

Being able to measure things is as important as being able to count – it means you can share things out fairly!

Objectives

By the end of this chapter, you will have learned how to ...

- Use appropriate units to measure length, mass and capacity.
- Know rough metric equivalents to imperial units.
- Read and interpret scales.
- Calculate the perimeter and area of a rectangle.
- Calculate the perimeter and area of a triangle.
- Calculate the area of a parallelogram and a trapezium.

Check in

Work out the calculations in questions **1–3**.

1. **a** 30×100
   b $560 \div 10$
   c 4.6×10
   d $8500 \div 1000$

2. **a** 60×2.2
   b 8×4.5
   c 5×1.6
   d 15×0.6

3. **a** $32 \div 1.6$
   b $20 \div 2.5$
   c $60 \div 0.6$
   d $18 \div 4.5$

4. Calculate the perimeter and the area of these shapes.
   Each square represents one square centimetre.

   a
   b
   c

Starter problem

A surveyor has 240 m of fencing. He wants
to mark out the largest area he can for the
construction of a house.

Investigate.

You can measure **length** using the metric units millimetre (mm), centimetre (cm), metre (m) and kilometre (km).

▲ Your finger is about 1 cm wide.

▲ A desk is about 1 m wide.

▲ You can walk about 1 km in 15 minutes.

1 cm = 10 mm
1 m = 1000 mm
1 m = 100 cm
1 km = 1000 m

The **mass** of something is how heavy it is. You can measure mass using grams (g), kilograms (kg) and tonnes (t).

1 kg = 1000 g
1 t = 1000 kg

▲ A paper clip weighs about $\frac{1}{2}$ g.

▲ A bag of sugar weighs 1 kg.

▲ A small car weighs about 1 tonne.

1· = 1000 ml
1· = 100 cl

Capacity is the amount of space a container can hold. You measure capacity using millilitres (ml), centilitres (cl) and litres (l).

▲ A teaspoon holds 5 ml.

▲ A can of drink holds 33 cl.

▲ A carton of fruit juice holds 1·.

Example

Convert these measurements into the units indicated in brackets.

a 5· (into ml) **b** 450 cm (into m)

a 5· = 5 × 1000 ml
    = 5000 ml

× 1000

1· = 1000 ml

÷ 1000

b 450 cm = 450 ÷ 100 m
    = 4.5 m

× 100

1 m = 100 cm

÷ 100

Exercise 2a

1 Copy and complete each sentence, using the most appropriate metric unit.

  a The amount of liquid in a mug is 25 _____.

  b The length of a room is 2.8 _____.

  c A bucket holds 9 _____ of water.

  d A teabag has a mass of 5 _____.

  e The width of my fingernail is 10 _____.

> **Useful approximations**
> Height of a door = 2 m
> Height of a house = 10 m
> Mass of 1 bag of sugar = 1 kg
> Mass of a small car = 1 tonne
> Capacity of a bottle of drink = 2 ·
> Time to walk 1 km = 15 min

2 Estimate the size of each of these measurements. Use the approximations to help you.

  a Distance across a road

  b Capacity of a rucksack

  c Mass of an elephant

  d Time to boil an egg

  e Mass of a small child

  f Height of a classroom

3 Calculate the number of metres in a 50 km race.

4 Convert these measurements to the units in the brackets.

  a 7500 g (kg) **b** 650 mm (cm)

  c 850 cl (·) **d** 500 m (km)

  e 2500 kg (t) **f** 8.5 m (cm)

  g 7 · (ml) **h** 19.5 kg (g)

  i 4 km (cm) **j** 100 ml (cl)

  k 1 000 000 mm (km)

Problem solving

5 Type A fence panels have a width of 75 cm. Type B fence panels have a width of 1.25 m.

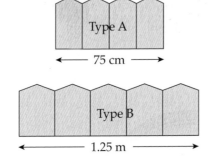

Find a combination of fence panels that will fit a seven metre gap.

6 A 250 ml bottle of hair shampoo costs 99p.
A one-litre bottle of the same shampoo costs £3.99.
Which bottle is better value for money?
Show your working to explain your answer.

7 **a** Which weighs more, you or one million paper clips? Explain your answer.

  b How many paper clips could you carry in one go? Explain your answer.

8 How long would it take you to walk from Lands End to John O'Groats? Explain your answer.

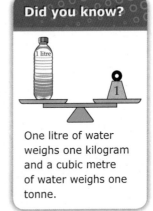

Did you know?

One litre of water weighs one kilogram and a cubic metre of water weighs one tonne.

2b Imperial measure

You can convert between **metric** and **imperial** units using this list of approximations.

- 1 inch ≈ 2.5 cm
- 1 yard is just less than 1 metre
- 1 mile ≈ 1.6 kilometres
- 1 kilogram ≈ 2.2 lb (pounds)
- 1 pint ≈ 0.6 litres
- 1 gallon ≈ 4.5 litres

Example

a Convert 50 kg to pounds (lb).

b Convert 100 cm to inches.

a 50 kg ≈ 50 × 2.2 lb
     ≈ 110 lb

× 2.2
1 kg ≈ 2.2 lb
÷ 2.2

b 100 cm ≈ 100 ÷ 2.5 inches
     ≈ 40 inches

× 2.5
1 inch ≈ 2.5 cm
÷ 2.5

You need to be able to read the scales on measuring instruments.

▲ A multimeter can have several scales.

Example

Write down the reading on each of the scales.

a
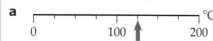
0   100 ↑ 200   °C

b

0
50
g

a 125°C
4 spaces represent 100°C
Each space represents 25°C

b 40 g
10 spaces represent 50 g
Each space represents 5 g

Exercise 2b

1 State the larger unit of measurement.

    a inch or centimetre

    b pound (lb) or kilogram

    c pint or litre

    d mile or kilometre

    e yard or metre

2 Convert these measurements to the units in brackets.

    a 5 kg (lb)   **b** 8 pints (litre)

    c 12 inches (cm)   **d** 70 kg (lb)

    e 36 inches (cm)   **f** 80 kg (lb)

    g 14 pints (litre)   **h** 0.5 kg (lb)

    i 2 feet (cm)   **j** 12 lb (kg)

3 Convert these measurements to the units in brackets.

    a 15 cm (inches)   **b** 99 lb (kg)

    c 12 litres (pints)   **d** 300 cl (pints)

    e 40 cm (inches)   **f** 132 lb (kg)

    g 50 cm (inches)   **h** 24 litres (pints)

    i 125 cm (inches)   **j** 4 gallons (litres)

4 Write down the readings on each scale.

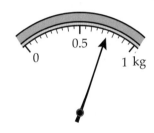

5 Write down the reading on this scale.

Problem solving

6 The sign below shows the distances in miles from Preston to other cities. Calculate the distances in kilometres.

🛣	
Manchester	30
Stoke	65
Birmingham	110
Bath	200

7 **a** A litre of petrol costs 130 pence. What will a gallon cost?

    b If you can drive 48 miles on one gallon, how far can you drive on one litre? Give your answer in

        i miles per litre

        ii kilometres per litre.

8 **a** Susan eats 40 g of cereal for breakfast every day.

        i How much will she eat in one year?

        ii When will she have eaten 50 kg of cereal?

    b Susan puts 125 ml of milk on each helping of her cereal. How many pints of milk does she need in a whole year?

9 An imperial pint is 20 fluid ounces. An American pint is 16 fluid ounces. A gallon is 8 pints. How many litres are there in an American gallon?

In this drawing, the wall goes around the **perimeter** of the lawn.
The grass covers the **area** of the lawn.

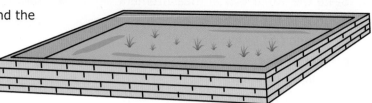

⬤ The **perimeter** is the distance around a two-dimensional shape.

You measure perimeter in units of length, such as mm, cm, m, km.

⬤ The **area** of a shape is the amount of surface it covers.

You measure area in squares, such as square centimetres (cm²) or square metres (m²).

▲ You can find the area of a shape by counting how many squares fit inside it.

⬤ You can find the area of a rectangle using a **formula**.
Area of a rectangle = length × width

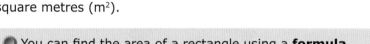

width

length

Example

Calculate the perimeter and area of the rectangle.

4 cm

6 cm

Perimeter = 6 cm + 4 cm + 6 cm + 4 cm
= 20 cm
Area = 6 × 4
= 24 cm²

Example

Calculate the perimeter and area of this shape.

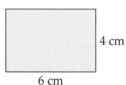

7 m

3 m

5 m

2 m

First split the shape into two rectangles and calculate the missing lengths.
7 − 2 = 5   5 − 3 = 2
Perimeter = 2 + 5 + 7 + 3 + 5 + 2 = 24 m
Area = 3 × 5 + 2 × 5
= 15 + 10
= 25 m²

Exercise 2c

1 Calculate the perimeter and area of these rectangles. State the units of your answers.

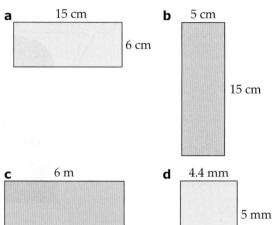

a 15 cm, 6 cm

b 5 cm, 15 cm

c 6 m, 5.5 m

d 4.4 mm, 5 mm

2 Calculate the perimeter of these rectangles.

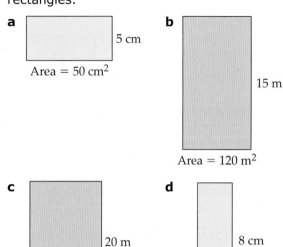

a 5 cm, Area = 50 cm²

b 15 m, Area = 120 m²

c 20 m, Area = 240 m²

d 8 cm, Area = 20 cm²

Problem solving

3 Calculate the perimeter and area of these shapes made from rectangles.
If necessary, draw the shapes on square grid paper.

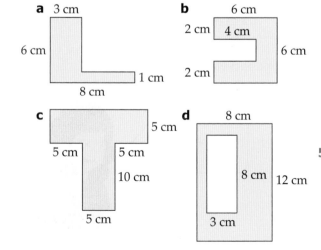

a 3 cm, 6 cm, 8 cm, 1 cm

b 6 cm, 2 cm, 4 cm, 6 cm, 2 cm

c 5 cm, 5 cm, 5 cm, 10 cm, 5 cm

d 8 cm, 8 cm, 12 cm, 3 cm

4 This is the national flag of Sweden.

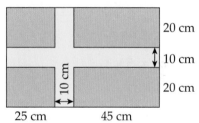

20 cm, 10 cm, 20 cm, 10 cm, 25 cm, 45 cm

Calculate
a the area of each blue rectangle
b the area of the yellow shape.

5 The national flag of Switzerland is square and symmetric.

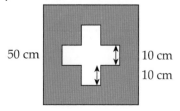

50 cm, 10 cm, 10 cm

Calculate
a the area of the white cross
b the area of the red background.

2d Area of a triangle

The area of this green triangle is half the area of the surrounding rectangle.

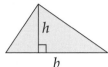 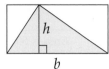 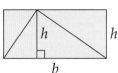

Area of the rectangle = $b \times h$

Perpendicular means 'at right angles to'.

The area of a triangle $= \frac{1}{2} \times b \times h$

$= \frac{1}{2} \times$ base $\times$ **perpendicular** height

The perpendicular height is not always inside the triangle.

Example

Calculate the area of these triangles.

a

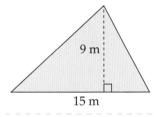

9 m

15 m

b

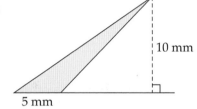

10 mm

5 mm

a Area $= \frac{1}{2} \times b \times h$

$= \frac{1}{2} \times 15 \times 9$

$= 67.5\,m^2$

b Area $= \frac{1}{2} \times b \times h$

$= \frac{1}{2} \times 5 \times 10$

$= 25\,mm^2$

If you know the area, you can use the **formula** to work backwards.

Example

The area of this triangle is 96 cm². Calculate the perpendicular height.

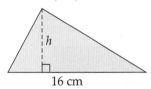

h

16 cm

Area $= \frac{1}{2} \times b \times h$

$96 = \frac{1}{2} \times 16 \times h$

$96 = 8 \times h$

$h = 12\,cm$

Remember to always write down the units.

Exercise 2d

1 Calculate the area of these triangles.
Each square represents 1 cm².

a   **b**

c   **d**

2 On square grid paper, draw a triangle with an area of 15 cm².

3 Calculate the area of these triangles.
State the units of your answers.

a 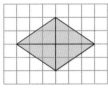   **b**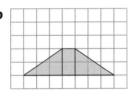

3 **c** 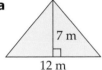   **d**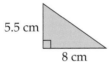

8 cm   16 cm   5 mm   7 mm

4 Calculate the unknown length in these triangles.

a
8 cm
Area = 20 cm²

b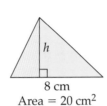
10 m
b
Area = 60 m²

c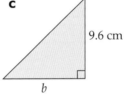
9.6 cm
b
Area = 48 cm²

d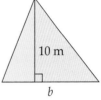
h
8 mm
Area = 30 mm²

Problem solving

5 Calculate the area of these shapes.
Each square represents 1 cm².

a 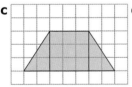   **b**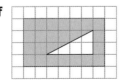

c **d**

e **f**

6 The surrounding rectangle is drawn around a kite.
The rectangle has a length of 20 cm and a width of 10 cm.
Calculate
a the area of the rectangle
b the area of the kite.
Explain your answers.

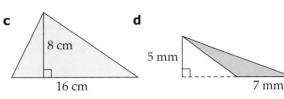
20 cm
10 cm

Did you know?

Triangles are very strong shapes, and because of this they are often used in architecture.

2e Area of a parallelogram and a trapezium

The **area** of the **parallelogram** is double the area of the triangle.

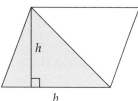

Area of the triangle $= \frac{1}{2} \times b \times h$

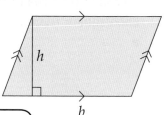

- Area of a parallelogram $= b \times h$
  $= $ base $\times$ perpendicular height

A trapezium has one pair of parallel sides.

A parallelogram has two pairs of **parallel** sides.

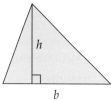

You can fit two **trapeziums** together to make a parallelogram.

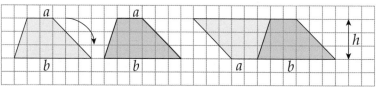

The area of the trapezium is half the area of the parallelogram.

Area of the parallelogram $= (a + b) \times h$

- The area of a trapezium $= \frac{1}{2} \times (a + b) \times h$

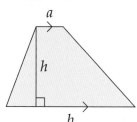

▲ a and b are the lengths of the parallel sides. h is the perpendicular height.

Example

Calculate the area of these shapes.

a

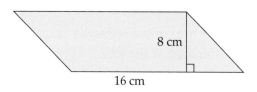

8 cm

16 cm

b

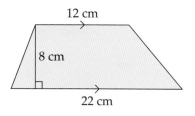

12 cm

8 cm

22 cm

a   Area $= b \times h$

     $= 16 \times 8$

     $= 128 \, cm^2$

b   Area $= \frac{1}{2} \times (a + b) \times h$

     $= \frac{1}{2} \times (12 + 22) \times 8$

     $= \frac{1}{2} \times 34 \times 8$

     $= 136 \, cm^2$

Exercise 2e

1 Calculate the area of these parallelograms. State the units of your answers.

a
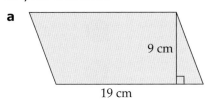
9 cm
19 cm

b
15 cm
24 cm

c
8.5 m
4 m

2 Calculate the area of these trapeziums.

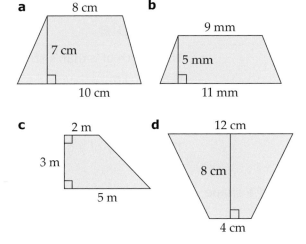

a
8 cm
7 cm
10 cm

b
9 mm
5 mm
11 mm

c
2 m
3 m
5 m

d
12 cm
8 cm
4 cm

3 Find the lengths b and h in these parallelograms. State the units of your answers.

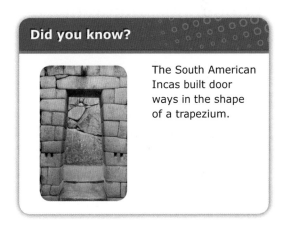

a
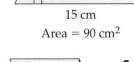
h
15 cm
Area = 90 cm^2

b
h
8 m
Area = 100 m^2

c
25 mm
b
Area = 750 mm^2

Did you know?

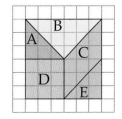

The South American Incas built door ways in the shape of a trapezium.

Problem solving

4 Copy the five-piece 'tangram' on square grid paper.

  a Calculate the area of the tangram.
     Cut out the five pieces.

  b Arrange shapes A, B, D and E to form
     i a rectangle
     ii a parallelogram
     iii an isosceles trapezium.

  c Calculate the area of each quadrilateral in part **b** using the appropriate formula.
     Show your working in each case.

  d Calculate the area of shape C using the appropriate formula.

2 MySummary

Check out

You should now be able to ...

Test it ➡

Questions

✓ Use appropriate units to measure length, mass and capacity and convert between metric units.	5	1, 2
✓ Know rough metric equivalents to imperial units.	5	3
✓ Read and interpret scales.	5	4
✓ Calculate the perimeter and area of a rectangle.	5	5–7
✓ Calculate the area of a triangle.	6	8
✓ Calculate the area of a parallelogram and a trapezium.	6	9, 10

Language	Meaning	Example
Length	How long something is	The length of a man's stride is about 1 m
Mass	How heavy something is	The mass of a bag of sugar is 1 kg
Capacity	How much something holds	The capacity of a drinks can is 330 ml
Perimeter	The distance around the edge of a shape	The perimeter of a square of side 5 cm is 20 cm
Area	The amount of space inside a 2D shape	The area of a square of side 5 cm is 25 cm²
Rectangle	A four-sided shape with four right-angles and two pairs of equal length sides	The shape of this book is a rectangle
Parallelogram	A four-sided shape with two pairs of parallel sides	
Trapezium	A four-sided shape with one pair of parallel sides	The cross-section of a trough is a trapezium

In the following questions you must state the units of your answer.

1 Write an appropriate metric unit for each measurement.

 a My sister is 0.9 .... tall.

 b The cross-country race was 5 .... long.

 c The ant is 3 .... long.

 d I weigh 45 ....

2 Convert

 a 27 km to cm   **b** 1250 g to kg

 c 550 cl to litres   **d** 5000 mm to km

3 Convert

 a 5 inches into cm

 b 10 pints into litres.

4 Write down the readings on this scale.

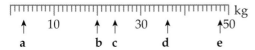

5 Calculate the area of this rectangle.

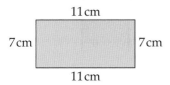

6 The area of this rectangle is 45 m². What is its perimeter?

7 Calculate the area of this shape which has been made using two rectangles.

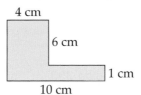

8 Calculate the area of these triangles.

 a

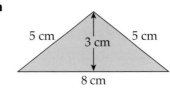

 b

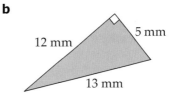

9 A parallelogram has a base of length 8 cm and an area of 48 cm². Calculate the height of the parallelogram.

10

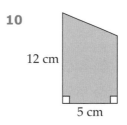

 a What is this shape called?

 b Calculate the area of the shape.

What next?

Score		
	0 – 3	Your knowledge of this topic is still developing. To improve look at Formative test: 2B-2; MyMaths: 1061, 1084, 1108, 1110, 1129 and 1191
	4 – 8	You are gaining a secure knowledge of this topic. To improve look at InvisiPen: 312, 313, 314, 315, 332 and 333
	9 – 10	You have mastered this topic. Well done, you are ready to progress!

2a

1 Copy and complete each sentence, using the most appropriate metric unit of length.

    a A banana weighs 150 ____.

    b I can walk 1 ____ in 15 minutes.

    c The weight of a football is just over 400 ____.

    d A ruler is 30 ____ long.

    e A small flask holds 300 ____ of liquid.

2 Convert these measurements to the units indicated in brackets.

    a 380 mm (cm)   **b** 4.5 kg (g)   **c** 6.5 ℓ (cl)

    d 3500 mm (m)   **e** 2500 kg (t)   **f** 500 ml (ℓ)

2b

3 Convert these measurements to the units indicated in brackets.

    a 8 inches (cm)   **b** 132 lbs (kg)   **c** 40 km (miles)

    d 5 pints (ℓ)   **e** 10 gallons (ℓ)   **f** 1 metre (inches)

4 Write down each reading on the scales.

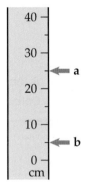
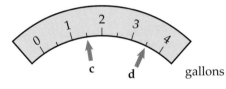
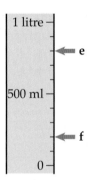

2c

5 Copy and complete the table for the rectangles.

	Length	Width	Perimeter	Area
a	15 cm	10 cm		
b	25 cm	20 cm		
c	9 cm			63 cm²
d	4.5 cm			18 cm²
e	5.5 cm		20 cm	
f	7.5 cm		26 cm	
g			28 cm	48 cm²

6 Calculate the perimeter and area of these shapes made from rectangles.

a
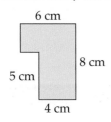
6 cm
8 cm
5 cm
4 cm

b
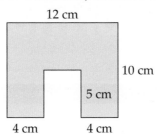
12 cm
10 cm
5 cm
4 cm   4 cm

c
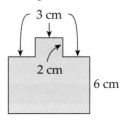
3 cm
2 cm
6 cm

7 Calculate the area of the shaded region.

a
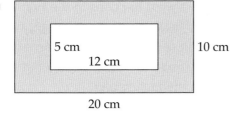
5 cm
12 cm
10 cm
20 cm

b
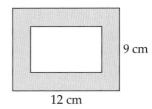
9 cm
12 cm
The shaded border is 2 cm wide.

8 On square grid paper, draw
a two different rectangles, each with an area of 6 cm²
b two different right-angled triangles, each with an area of 6 cm²
c two different triangles, neither of them right-angled each with an area of 6 cm².

9 Calculate the area of these parallelograms.

a
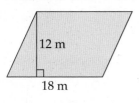
12 m
18 m

b
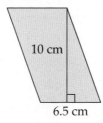
10 cm
6.5 cm

c
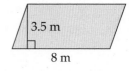
3.5 m
8 m

10 Calculate the area of these trapeziums.

a
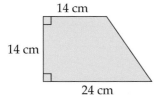
14 cm
14 cm
24 cm

b
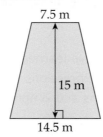
7.5 m
15 m
14.5 m

c
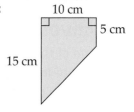
10 cm
5 cm
15 cm

MyMaths.co.uk

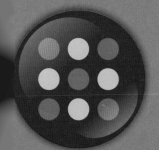

3 Expressions and formulae

Introduction

Engineers use algebraic formulae to represent the flight of a spacecraft, such as NASA's Voyager 1 space probe, launched in 1977. It has now recently left our solar system, the first man-made object ever to have done so. These formulae are often very complex, and they have allowed people on the ground to predict and control the spacecraft's progress with great accuracy.

What's the point?

Without the use of formulae to model and predict what happens in the real world, we would have no idea what might happen next in complex situations. An expensive space rocket would probably not even leave the launch pad!

Objectives

By the end of this chapter, you will have learned how to ...

- Substitute into simple algebraic expressions.
- Use indices to simplify expressions and simplify by collecting like terms.
- Expand brackets.
- Substitute into formulae.
- Construct a formula for different situations.

Check in

1 You have four boxes with twelve pencils in each box. You also have three packets with six coloured pencils in each packet. How many pencils do you have altogether?
2 Do these multiplications without using a calculator.

    a $2 \times 2 \times 2 \times 2$ **b** $2 \times 5 \times 2 \times 5$ **c** $2 \times 2 \times 3 \times 3 \times 5$

Starter problem

Here are some staircases made from wooden blocks.
How many blocks would you need to make a staircase with 35 steps?

2 steps
3 blocks

3 steps
6 blocks

4 steps
10 blocks

You can use letters to stand for unknown numbers.

If x is a number, four lots of the number is written as an **expression**:

$x + x + x + x$

You can **simplify** this expression:

$x + x + x + x = 4 \times x = 4x$

Half of the number is written

$x \div 2 = \frac{1}{2}x = \frac{x}{2}$

> An **expression** is formed when letters and numbers are combined.

Here are some expressions:

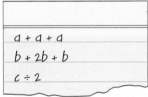

$a + a + a$
$b + 2b + b$
$c \div 2$

This is what they look like simplified:

$3a$
$4b$
$\frac{c}{2}$

You can **substitute** a number for a letter.

If $x = 12$, then $4x = 4 \times 12 = 48$ and $\frac{1}{2}x = \frac{1}{2} \times 12 = 6$

Example

If $p = 15$, find the values of

a $p + 5$ **b** $p - 6$ **c** $2p$ **d** $\frac{1}{3}p$

---

a $p + 5 = 15 + 5 = 20$

c $2p = 2 \times p = 2 \times 15 = 30$

b $p - 6 = 15 - 6 = 9$

d $\frac{1}{3}p = \frac{1}{3} \times 15 = 15 \div 3 = 5$

Example

A carpenter uses 4 screws weighing x grams each and 5 screws weighing y grams each. The total weight of the screws, T is $4x + 5y$.

Find the value of T when $x = 20$ and $y = 100$.

Hence find the total weight of screws.

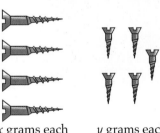

x grams each y grams each

$T = 4x + 5y = 4 \times 20 + 5 \times 100 = 80 + 500 = 580$

The total weight of screws is 580 g.

Exercise 3a

1 Write these expressions in a simpler way.
Here is an example: $a + a + a + a = 4a$

   a $x + x + x + x + x$ **b** $y + y + y$

   c $z + z + z + z$ **d** $3 \times z$

   e $8 \div x$ **f** $y \times 5$

   g $x \div 2$ **h** $y \div 5$

   i $z \div 3$ **j** $y + y + 2y$

2 Find the value of each of the expressions in question **1** if $x = 10$, $y = 5$ and $z = 6$.

3 Find the value of the expression $3x - 2y$
when **a** $x = 2$ and $y = -1$

            b $x = -2$ and $y = 1$

            c $x = -2$ and $y = -3$

Problem solving

4 A bus has x passengers. Another four passengers get on.

   a   Write an expression for the number of passengers on the bus now.

   b   If $x = 12$, how many passengers are on the bus now?

5 A train has y passengers. At the next station, twelve passengers get off and another two passengers get on.

   a   Write an expression for the number of passengers after this station.

   b   If $y = 50$, how many passengers are on the train after the next station?

6 A box holds n glasses. You have four of these boxes.

   a   Write an expression for the total number of glasses in all the boxes.

   b   If $n = 6$, how many glasses have you altogether?

7 A square flower bed has sides y metres long.

   a   Write an expression for its perimeter.

   b   If $y = 12$, how long is its perimeter?

8 A football pitch is r metres long and s metres wide.

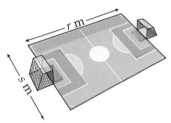

   a   Write down an expression for its perimeter.

   b   If $r = 25$ and $s = 60$, find the length of its perimeter.

9 Here is a street map of part of an American city. It shows the court house C and the police department P. Each rectangle of the grid of streets is x cm by y cm. How long are the shortest routes from C to P in terms of x and y? How many of these shortest routes are there?

If $x = 5$ and $y = 8$, how long are the shortest routes in cm?

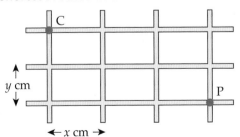

3b Indices

⟨ p.14

$2 \times 2 \times 2 \times 2 \times 2 = 2^5$

This is the **index** or **power**.

> You can say '2 to the power 5'.

> Any number or letter multiplied by itself can be written using an **index** or **power**.

$2 \times 2 \times 2 = 2^3$

> You can say '2 to the power 3' or '2 cubed'.

Example

Work out the value of $2^4 \times 5^2$.

$2^4 \times 5^2 = 2 \times 2 \times 2 \times 2 \times 5 \times 5$

$\qquad = 16 \times 25$

$\qquad = 400$

> The plural of 'index' is indices.

You can simplify an **expression** using **indices**.

Example

a Simplify $s \times s \times s \times t \times t \times t \times t \times u$.

b Simplify $a \times a \times c \times b \times a \times b \times b \times c$

c Simplify $6^3 \times 6^4$, giving your answer as a power of 6.

> You should write u not u^1.

a $s \times s \times s \times t \times t \times t \times t \times u = s^3 \times t^4 \times u^1$

$\qquad\qquad\qquad\qquad\qquad = s^3\, t^4\, u$

b $a \times a \times c \times b \times a \times b \times b \times c = a \times a \times a \times b \times b \times b \times c \times c$

$\qquad\qquad\qquad\qquad\qquad\qquad = a^3 \times b^3 \times c^2$

c $6^3 \times 6^4 = (6 \times 6 \times 6) \times (6 \times 6 \times 6 \times 6)$

$\qquad\quad = 6^7$

> Notice that $3 + 4 = 7$.

Example

Simplify $z^3 \times z^2 \times z^4$.

$z^3 \times z^2 \times z^4 = (z \times z \times z) \times (z \times z) \times (z \times z \times z \times z)$

$\qquad\qquad\quad = z^9$

Exercise 3b

1 Simplify these expressions by using indices. Do not work out any values.

Examples: $3 \times 3 \times 3 \times 3 = 3^4$

$\qquad a \times a \times a = a^3$

a $2 \times 2 \times 2 \times 2$

b $7 \times 7 \times 7 \times 7 \times 7$

c $9 \times 9 \times 9 \times 9 \times 9 \times 9$

d $n \times n \times n$

e $y \times y \times y \times y \times y \times y \times y$

f $z \times z$

2 Simplify these expressions. Do not work out any values.

a $4 \times 4 \times 4 \times 5 \times 5 \times 5 \times 5$

b $8 \times 8 \times 6 \times 6 \times 6 \times 6 \times 6$

c $2 \times 3 \times 2 \times 3 \times 2 \times 3 \times 3$

d $5 \times 9 \times 9 \times 5 \times 5$

e $6 \times 4 \times 4 \times 6 \times 6 \times 6$

f $3 \times 3 \times 3 \times 3 \times n \times n$

g $r \times s \times s \times s \times s \times r \times s$

h $a \times b \times c \times a \times b \times c \times c$

3 Write these quantities out in full and then find their values.

a 2^4 **b** 3^3

c 5^2 **d** 2^5

e 1^6 **f** $2^2 \times 3^2$

g $2^3 \times 5^2$ **h** $1^4 \times 6^2$

i $10^4 \times 3^2$ **j** $0^5 \times 7^3$

4 Simplify each of these quantities. Use indices in your answers. Do not work out the actual values.

a $6^4 \times 6^3$ **b** $8^2 \times 8^4$

c $2^4 \times 2^5$ **d** $3^7 \times 3^2$

e $5^5 \times 5^3$ **f** $7^4 \times 7^8$

g $10^2 \times 10^4 \times 10^3$ **h** $3^3 \times 3^4 \times 3^2$

i $5 \times 5^2 \times 5^4$ **j** $6 \times 6^5 \times 6^2$

k $4 \times 4 \times 4^8$ **l** $10 \times 10^6 \times 10$

5 Simplify these expressions. Write your answers using indices.

a $2^2 \times 3^3 \times 3^4 \times 2^5$

b $9^5 \times 7 \times 5^2 \times 7^4 \times 9^2 \times 5^3$

Problem solving

6 Find the value of n in each of these statements.

a $2^n = 8$ **b** $3^n = 9$ **c** $10^n = 1000$

d $5^n = 125$ **e** $4^n = 64$ **f** $3^n = 243$

7 A litre of water fills this hollow cube.

a Write the volume of water in cm³ as a power of 10.

b Write how many cm³ there are in 1 litre.

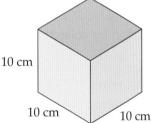

10 cm

10 cm   10 cm

8 a Find the area of this square and the volume of this cube.

b Can you see why we say 'squared' and 'cubed'?

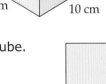

x cm x cm

9 A million is $10 \times 10 \times 10 \times 10 \times 10 \times 10 = 10^6 = 1\,000\,000$.

Find the meaning of *billion, trillion* and *quadrillion*.

Can you find any other names for very large numbers?

How did the numbers *googol* and *googolplex* get their names?

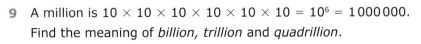

MyMaths.co.uk

Expressions are made up of terms separated by plus or minus signs.

$$3x - 2y + 4z$$

The terms are $3x$, $-2y$ and $4z$.

There are lots of little rules for simplifying algebraic expressions. You need to remember them!

- **Like terms** contain the same letter. a and $2a$ are like terms.

- You can **simplify** an expression by collecting like terms. $a + 2a = 3a$

- Terms that use different letters are not like terms. a and $2b$ are *not* like terms.

- Terms which use different powers are not like terms. a and a^2 are *not* like terms.

Two pipes of length $5a$ and $3a$ are joined together.

5a 3a

The total length $= 5a + 3a = 8a$

This necklace is made from two kinds of beads of lengths a cm and b cm.

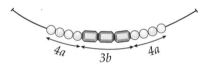

4a 3b 4a

The total length $= 4a + 3b + 4a$
$$= 8a + 3b$$

Simplify this expression by collecting like terms.
$5x + 4y + 2x - 3x + y$

The terms in x are like terms. $5x + 2x - 3x = 4x$
The terms in y are like terms. $4y + y = 5y$
$5x + 4y + 2x - 3x + y = 4x + 5y$

Simplify this expression.
$3x^2 + 2x - x^2 + x^2 + 4x + 5x^2$

Collect terms in x. $2x + 4x = 6x$
Collect terms in x^2. $3x^2 - x^2 + x^2 + 5x^2 = 8x^2$
$3x^2 + 2x - x^2 + x^2 + 4x + 5x^2 = 6x + 8x^2$

Exercise 3c

1 Write the total lengths of these pipes when the parts are joined together.

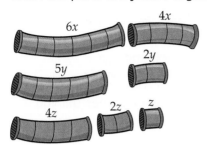

a $6x + 4x = \square$ b $5y + 2y = \square$

c $4z + 2z + z = \square$

2 Simplify these expressions.

a $2n + 3n + n$ b $6m + 4m + 2m$

c $4p + 3p - 2p$ d $8q - 2q - 3q$

e $5t + 3t + 4t$ f $7r + r - 5r$

g $6s - 4s - 2s$ h $8x - 5x - 2x$

i $5x - 6x + 3x$ j $6y - 8y + 9y$

k $z - 3z + 4z$ l $9m - 5m - 4m$

3 Necklaces are made from two kinds of beads of length x cm and y cm.

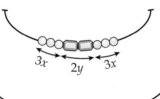

Write the total lengths of these two necklaces as simply as you can.

a $3x + 2y + 3x = \square$

b $2x + 3y + 2x + 3y = \square$

4 Simplify these expressions by collecting like terms.

a $2x + 3x + 6y - 4y$

b $5x + 2y - 3x + 6y$

c $4x + 2y + 3y - 2x$

d $5s + s + 7t - t$

e $u + u + 8v - v$

f $3r + 4r + 5s - 2s$

g $4x + x - 3y + 5y$

h $6a - 2a + a + 3b$

i $3a + 2b + 4a - 5a$

5 Simplify these expressions.
Collect terms with the same indices.

a $2x + 4x + 3x^2 + 5x^2$

b $7y + 2y + 6y^2 - 3y^2$

c $4z + 2z^2 + 3z + 2z^2$

d $8u + 5u^2 - 3u - 2u^2$

e $5v + 2v^2 - 3v + v^2$

f $8x + x^2 + 4x^2 - 2x$

g $3z + 2z^3 - z - 2z^3$

h $9h^3 - 2h - h + 5h$

i $j^2 - 3j + j^2 + 4j$

6 Simplify these expressions.

a $4a + b^2 + 3b^2 + 2a$

b $u^2 + 7v - u + 6v$

c $x - 2y^2 + 4x^2 - 4x + 3y^2$

d $-4s^2 + t^2 - 2s + 4t^2 - 3s^2$

e $2p - 3q^2 + 4r - 3q^2 + 2p$

f $4n^2 + 2m + 2n - 3m^2$

Problem solving

7 This path is laid using square and rectangular slabs.
Write an expression in x and y for

a the area of the path

b the perimeter of the path.

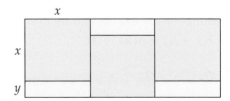

8 A necklace is made up of five beads. Three beads each have a length a cm. The other two each have a length b cm. The beads can be threaded in any order. How many different necklaces of length $3a + 2b$ cm can be made?

3d Expanding brackets

Here are two identical rectangles with sides in cm.

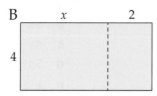

A

$x + 2$

4

Area A $= 4 \times (x + 2)$
$= 4(x + 2)\,\text{cm}^2$

B

x 2

4

Area B $= 4 \times x + 4 \times 2$
$= 4x + 8\,\text{cm}^2$

So $4\overparen{(x + 2)} = 4x + 8$
You can use this method to expand $3(p + 1)$, $2(2q + 3)$ or $6(z - 3)$.

The curved lines tell you which terms to multiply.

⬤ When you multiply a term by a bracket, you multiply it by everything within the bracket.

▶ This process is often called **expanding** the brackets.

p.183 >

You don't need to draw rectangles to multiply a term by a bracket, just multiply each term inside by what's outside.

$4\overparen{(2x - 3)} = 4 \times 2x + 4 \times \text{-}3$ —— $\boxed{4 \times 2x = 8x}$
$= 8x + \text{-}12$
$= 8x - 12$ ———— $\boxed{+ - \text{ makes } -}$

Example

Expand these brackets.

a $3(2x - 4)$

b $x(x + 5)$

a $3\overparen{(2x - 4)} = 3 \times 2x - 3 \times 4$
$= 6x - 12$

b $x\overparen{(x + 5)} = x \times x + x \times 5$
$= x^2 + 5x$

Try not to get confused between x and the multiply sign!

⬤ An **expression** can have several pairs of brackets.
Expand each pair separately and then collect 'like terms'.

Example

Simplify the expression by first expanding brackets.
$2(z + 5) + 4(2z + 3)$

$2\overparen{(z + 5)} + 4\overparen{(2z + 3)} = 2z + 10 + 8z + 12$ Expand brackets
$= 10z + 22$ Collect like terms

Exercise 3d

1 Expand these brackets using the diagrams to help you.

a
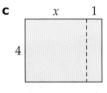
$3(x + 2) = \ldots$

b
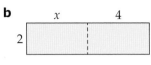
$2(x + 4) = \ldots$

c

$4(x + 1) = \ldots$

d
$x(x + 2) = \ldots$

2 Expand these brackets.

a	$5(x + 3)$	**b**	$5(2x + 5)$
c	$5(x + 3)$	**d**	$5(2x - 5)$
e	$6(3u + 2)$	**f**	$3(v - 4)$
g	$5(2a - 3)$	**h**	$4(3b - 1)$
i	$5(3 - 2c)$	**j**	$6(2b - 3)$

3 Expand these brackets.
Take care with the powers of x.

a	$x(x + 3)$	**b**	$x(5x + 3)$
c	$x(2x + 4)$	**d**	$x(3x - 2)$
e	$x(4x - 5)$	**f**	$x(2x - 7)$
g	$x(4 - 5x)$	**h**	$x(2 + x)$
i	$x(7 + 3x)$	**j**	$x(7 - 2x)$

4 Expand these brackets and collect like terms.

a $3(2x + 1) + 2(4x + 3)$

b $5(3x + 4) + 4(3x - 4)$

c $5(x + 4) + 6(2x - 3)$

d $4(x - 3) + 3(2x + 5)$

e $5(2x - 1) + 2(3x - 2)$

f $4(3x + 1) + 3(x - 4)$

g $8(2x + 3) - 5(x + 2)$

h $7(4 - 2x) + 3(4 - x)$

i $3(9x + 4) - 6(4x - 9)$

j $2(4 - 3x) - 4(6 - 4x)$

Problem solving

5 A metal casting weighing x kg is packed in a crate weighing 8 kg.
Four of these castings are loaded in their crates on a lorry.

a Use brackets to write an expression for the total mass of the load.

b Expand the brackets in your expression.

6 A biscuit tin weighs 150 grams. It contains 20 biscuits weighing y grams each. Mrs Hooper buys 3 tins.

a Use brackets to write an expression for the total mass of her purchase.

b Expand the brackets.

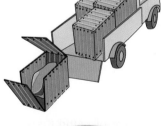

7 When you expand $2(6x + 12)$, you get an answer of $12x + 24$.
How many other ways can you use brackets so that you get the answer $12x + 24$ when you expand them?

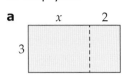

Claire drives a taxi cab. She calculates the fare £F depending on the length of the journey, M miles, using $F = 3 + 2M$.

A **formula** can often help you work out values in a real-life situation.

Claire can **substitute** a value for M to find the fare F.
A journey of 10 miles has $M = 10$.
$$F = 3 + 2M$$
$$= 3 + 2 \times 10$$
$$= 3 + 20$$
$$= 23$$
The fare is £23.

The amount of sleep that a child needs, H hours, depends on its age, A years, and is given by the formula $H = 16 - \frac{1}{2}A$.

Find the amount of sleep recommended for

a David, aged six

b his sister Jessica, aged twelve.

a When $A = 6$, $H = 16 - \frac{1}{2} \times 6$
$$= 16 - 3$$
$$= 13$$
David needs 13 hours sleep.

b When $A = 12$, $H = 16 - \frac{1}{2} \times 12$
$$= 16 - 6$$
$$= 10$$
Jessica needs 10 hours sleep.

The cost C pence of using Kieran's radio depends on how long he uses it with batteries, x hours, and how long he uses it with mains electricity, y hours.
If $C = 2(3x + y)$, find C when

a $x = 2$, $y = 8$ **b** $x = 10$, $y = 0$.

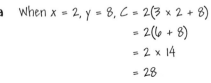

a When $x = 2$, $y = 8$, $C = 2(3 \times 2 + 8)$
$$= 2(6 + 8)$$
$$= 2 \times 14$$
$$= 28$$
It costs 28 pence.

b When $x = 10$, $y = 0$, $C = 2(3 \times 10 + 0)$
$$= 2(30 + 10)$$
$$= 2 \times 30$$
$$= 60$$
It costs 60 pence.

Exercise 3e

1 A plumber charges £C for a call that lasts *h* hours where $C = 20 + 30h$.
Find the value of C when
a $h = 1$ **b** $h = 2$ **c** $h = 5$

2 A car travelling at 20 mph begins to accelerate. Its speed *v* after *t* seconds is given by $v = 20 + 3t$.
Find the value of *v* when
a $t = 10$ **b** $t = 5$ **c** $t = 1$
d $t = 100$ **e** $t = 0$ **f** $t = 50$

3 The time *T* minutes for a cyclist to ride *U* km uphill and then *D* km downhill is given by $T = 12U + 2D$.

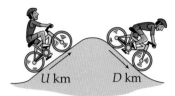

Find *T* when
a $U = 2, D = 5$ **b** $U = 6, D = 8$
c $U = 3, D = 12$ **d** $U = 5, D = 5$

Problem solving

4 The time taken, *t* minutes, for Sara to get to school depends on how far she walks, *w* km, and how far she goes by bus, *b* km.

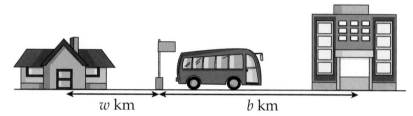

If $t = 5(2w + b)$, find the amount of time it takes for Sara to get to school when
a $w = 1, b = 8$ **b** $w = 2, b = 2$ **c** $w = 3, b = 4$

5 The cost £C of framing a picture depends on its length *L* cm and its height *H* cm, where
$C = \dfrac{3L + 2H}{10}$.
Find C when
a $L = 50, H = 20$ **b** $L = 30, H = 25$ **c** $L = 40, H = 30$

6 The number of small cakes, *n*, bought for a child's birthday party depends on the number of boys *B* and the number of girls *G* who are invited.
If $n = 2(3B + 2G)$, find *n* when
a $B = 4, G = 2$ **b** $B = 2, G = 3$ **c** $B = 5, G = 0$

7 The USA measures temperature in °F. Europe uses °C. You can change °F to °C using the formula $C = \dfrac{5}{9}(F - 32)$.
a Change 212 °F and 32 °F to °C. What is special about these two temperatures?
b What do these five surnames of famous scientists have in common?
Fahrenheit   Celsius   Kelvin   Réaumur   Rankine

3f Writing a formula

⟨ p.30

The perimeter of this quadrilateral is $P = (6 + 4 + 7 + x)$ cm

$$= (17 + x) \text{ cm}$$

You can use this **formula** for P if you know the value of x.

If $x = 6$, then $P = 17 + 6$

$$= 23.$$

The perimeter is 23 cm.

Draw your own shapes and create formulae for their perimeters.

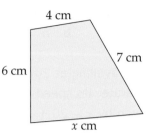

4 cm

7 cm

6 cm

x cm

Example

This isosceles triangle has two equal angles, x.

a Find a formula for the third angle, A.

b Find the value of A when $x = 50°$.

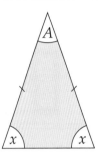

a The angles of a triangle add up to 180°.

So, $A = 180 - x - x$

$$= 180 - 2x$$

The formula is $A = 180 - 2x$.

b When $x = 50$, $A = 180 - 2 \times 50$

$$= 180 - 100 = 80$$

The third angle, A is 80°.

You can **write a formula** to describe a real life situation.

Example

A trailer weighs 50 kg. The trailer carries n crates, each weighing 20 kg.

a Write a formula for the total mass of the loaded trailer.

b Find the total load if there are 10 crates.

n crates

a The mass of all the crates is $20 \times n$. A formula for the total load is $L = 20n + 50$, where L is the mass of the load in kg.

b If $n = 10$, $L = 20 \times 10 + 50$

$$= 200 + 50$$

$$= 250.$$

So, with 10 crates, the total load is 250 kg.

You should always write down what any letter you use stands for.

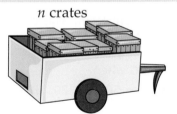

Algebra Expressions and formulae

Exercise 3f

1 a Find a formula for the perimeter *P* of each of these shapes. The sides are all measured in cm.

i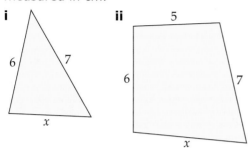

ii

iii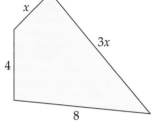

b Find the value of each perimeter *P* if *x* = 4.

2 The angles *x* and *y* make a straight angle of 180°.

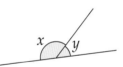

a Write a formula for *y* in terms of *x*.
b If *x* = 60°, find the value of *y*.

3 This isosceles triangle has sides *x* cm and (*x* + 5) cm long. Find a formula for its perimeter *P*. Find the value of *P* when *x* = 6.

4 This shape is made from two rectangles.

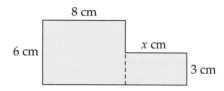

a Write the area of each rectangle in cm².
b Write a formula for the total area *A* of the whole shape.
c Find the value of *A* when *x* = 5.

5 This rectangle has sides *n* cm and (*n* + 2) cm long. Find a formula for
a its perimeter, *P*
b its area, *A*.
c Use the **formulae** to find *P* and *A* when *n* = 5.
d Find *n* when *P* = 20.

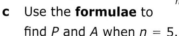

6 Repeat question **5** for a rectangle with sides of length 2*x* − 1 and 3*x* + 6.

Problem solving

7 A school trip to the zoo uses four full coaches, each carrying *p* children. Another six children meet the coaches at the zoo.
a Write a formula for the total number of children *C* that visit the zoo.
b How many children visit the zoo
 i if *p* = 30   **ii** if *p* = 35?

8 A rectangular sheet has a square hole cut in it.
a Find a formula for the shaded area *A* that is left.
b If *x* = 6, find the value of *A*.

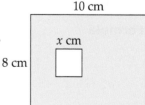

3 MySummary

Check out

You should now be able to ...

Test it ➡

		Questions
✓ Simplify algebraic expressions.	5	1
✓ Substitute into simple algebraic expressions.	5	2
✓ Use indices to simplify expressions and simplify by collecting like terms.	5	3, 4
✓ Expand brackets.	5	5, 6
✓ Substitute into formulae.	5	7, 8
✓ Construct a formula for different situations.	5	9, 10

Language	Meaning	Example
Expression	A series of letters and numbers in algebra	$2a$, $4a - 3b$ and $2x^2$ are all expressions
Substitute	To replace a letter in an algebraic expression with a number	Substituting $x = 2$ into $3x - 1$ gives $3 \times 2 - 1 = 5$
Index	Another name for a **power** such as 'squared' or 'to the power of 5' (plural: indices)	5 is the index in x^5
Like terms	Algebraic terms which have the same combination of letters in them	$3a$ and $4a$ are like terms but $5b$ and $2c$ are not
Simplify	Collect like terms in an algebraic expression	$2a + 6a = 8a$
Expand	To multiply out a bracket in algebra	$2(3a + 1) = 6a + 2$
Formula	An algebraic statement that connects things (plural: formulae)	$d = s \times t$, distance = speed $\times$ time

1 Simplify these expressions.

   a $b \times 5$ **b** $t + t + t$

   c $k \div 2$ **d** $2f + f$

2 If $s = 8$, evaluate these expressions.

   a $s + 4$ **b** $4 - s$

   c $s \div 2$ **d** $5s$

3 Use indices to simplify these expressions.

   a $3^5 \times 3^4$ **b** 5×5^6

4 Simplify these expressions.

   a $3n + 4m - n + 2m$

   b $6g - 8h + 5h - 8g$

   c $3y + 4y^2 + 5y + y^2$

5 Expand these brackets.

   a $9(p + q)$ **b** $3(2v - 4)$

   c $x(x + 1)$ **d** $x(3x - 4)$

6 Expand the brackets and collect like terms in these expressions.

   a $3(u + 4) + 2(2u - 1)$

   b $8(3v - 5) - 7(4v + 3)$

7 A number of tables, T, are arranged in such a way that the number of chairs required is given by C where

   $C = 4T + 2$.

   Calculate the number of chairs needed when there are five tables.

8 The number of sandwiches, s, needed for a primary school picnic is calculated using this formula:

   $s = 3a + 2c$

   where a = the number of adult

     and c = the number of children.

   How many sandwiches are needed if there are five adults and 30 children?

9 Find a formula for the perimeter, P, of each shape.

   Simplify your answers.

   a

   b 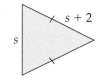   **c**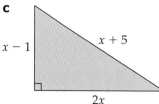

10 A taxi costs £2.50 to hire plus 50p per mile for the journey. If your journey is x miles long

   a write a formula for the cost of the journey

   b find the cost of a 7 mile journey.

What next?

Score		
	0 – 3	Your knowledge of this topic is still developing. To improve look at Formative test: 2B–3; MyMaths: 1158, 1179, 1187 and 1247
	4 – 7	You are gaining a secure knowledge of this topic. To improve look at InvisiPen: 211, 212, 214, 221, 252 and 254
	8 – 10	You have mastered this topic. Well done, you are ready to progress!

1 Write these expressions in a simpler way.

   a $x + x + x$ **b** $y + y + y + y$ **c** $2 \times 3 \times z$

2 There are x biscuits in a packet. You buy five packets.

   a How many biscuits do you buy?

   b You open one of the packets and eat six biscuits. How many biscuits do you now have altogether?

   c If $x = 10$, how many biscuits are you left with?

3 If $p = 12$ and $q = 4$, find the values of

   a $p + 2q$ **b** $2p - q$ **c** $\dfrac{p}{q}$ **d** $\dfrac{5q + 4}{p}$

4 Find the values of

   a $3 \times 3 \times 3$ **b** 2^4 **c** 10^2 **d** $5^2 \times 10^3$

5 Simplify each of these, using indices in your answers.

   a $a \times a \times a \times b \times b \times c \times c \times c$ **b** $3^4 \times 3^2$ **c** $6^5 \times 6^3$

6 What values of n makes these statements true?

   a $2^n = 16$ **b** $5^3 \times 5^n = 5^7$ **c** $3^6 \times 3^n \times 3^2 = 3^{10}$

7 A necklace is made from two kinds of beads of length x cm and y cm.

Write the total length of this necklace as simply as you can.

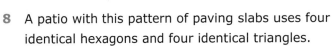

$3x + 2y + 2x + 3y = \square$

8 A patio with this pattern of paving slabs uses four identical hexagons and four identical triangles.

Write an expression for the perimeter of the shape in terms of x and y.

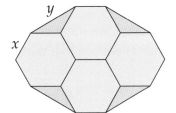

9 Simplify these expressions by collecting like terms.

   a $3p + 2p + 5q - 2q$ **b** $4m + 2n + m - 3n$

   c $3x^2 + 4x + 6x^2 - 5x$ **d** $z^2 + 5z + z^2 - 2z - 2z^2 - 3z$

10 a Find the total area of rectangles A and B together.

   b Expand this bracket. $5(x + 2)$

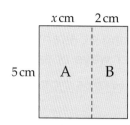

11 a Expand these brackets. **i** $4(x + 3)$ **ii** $3(5x + 4)$

   b Expand these brackets and simplify your answers by collecting like terms.

    i $2(y + 3) + 4(5y + 2)$ **ii** $3(2z + 4) + 2(z - 5)$

12 a A box weighing 20 grams contains 10 screws weighing x grams each. Write an expression for the total weight of the box and its contents.

   b Mr Sturman buys five of these boxes. Write an expression (using brackets) for the total weight of these five boxes and their contents.

   c Expand this bracket.

13 The time T hours to cook a turkey weighing W pounds is given by $T = \dfrac{W}{3} + 1$. Find T when

   a $W = 12$ **b** $W = 18$ **c** $W = 20$

14 The charge £C for excess baggage when you fly depends on the weight W kg of your luggage where $C = 5(W - 20)$.

   Find C when

   a $W = 32$ **b** $W = 65$ **c** $W = 20$

15 If $p = 4$, $q = 2$ and $r = 5$, find the values of

   a $2p + q$ **b** $4r - 5p$ **c** $3(p + 2q - r)$

16 This trapezium has two sides of 8 cm and 5 cm and two equal unknown sides.

   a Write a formula for its perimeter P.

   b Find the value of P when $x = 4$ cm.

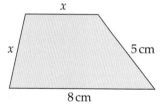

17 A triangle has three angles x, y and A.

   a Write a formula for angle A in terms of x and y.

   b Find the value of A when $x = 60°$ and $y = 45°$.

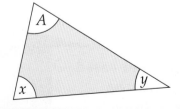

With headlines like these, many people are looking at alternative forms of energy and other ways of saving energy in their homes.

ELECTRICITY PRICE SHOCK!

Oil cost hits new high

Gas price explodes

Solar power

Save up to 70% on your yearly hot water bill. Save money on your electricity bill forever. Cut your CO_2 emissions. Use an everlasting FREE source of energy!

Loft insulation
Cost £350
Save £200 per year

Task 1

a Look at all the green labels. Work out how long it would take for the savings to repay the cost of installing the item.

b i Which things do you think are most cost effective?

   ii Which are not so cost effective?

c Would the length of time you are going to live in the same house alter your decisions?

Lagging hot water tank
Cost £20
Save £50 per year

Efficient A rated boiler
Cost £2000
Save £150 per year

New heating controls
Cost £150
Save £50 per year

Ground based heat pump
Cost £12000
Save £800 per year

Double glazing
Cost £3500
Save £100 per year

Solar water heating
Cost £5000
Save £100 per year

Small wind generator
Cost £5000
Save £250 per year

Solar panels
Cost £6000 per panel
Save £120 per panel per year

Cavity wall insulation
Cost £350
Save £200 per year

Energy efficient light bulbs

Draught proofing
Cost £120
Save £50 per year

Task 2

An average house in the UK uses around 3300 kWh of electricity in a year.

A typical solar panel will generate 825 kWh per year. The costs and saving are shown below

a How many solar panels would a house need to meet all of its electricity demands?

b What would be the total cost of fitting these solar panels?

c How long would it take to make a saving on having solar panels fitted?

Task 3

A **standard** light bulb can last up to 1000 hours switched on.

A typical **energy efficient** bulb can last up to 15000 hours.

a Think about a light bulb in your house.

   i How many hours would it be switched on per day on average?

   ii Estimate how many hours it would be switched on per year.

b How long would this bulb last **i** if it is energy-efficient **ii** if it is standard?

c In reality, an energy-efficient bulb might typically last for only 40% of this time.

Using your answer to **b**, estimate how long in years a typical energy-efficient bulb might last.

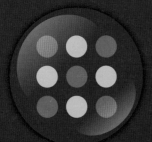

4 Fractions, decimals and percentages

Introduction

You use fractions in your everyday life. Although you might not actually use the word fraction in your sentences, the coins you use to buy things are all fractions of a pound, the measurements you use for distance are fractions of a metre, and when you are telling the time you do actually say the fractions out loud!

What's the point?

Using fractions allows you to describe amounts that are not a whole number.

Objectives

By the end of this chapter, you will have learned how to …
- Understand, compare and order decimals.
- Convert between decimals, fractions and percentages.
- Order fractions.
- Add and subtract fractions.
- Find a fraction of a quantity.
- Express one number as a fraction of another.
- Calculate percentages of amounts.
- Express one number as a percentage of another.

Check in

1 Write these numbers as decimals.

   a 3 tenths   **b** 7 units and 4 tenths   **c** 5 hundredths

2 Write these numbers in order starting with the smallest.

   0.4   0.39   0.3   0.23   0.35

3 Calculate these percentages using a mental method.

   a 50% of £60   **b** 10% of 35 kg   **c** 1% of 1800 m

Starter problem

Andy buys a new car for £12 000.

He borrows the money from a bank.

The bank charges a fee of 15% per year in interest.

Andy pays back £1200 per year.

Investigate what happens.

You can write tenths, hundredths and thousandths using **decimals**.

11 seconds and 45 hundredths of a second.
= 11 seconds + 4 tenths + 5 hundredths
= 11.45 seconds

To compare decimals, digits in the same position must be compared, beginning with the first non-zero digit.

Example

Which of these numbers is the smallest: 0.047 or 0.0462?

Re-write the numbers vertically, making sure that the decimal points are lined up.

0.047	has a thousandths digit of 7
0.0462	has a thousandths digit of 6
0.0462 < 0.047	

The hundredths digits are the same, so compare the thousandths.

< means that 0.0462 is smaller than 0.047.

You can use inequality signs to sort data involving decimal numbers.

Example

Didier records the time it takes ten students to run 100 m.

13.7	16.4	19.8	17.5	21.3
13.9	14.14	18.6	19.3	20.0

Put this data into a frequency table.

Time t (seconds)	Frequency
$12 \leq t < 14$	2
$14 \leq t < 16$	1
$16 \leq t < 18$	2
$18 \leq t < 20$	3
$20 \leq t < 22$	2

$18 \leq t < 20$ means greater than or equal to 18 seconds but less than 20 seconds.
The time 20.0 goes into the next group, $20 \leq t < 22$.

p.138 >

Exercise 4a

1 Write the value of the digit 7 in each of these numbers.

Write your answer in words, in figures and as a fraction where appropriate.

a 3730 **b** 17140

c 108 373 **d** 765 283

e 1703 018 **f** 37.2

g 28.74 **h** 62.057

2 Place $<$ or $>$ between each pair of numbers to show which number is the larger.

a 0.37 ☐ 0.4 **b** 1.52 ☐ 1.51

c 5.284 ☐ 5.293 **d** 3.35 ☐ 3.3

e 4.37 ☐ 4.35 **f** 1.654 ☐ 1.66

3 Write these numbers in order starting with the smallest.

a 3.4 3.39 3.3 3.23 3

b 3.74 3.757 3.72 3.88 3.8

c 0.033 0.035 0.03 0.0362 0.0351

4 Copy these and place $<$ or $>$ between each pair of numbers to show which number is the larger.

a 3.2 m ☐ 325 cm **b** 25 mm ☐ 2.4 cm

c 1.95 kg ☐ 1960 g **d** 4.5 m ☐ 46 cm

> Remember to change the measurements to the same units first.

Problem solving

5 Haroon records the heights in metres of twenty students in his class.

1.34   1.56   1.75   1.65   1.39

1.5   1.67   1.55   1.4   1.31

1.45   1.62   1.71   1.58   1.52

1.47   1.61   1.6   1.45   1.7

Copy and complete his frequency table.

Which numbers are the most difficult to place in Haroon's table? Explain your answer.

Height h (metres)	Frequency
$1.3 \leq h < 1.4$	
$1.4 \leq h < 1.5$	
$1.5 \leq h < 1.6$	
$1.6 \leq h < 1.7$	
$1.7 \leq h < 1.8$	

6 a Collect some data you can measure on the students in your class.

For example, the heights of each student in metres; the distance they live from school in km.

b Put your data into a frequency table using inequalities for each group.

7 Identify the value of the letter by its description.

a $5.7 < x < 5.9$

x has 1 decimal place.

b y is halfway between 0.2 and 0.7.

8 The value of x satisfies these conditions

$4 < x \leq 7$ and $5 \leq x < 8$

What are the possible values of x?

The number 0.357 stands for 3 tenths, 5 hundredths and 7 thousandths. You can use this idea to convert **terminating** decimals into fractions.

A terminating decimal has a fixed number of decimal places.

$$0.357 = \frac{3}{10} + \frac{5}{100} + \frac{7}{1000}$$
$$= \frac{300}{1000} + \frac{50}{1000} + \frac{7}{1000}$$
$$= \frac{357}{1000}$$

Example

Convert these decimals into fractions.

a 0.8   **b** 0.64   **c** 0.217

a $0.8 = \frac{8}{10}$

$\frac{8}{10} \overset{\div 2}{\underset{\div 2}{=}} \frac{4}{5}$

$0.8 = \frac{4}{5}$

b $0.64 = \frac{64}{100}$

$\frac{64}{100} \overset{\div 4}{\underset{\div 4}{=}} \frac{16}{25}$

$0.64 = \frac{16}{25}$

c $0.217 = \frac{217}{1000}$

$\frac{217}{1000}$ cannot be simplified

$0.217 = \frac{217}{1000}$

- You can order fractions by converting them to decimals.
- You convert a fraction into a decimal by dividing the **numerator** by the **denominator**.

Example

Put these fractions in order from lowest to highest: $\frac{2}{5}$ $\frac{3}{8}$ $\frac{1}{3}$

$\frac{2}{5} = 2 \div 5 = 0.4$ $\frac{3}{8} = 3 \div 8 = 0.375$ $\frac{1}{3} = 1 \div 3 = 0.333...$

Putting the decimals in order   0.333...   0.375   0.4

      ↓   ↓   ↓

Putting the fractions in order $\frac{1}{3}$ $\frac{3}{8}$ $\frac{2}{5}$

The decimal 0.333... is called a **recurring** decimal. It can be written $0.\dot{3}$

Exercise 4b

1 Which of these are terminating decimals?

    a 0.325   **b** 0.666...

    c 0.1212...   **d** 0.4785

    e 0.999

2 Write these decimals as fractions in their simplest form.

    a 0.3   **b** 0.6   **c** 0.75

    d 0.28   **e** 0.66   **f** 0.05

    g 0.375   **h** 0.185   **i** 0.095

    j 0.008

3 Write these fractions as decimals without using a calculator.

    a $\frac{1}{10}$ **b** $\frac{13}{20}$ **c** $\frac{7}{25}$ **d** $\frac{33}{50}$

    e $\frac{15}{25}$ **f** $\frac{3}{5}$ **g** $\frac{19}{20}$ **h** $\frac{3}{4}$

    i $\frac{7}{10}$ **j** $\frac{11}{50}$

4 Copy these and place $<$ or $>$ between each pair of numbers to show which number is the larger.

    a 0.3 $\square$ 0.28   **b** $\frac{7}{8}$ $\square$ $\frac{4}{5}$

4 **c** $\frac{5}{8}$ $\square$ $\frac{7}{16}$ **d** 0.37 $\square$ $\frac{5}{16}$

    e $\frac{3}{5}$ $\square$ $\frac{5}{7}$ **f** 0.54 $\square$ $\frac{6}{11}$

    g $\frac{4}{9}$ $\square$ $\frac{3}{7}$ **h** 0.114 $\square$ $\frac{1}{9}$

5 Put these fractions in order from lowest to highest.

    a $\frac{3}{7}$ $\frac{4}{5}$ $\frac{7}{8}$ $\frac{3}{4}$

    b $\frac{1}{3}$ $\frac{2}{9}$ $\frac{3}{13}$ $\frac{4}{19}$

    c $\frac{2}{5}$ $\frac{4}{9}$ $\frac{7}{16}$ $\frac{9}{20}$

6 Write these decimals as fractions in their simplest form.

    a 1.5   **b** 2.75

    c 3.4   **d** 1.35

    e 1.475   **f** 2.525

7 Write these fractions as decimals using an appropriate method.

    a $1\frac{7}{10}$ **b** $1\frac{3}{4}$ **c** $1\frac{7}{20}$

    d $2\frac{5}{16}$ **e** $3\frac{11}{25}$ **f** $4\frac{13}{40}$

Problem solving

8 Calvin thinks that only fractions with a denominator of 2, 4, 5, 10 and 20 will change into terminating decimals. See if he is correct by converting every **unit fraction** from $\frac{1}{2}$ up to $\frac{1}{25}$ into a decimal using your calculator. Try to explain your findings.

A **unit fraction** has a numerator of 1.

Did you know?

The ancient Egyptians preferred to use unit fractions. For our $\frac{2}{5}$ they used $\frac{1}{3} + \frac{1}{15}$ which they wrote as 3 and 15 with a `mouth´ symbol above them.

● You can add and subtract fractions that have the same denominator.

Francis eats $\frac{1}{5}$ of a pizza, and Georgia eats $\frac{3}{5}$ of the pizza. What fraction of the pizza has been eaten?

Francis and Georgia eat $\quad \frac{1}{5} + \frac{3}{5} = \frac{1+3}{5} = \frac{4}{5}$

They eat $\frac{4}{5}$ of the pizza.

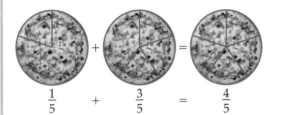

$\frac{1}{5} \quad + \quad \frac{3}{5} \quad = \quad \frac{4}{5}$

When the **denominators** are the same you can just add the **numerators**.

● You can add or subtract fractions with different denominators by first writing them as **equivalent fractions** with the same denominator.

Example

Calculate

a $\frac{2}{3} + \frac{1}{4}$

b $\frac{3}{5} - \frac{5}{10}$

Re-write as equivalent fractions with the same denominator.

a
$$\frac{2}{3} \overset{\times 4}{=} \frac{8}{12} \quad \frac{1}{4} \overset{\times 3}{=} \frac{3}{12}$$
(×4, ×3)

b
$$\frac{3}{5} \overset{\times 2}{=} \frac{6}{10}$$
(×2)

‹ p.11

The common denominator is 12. This is the **lowest common multiple** of 3 and 4.

The common denominator is 10. This is the **lowest common multiple** of 5 and 10.

Add the numerators.

$$\frac{8}{12} + \frac{3}{12} = \frac{8+3}{12}$$
$$= \frac{11}{12}$$

Subtract the numerators.

$$\frac{6}{10} - \frac{5}{10} = \frac{6-5}{10}$$
$$= \frac{1}{10}$$

Exercise 4c

1 Find the missing number in each of these pairs of equivalent fractions.

a $\dfrac{1}{4} = \dfrac{\square}{12}$ **b** $\dfrac{2}{5} = \dfrac{\square}{25}$

c $\dfrac{3}{7} = \dfrac{\square}{28}$ **d** $\dfrac{4}{9} = \dfrac{\square}{63}$

e $\dfrac{5}{8} = \dfrac{45}{\square}$ **f** $\dfrac{6}{11} = \dfrac{\square}{88}$

g $\dfrac{7}{12} = \dfrac{\square}{36}$ **h** $\dfrac{8}{15} = \dfrac{\square}{150}$

2 Calculate each of these, giving your answer as a fraction in its simplest form.

a $\dfrac{2}{7} + \dfrac{3}{7}$ **b** $\dfrac{1}{8} + \dfrac{5}{8}$ **c** $\dfrac{4}{5} - \dfrac{1}{5}$

d $\dfrac{7}{8} - \dfrac{5}{8}$ **e** $\dfrac{3}{11} + \dfrac{5}{11}$ **f** $\dfrac{9}{13} - \dfrac{6}{13}$

g $\dfrac{5}{3} - \dfrac{1}{3}$ **h** $\dfrac{8}{5} - \dfrac{4}{5}$ **i** $\dfrac{1}{6} + \dfrac{5}{6}$

j $\dfrac{7}{9} - \dfrac{1}{9}$ **k** $\dfrac{11}{15} - \dfrac{2}{15}$ **l** $\dfrac{3}{16} + \dfrac{5}{16}$

m $\dfrac{8}{21} + \dfrac{6}{21}$ **n** $\dfrac{21}{40} - \dfrac{13}{40}$ **o** $\dfrac{29}{49} - \dfrac{8}{49}$

p $\dfrac{2}{51} + \dfrac{1}{51}$

3 Copy the grids and use them to show how to add each of these pairs of fractions.

a $\dfrac{1}{2} + \dfrac{1}{5}$

b $\dfrac{2}{3} + \dfrac{1}{4}$

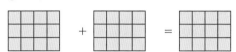

c $\dfrac{2}{5} + \dfrac{1}{3}$

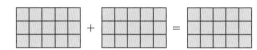

4 Calculate each of these additions and subtractions, giving your answer as a fraction in its simplest form.

a $\dfrac{1}{3} + \dfrac{1}{4}$ **b** $\dfrac{2}{3} + \dfrac{1}{5}$ **c** $\dfrac{1}{6} + \dfrac{1}{5}$

d $\dfrac{2}{5} + \dfrac{1}{3}$ **e** $\dfrac{5}{8} + \dfrac{1}{3}$ **f** $\dfrac{3}{10} + \dfrac{1}{3}$

g $\dfrac{8}{9} - \dfrac{3}{5}$ **h** $\dfrac{9}{11} - \dfrac{2}{3}$

Problem solving

5 Kyle owns lots of computer games. Exactly $\dfrac{2}{5}$ of his games are sports games and $\dfrac{1}{4}$ of his games are action games. The rest of his games are adventure games. What fraction of Kyle's computer games are adventure games?

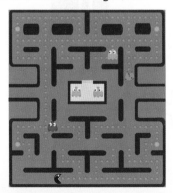

6 Jameela and Ursula are working out $\dfrac{2}{9} + \dfrac{4}{7}$

a Explain what Ursula has done wrong.

b Explain how Jameela knows the answer is more than a half.

c Work out the correct answer.

Ursula says   Jameela says

The answer is $\dfrac{6}{16}$.

The answer must be more than a half.

4d Fraction of a quantity

You can often find a fraction of an amount by using a mental or a written method.

To calculate $\frac{2}{5}$ of £80
first find $\frac{1}{5}$ of £80.

$\frac{1}{5}$ of £80 = 80 ÷ 5
= £16

Now double it:

$\frac{2}{5}$ of £80 = 2 × £16
= £32

Find **a** $\frac{3}{4}$ of 60 kg   **b** $\frac{3}{8}$ of 10 miles

a $\frac{3}{4}$ of 60 = $\frac{1}{4}$ × 3 × 60

$= \frac{1 \times 180}{4}$

$= \frac{180}{4}$

= 45 kg

b $\frac{3}{8}$ of 10 = $\frac{1}{8}$ × 3 × 10

$= \frac{1 \times 30}{8}$

$= \frac{30}{8}$

$= 3\frac{6}{8} = 3\frac{3}{4}$ miles

You can write one number as a fraction of another number.

Pritti and Gina share £80 between them. Pritti receives £32 and Gina gets the rest.
a What fraction of the money does Pritti have?
b What fraction of the money does Gina get?

a There is £80 altogether.
Pritti receives £32 of the money.

$$\text{Fraction} = \overset{\div 16}{\underset{\div 16}{\frac{32}{80}}} = \frac{2}{5}$$

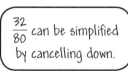

$\frac{32}{80}$ can be simplified by cancelling down.

Pritti has $\frac{2}{5}$ of the money.

b Gina gets 80 − 32 = £48

$$\overset{\div 16}{\underset{\div 16}{\frac{48}{80}}} = \frac{3}{5}$$

$\frac{3}{5}$ is the same as $1 - \frac{2}{5}$

Gina gets $\frac{3}{5}$ of the money.

Number Fractions, decimals and percentages

Exercise 4d

1 Use a mental method to calculate

  a $\frac{1}{3}$ of £15   **b** $\frac{1}{10}$ of 50 MB

  c $\frac{1}{8}$ of 32 DVDs   **d** $\frac{1}{6}$ of 30 pupils

  e $\frac{4}{5}$ of 25 shops   **f** $\frac{2}{3}$ of 120 g

2 Calculate each of these, leaving your answer in its simplest form and as a mixed number where appropriate.

  a $4 \times \frac{1}{9}$ **b** $6 \times \frac{1}{12}$

  c $12 \times \frac{1}{18}$ **d** $2 \times \frac{2}{3}$

  e $2 \times \frac{7}{8}$ **f** $\frac{5}{6} \times 4$

3 Calculate these, leaving your answer as a mixed number where appropriate.

  a $\frac{3}{4}$ of 7 feet   **b** $\frac{2}{3}$ of 14 million

  c $\frac{5}{8}$ of 30 km   **d** $\frac{3}{10}$ of 400 kg

  e $\frac{5}{7}$ of 25 m   **f** $\frac{7}{25}$ of 40 mm

4 Use an appropriate method to calculate these amounts. Where possible give your answer to 2 decimal places.

  a $\frac{3}{5}$ of 148 kg   **b** $\frac{5}{12}$ of £295

  c $\frac{3}{11}$ of 25 km   **d** $\frac{4}{7}$ of 5 kg

  e $\frac{4}{9}$ of 200 litres   **f** $\frac{3}{20}$ of 360°

Did you know?

The average family in the UK spends between $\frac{1}{6}$ and $\frac{1}{10}$ of their income on food. In Sierra Leone the fraction is around $\frac{2}{3}$.

Problem solving

5 **a** A DVD costs £12.95. In a sale all prices are reduced by $\frac{3}{10}$. What is the sale price of the DVD?

  b Isaac earns £28 a week from his paper round. He spends £10 and saves the rest. What fraction of his money does he save?

6 **a** What fraction of 30 is 12?

  b What fraction of 1 hour is 55 minutes?

  c What fraction of 1 foot is 8 inches?

  d What fraction of July is 1 week?

7 Ian spends $\frac{1}{3}$ of his life sleeping and $\frac{1}{4}$ of it at work. He lives to be 84.

  a How many years does Ian spend

    i in bed   **ii** at work?

  b How many years does Ian spend not in bed or at work?

  c What fraction of his life is this?

8 An oak tree is 60 feet tall. Each year the tree increases in height by $\frac{1}{10}$.

  a What is the height of the tree after one year?

  b What is the height of the tree after two years?

  c In how many years will the tree be over 100 feet tall?

60 feet

You can calculate **percentages** by using an equivalent fraction or decimal.

Example

Calculate   **a**   65% of 80 kg   **b**   35% of £180

a 50% of $80\,kg = \frac{1}{2}$ of 80
          $= 40$

   10% of $80\,kg = \frac{1}{10}$ of 80
          $= 8$

   5% of $80\,kg = \frac{1}{2}$ of 8
          $= 4$

   ....

   65% of $80\,kg = 40 + 8 + 4$
          $= 52\,kg$

b 25% of $180 = \frac{1}{4}$ of 180
          $= 45$

   10% of $180 = \frac{1}{10}$ of 180
          $= 18$

   ....

   35% of £180 $= 45 + 18$
          $= £63$

With harder percentages, you might want to use a written method or a calculator.

Example

p.277 >

Calculate 12% of £68.

Using an equivalent fraction:

12% of $68 = \frac{12}{100}$ of 68
$= \frac{12 \times 68}{100}$
$= \frac{816}{100}$
$= £8.16$

Using an equivalent decimal:

12% of $68 = \frac{12}{100}$ of 68
$= 12 \div 100 \times 68$
$= 0.12 \times 68$
$= £8.16$

You could use a calculator to work out 0.12×68.

Exercise 4e

1 Calculate these percentages using a mental method.

   a 50% of £70   **b** 10% of 45 kg

   c 1% of 1500 m   **d** 25% of 256 MB

   e 10% of £100   **f** 100% of 10 cm

   g 50% of 84 kg   **h** 25% of 76 m

2 Calculate these percentages using a mental method.

   a 20% of £40   **b** 5% of 60 DVDs

   c 2% of 150 MB   **d** 40% of £75

   e 60% of £700   **f** 15% of 180°

   g 11% of £5500   **h** 30% of 250 N

   i 8% of 240 ml   **j** 35% of £20 000

   k 65% of 440 yards   **l** 95% of 400 kJ

3 Calculate these using a mental, written or calculator method, giving your answers to 2 decimal places where appropriate.

   a 18% of £40   **b** 7% of 71 kg

   c 11% of 58 km   **d** 16% of 85 euros

   e 3% of 75 mm   **f** 24% of 55 kB

   g 29% of 18 litres   **h** 35% of 92 mph

   i 46% of 46 m   **j** 49% of 90 MB

   k 63% of 15 cm   **l** 77% of 90°

4 Calculate these using a calculator. Show all the steps of your working out, and give your answer to 2 decimal places where appropriate.

   a 12% of £148   **b** 35% of 96 kg

   c 52% of 512 MB   **d** 86% of 355 km

   e 4% of 185 mm   **f** 55% of 420 ml

   g 2.5% of £800   **h** 47% of 925 g

   i 12.5% of 48 N   **j** 41% of £8000

   k 73% of 840 kJ   **l** 110% of 5 million

Problem solving

5 **a** Naheeda scores 45% in her English exam. The maximum score on the exam is 120. How many marks did Naheeda score on the exam?

   b Gavin starts to download an 8 GB file from the internet. He downloads 65% of the file in 10 minutes. How much of the file has he downloaded?

   c The label on the back of a 150 g packet of crisps says that the crisps are 6% fat. How much fat is that in grams?

   d Fiona has a box containing 36 chocolates. She eats 25% of the chocolates. How many does she have left?

6 **a** Sheena eats 240 g of baked beans. The beans contain

Sugar	5%
Fat	0.2%
Protein	4.9%
Carbohydrates	13%

Calculate how much sugar, fat, protein and carbohydrate Sheena has eaten.

   b What weight of the product is **not** sugar, fat, protein or carbohydrates?

You can convert between **fractions**, **decimals** and **percentages**.

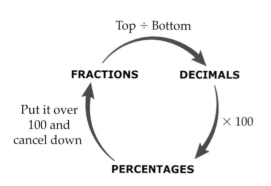

Top ÷ Bottom

FRACTIONS → **DECIMALS**

Put it over 100 and cancel down

× 100

PERCENTAGES

Use place value and cancel down

FRACTIONS ← **DECIMALS**

Write as a decimal and × 100

÷ 100

PERCENTAGES

Example

Convert 0.64 into **a** a fraction **b** a percentage.

a

$$0.64 = \frac{64}{100} \overset{\div 4}{\underset{\div 4}{=}} \frac{16}{25}$$

b $0.64 = \frac{64}{100} = 64\%$

Example

Convert 45% into **a** a decimal **b** a fraction

a $45\% = 0.45$

b

$$45\% = \frac{45}{100} \overset{\div 5}{\underset{\div 5}{=}} \frac{9}{20}$$

Example

Kira weighs 52 kg. Jack weighs 80 kg.
What percentage of Jack's weight is Kira?

Jack weighs 80 kg.
Kira weighs 52 kg.

$$\text{Fraction} = \frac{52}{80} = 52 \div 80$$
$$= 0.65$$
$$= 65\%$$

Kira is 65% of Jack's weight.

This fraction can be changed into a decimal using a calculator.

Exercise 4f

1 This number line is split into twentieths.

   a Match each of the fractions, decimals and percentages to the letters on the number line.

   b Write each letter with its percentage, fraction and decimal equivalent.

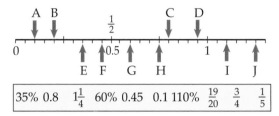

35% 0.8 $1\frac{1}{4}$ 60% 0.45 0.1 110% $\frac{19}{20}$ $\frac{3}{4}$ $\frac{1}{5}$

2 Write these percentages as fractions in their simplest form.

   a 40%   **b** 75%   **c** 85%

   d 45%   **e** 32%   **f** 5%

   g 1%   **h** 125%   **i** 105%

   j 2.5%   **k** 15%   **l** 140%

3 Write these percentages as decimals.

   a 80%   **b** 25%   **c** 8%

   d 35%   **e** 99%   **f** 130%

   g 23.5% **h** 7.2%   **i** 4.75%

   j 145%   **k** 150%   **l** 175%

4 Write these fractions as percentages without using a calculator.

   a $\frac{3}{10}$ **b** $\frac{29}{50}$ **c** $\frac{14}{25}$ **d** $\frac{7}{4}$

   e $\frac{13}{40}$ **f** $1\frac{3}{5}$ **g** $1\frac{11}{25}$ **h** $\frac{23}{20}$

   i $\frac{47}{40}$ **j** $2\frac{3}{8}$ **k** $3\frac{1}{5}$ **l** $6\frac{4}{5}$

5 Write these fractions as percentages. Give your answers to 1 decimal place where appropriate.

   a $\frac{9}{16}$ **b** $\frac{27}{40}$ **c** $\frac{17}{25}$

   d $\frac{5}{4}$ **e** $\frac{13}{25}$ **f** $\frac{7}{8}$

   g $\frac{7}{9}$ **h** $\frac{27}{20}$ **i** $\frac{5}{6}$

   j $\frac{2}{3}$ **k** $\frac{1}{9}$ **l** $\frac{8}{9}$

6 Write these decimals as percentages.

   a 0.58   **b** 0.08   **c** 0.8

   d 1.08   **e** 1.8   **f** 0.035

   g 0.415   **h** 1.05   **i** 1.555…

   j 0.999   **k** 1.26   **l** 3.02

Problem solving

7 **a** Avril scored 48 out of 80 in her maths test. What percentage of the test did she answer correctly?

   b In Ken's class there are 12 boys and 18 girls. What percentage of the class are girls?

8 These are the marks scored by Boris in his recent exams.

   a In which subject did he do the best? Explain your answer.

   b In which subject did he do the worst? Explain your answer.

   c Put the subjects in order from Boris' worst subject to his best.

REPORT CARD

English	14/20
Maths	72%
Science	31/40
French	11/15
History	24/35
Geography	31/45
RE	69%

Check out

You should now be able to ...

Test it ➡

Questions

✓ Understand, compare and order decimals.	4	1, 11–13
✓ Convert between decimals, fractions and percentages.	5	2, 3
✓ Order fractions.	5	4
✓ Add and subtract fractions.	6	5
✓ Find a fraction of a quantity.	6	6, 7
✓ Express one number as a fraction of another.	5	8
✓ Calculate percentages of amounts.	5	9, 10
✓ Express one number as a percentage of another.	5	14

Language	Meaning	Example
Decimal	A number which has digits after the decimal point, representing tenths, hundredths, thousandths, etc	$1.27 = 1 + \frac{2}{10} + \frac{7}{100}$ is a decimal
Terminating decimal	A decimal which has a fixed number of decimal places	$0.125 = \frac{1}{8}$ has three decimal places
Recurring decimal	A decimal which goes on for ever and has a repeating pattern	$0.333... = \frac{1}{3}$ has the number 3 repeating forever
Fraction	A fraction is written as the *ratio* of the numerator and the denominator	$\frac{3}{4}$ is a fraction with numerator 3 and denominator 4
Equivalent fractions	Fractions which have the same value	$\frac{1}{3}, \frac{2}{6}, \frac{3}{9}$ and $\frac{10}{30}$ are all equivalent fractions
Percentages	A number which means 'out of 100'	85% means $\frac{85}{100}$

1 Write these decimals in order starting with the smallest.
   a 2.5   2.57   2.45   2.56
   b 0.07   0.077   0.008   0.0078

2 Write these fractions as decimals without using a calculator.
   a $\dfrac{3}{10}$ **b** $\dfrac{4}{5}$ **c** $\dfrac{3}{20}$ **d** $\dfrac{7}{25}$

3 Write these decimals as fractions in their simplest form.
   a 0.7   **b** 0.02   **c** 0.008   **d** 1.75

4 Order these fractions from lowest to highest.
   $\dfrac{2}{5}$ $\dfrac{3}{10}$ $\dfrac{3}{8}$ $\dfrac{1}{4}$

5 Calculate each of these, giving your answer as a fraction in its simplest form.
   a $\dfrac{11}{12} - \dfrac{9}{12}$ **b** $\dfrac{2}{5} + \dfrac{4}{15}$
   c $\dfrac{8}{9} - \dfrac{1}{6}$ **d** $\dfrac{6}{7} + \dfrac{5}{8}$

6 Use a mental method to calculate
   a $\dfrac{1}{5}$ of £20   **b** $\dfrac{3}{8}$ of 32 students.

7 Calculate these using a suitable method.
   a $12 \times \dfrac{3}{4}$ **b** $\dfrac{3}{10} \times 15$

8 Give your answers to these questions in their simplest form.
   a What fraction of 72 is 48?
   b What fraction of a day is four hours?

9 Calculate these percentages using a mental method.
   a 5% of 50   **b** 40% of 140
   c 15% of 660   **d** 99% of 800

10 Calculate these percentages using a written or calculator method. Give your answers to two decimal places.
   a 37% of 44   **b** 112% of 320

11 Write these fractions and decimals as percentages without using a calculator.
   a $\dfrac{3}{5}$ **b** $\dfrac{8}{40}$ **c** 0.04   **d** 1.2

12 Write these percentages as decimals.
   a 73%   **b** 16.5%

13 Write these percentages as fractions in their simplest forms.
   a 65%   **b** 8%

14 a What percentage of 90 is 36?
   b A pet shop has 17 cats and 8 dogs. What percentage of the pets are dogs?

What next?

Score		
	0 – 4	Your knowledge of this topic is still developing. To improve look at Formative test: 2B-4; MyMaths: 1015, 1016, 1017, 1018, 1029, 1031 and 1072
	5 – 11	You are gaining a secure knowledge of this topic. To improve look at InvisiPen: 111, 142, 145, 161 and 162
	12 – 14	You have mastered this topic. Well done, you are ready to progress!

1 Write these numbers in order starting with the smallest.

a 4.5	4.48	4.4	4.34	4
b 5.96	5.979	5.94	6	5.9
c 0.066	0.068	0.06	0.0695	0.0684
d 2.8	2.771	2.16	2.776	2.77

2 Copy these and place < or > between each pair of numbers to show which number is the larger.

a 0.46 ☐ 0.5   **b** 1.61 ☐ 1.6   **c** 4.375 ☐ 4.384   **d** 5.24 ☐ 5.2

e 7.13 ☐ 7.14   **f** 2.753 ☐ 2.76   **g** 8.0444 ☐ 8.044   **h** 6.999 ☐ 7.1

3 Rebecca measured the weight, in kilograms, of 20 people in her maths class.
Make a copy of this table and help Rebecca by filling in the frequencies.

45.20, 39.75, 51.09, 46.49, 35.21, 33.00, 38.19, 42.83, 35.50, 53.61, 44.29, 46.38, 37.01, 32.76, 43.35, 49.81, 30.57, 41.72, 46.85, 41.29

Weight, W(kg)	Frequency
$30 \leqslant W < 35$	
$35 \leqslant W < 40$	
$40 \leqslant W < 45$	
$45 \leqslant W < 50$	
$50 \leqslant W < 55$	

4 Change these fractions into decimals using division.
Use an appropriate method.

a $\dfrac{7}{8}$ **b** $\dfrac{7}{16}$ **c** $\dfrac{7}{20}$ **d** $\dfrac{1}{6}$ **e** $\dfrac{5}{9}$ **f** $\dfrac{11}{40}$ **g** $\dfrac{7}{15}$

5 Put these fractions in order from lowest to highest.

a $\dfrac{2}{9}$ $\dfrac{1}{4}$ $\dfrac{3}{10}$ $\dfrac{4}{13}$ **b** $\dfrac{2}{3}$ $\dfrac{3}{4}$ $\dfrac{13}{18}$ $\dfrac{11}{15}$

c $\dfrac{3}{5}$ $\dfrac{5}{9}$ $\dfrac{9}{16}$ $\dfrac{13}{20}$ **d** $\dfrac{2}{7}$ $\dfrac{6}{25}$ $\dfrac{3}{10}$ $\dfrac{3}{11}$

6 Write these decimals as fractions in their simplest forms.

a 0.125   **b** 0.55   **c** 1.75   **d** 0.05   **e** 2.$\dot{6}$ **f** 3.15

7 Find the missing number in each of these pairs of equivalent fractions.

a $\dfrac{2}{3} = \dfrac{\square}{15}$ **b** $\dfrac{3}{7} = \dfrac{\square}{21}$ **c** $\dfrac{4}{9} = \dfrac{\square}{36}$ **d** $\dfrac{5}{7} = \dfrac{\square}{49}$

e $\dfrac{4}{11} = \dfrac{44}{\square}$ **f** $\dfrac{3}{13} = \dfrac{\square}{39}$ **g** $\dfrac{5}{12} = \dfrac{\square}{72}$ **h** $\dfrac{7}{16} = \dfrac{\square}{80}$

8 Calculate each of these additions and subtractions, giving your answer as a fraction in its simplest form.

a $\frac{2}{5} + \frac{1}{4}$ b $\frac{3}{7} + \frac{1}{5}$ c $\frac{1}{3} + \frac{1}{5}$ d $\frac{3}{4} + \frac{1}{9}$

e $\frac{3}{15} + \frac{9}{20}$ f $\frac{5}{6} - \frac{4}{9}$ g $\frac{5}{8} + \frac{7}{12}$ h $\frac{6}{7} - \frac{2}{21}$

9 Use an appropriate method to calculate these amounts. Where appropriate give your answer to 2 decimal places.

a $\frac{2}{7}$ of 236 g   b $\frac{7}{16}$ of £500   c $\frac{4}{7}$ of 18 km   d $\frac{8}{5}$ of 47 miles

e $\frac{5}{12}$ of 48 hours   f $\frac{3}{5}$ of $25   g $\frac{7}{9}$ of 25 tonnes   h $\frac{2}{5}$ of 360°

10 a In Karla's class there are 14 boys and 21 girls. What fraction of the class are boys?

b Spencer has 12 music CDs, 10 of which are classical music. What fraction of Spencer's CDs are not classical music?

11 Calculate these using an appropriate method, giving your answers to 2 decimal places where appropriate.

a 7% of £50   b 12% of 45 kg   c 31% of 18 km

d 57% of 39 euros   e 29% of £87   f 41% of 63 kg

12 A packet of sausages weighs 275 g. The label says it contains 75% meat, 11% bread crumbs and 2% salt.

What weight of meat, breadcrumbs and salt does the packet contain?

13 Bethany's form teacher has been supplied with the following marks from her subject teachers.

a Convert all the marks into percentages and list Bethany's subjects in order from best to worst.

b Write a sentence to summarize her results.

Subject	Mark
Art	66/100
Maths	59%
PE	28/40
Science	17/50
History	18/25
English	51/70

MyMaths.co.uk

These questions will test you on your knowledge of the topics in chapters 1 to 4.
They give you practice in the types of questions that you may eventually be given in your GCSE exams. There are 100 marks in total.

1 Calculate
  a -6 − -3 **b** -16 + -24 **c** -9 × -4
  d -35 ÷ -7 **e** 7 × -3 **f** -42 ÷ 6 (6 marks)

2 Place these decimals in order of size from largest to smallest.
  0.014   -0.052   0.01   -1.099   1.109   -0.555 (2 marks)

3 Which one of these numbers does **not** have 9 as one of its factors?
  189   801   739   486   639   2052 (2 marks)

4 Find the HCF and LCM of 81 and 36. (3 marks)

5 Work out the value of
  a 7^2 **b** $(-8)^3$ **c** 5^3 **d** $(-2.5)^2$ (4 marks)

6 a Find two consecutive numbers with a product of 3080. (2 marks)
  b Briefly explain your method for solving this problem. (1 mark)

7 Convert these measurements to the units in the brackets.
  a 1750 kg (tonnes) **b** 560 cl (litres) **c** 24 litres (pints)
  d 33 lb (kg) **e** 32 km (miles) **f** 8 gallons (litres) (6 marks)

8 The flag of Denmark is being made.

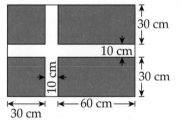
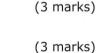

  a Calculate the area of the white material. (3 marks)
  b Calculate the area of the red material. (3 marks)
  c What is the total area of the flag? (1 mark)

9 The flag of Eritrea is made from three triangles

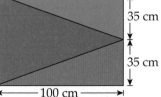

  a Calculate the area shaded green. (2 marks)
  b Calculate the area shaded red. (3 marks)
  c Work out the total area of the flag. (3 marks)

10 The parallelogram is split into two trapeziums.

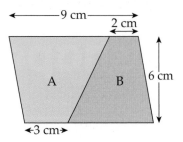

  a Find the area of the parallelogram. (2 marks)
  b Find the areas of the two trapeziums and show that one trapezium is $\frac{4}{9}$ ths of the area of the parallelogram. (3 marks)

11 a Write these expressions in their simplest form.
  i $5 \times x$ **ii** $x + x + x$ **iii** $y \div 4$ **iv** $x \times y$ **v** $x + y + x + y + y$ (5 marks)
  b Find the value of these expressions if $x = 7$ and $y = 8$. (5 marks)

12 Simplify these expressions.
  a $5^3 \times 5^8$ **b** $10^6 \times 10^3 \times 10^8$ **c** $z^2 \times z^5 \times z^{12}$ **d** $s^6 \times t^3 \times u^8$ (4 marks)

13 Simplify these expressions by collecting like terms with the same indices.
  a $4p + 8p - 2p - p$ **b** $12q - 4q + 16q - q$
  c $3z + 2z^2 - 7z + 5z^2$ **d** $6t^2 - 6t^3 + 3t^2 - 6t$ (4 marks)

14 Expand these brackets.
  a $5(2x + 5)$ (2 marks) **b** $p(7p - 3)$ (2 marks)
  c $3(2y - 1) + 2(3y + 1)$ (3 marks) **d** $u(3u + 2) + 2u(u - 1)$ (3 marks)

15 a Find a formula for the perimeter, P, of this quadrilateral. (2 marks)
  b If $x = 4$ find the value of the perimeter. (1 mark)
  c Find an equation for the fourth angle, y, and solve this to find y. (3 marks)

16 a Write the value of the digit 3 in words in each of these numbers.
  i 0.437 **ii** 0.034 **iii** 0.374 **iv** 0.473 **v** 0.043 (5 marks)
  b Place these numbers in order from smallest to largest. (2 marks)

17 A stamp is $2\frac{3}{5}$ cm high and $1\frac{2}{3}$ cm wide.
  a Work out the perimeter of the stamp. (2 marks)
  b What is the difference between the height and width of the stamp? (2 marks)

18 Using a calculator work out the following.
  a 56% of 450 ml **b** $\frac{5}{9}$ of 3.6 km **c** 0.65 of 800 MB **d** 2% of 5200 g (4 marks)

19 In a recent test only seven students out of 42 gained a grade A.
  a Write this as **i** a fraction in its simplest terms
         ii a decimal to 2 decimal places
         iii a percentage to 1 decimal places. (3 marks)
  b Twelve students gained a B grade. What percentage of the students gained a grade A or B (give your answer to one decimal place)? (2 marks)

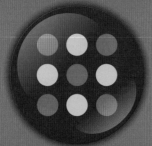

5 Angles and shapes

Introduction

In computer games, 3D characters and objects are made from thousands of triangles. Computer programmers write a piece of computer code to represent a triangle and then repeat this over and over again to represent much more complex shapes. The triangles are then given different colours to create the illusion of three dimensions.

What's the point?

The triangle is the most basic polygon. By understanding triangles, people can create highly sophisticated shapes in computer technology and in architecture.

Objectives

By the end of this chapter, you will have learned how to …

- Work with angles at a point and on a line.
- Work with angles in a triangle.
- Work with angles on parallel and intersecting lines.
- Recognise quadrilaterals and know their properties.
- Know and use some properties of polygons.
- Recognise congruent shapes.

Check in

1 Match each angle with the correct description from the box.

a **b** **c** **d** **e**

reflex
straight
right
obtuse
acute

2 Solve these equations.

a $2a = 180$ **b** $3b + 30 = 180$ **c** $5c = 360$

Starter problem

You will need a 3 × 3 pinboard or a 3 × 3 dotted grid.

Make as many different quadrilaterals as you can.

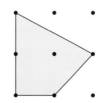

An **angle** is a measure of turn. You can measure the angle of the turn in degrees.

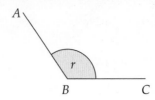

You can describe this angle in different ways.

angle *ABC*
or angle *CBA*
or angle *B*
or *r*

▲ There are 360° in a full turn at a **point**.

▲ There are 180° on a **straight line**.

▲ There are 90° in a **right angle**.

Example

Calculate the values of *a* and *b*.

a

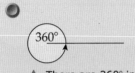

b

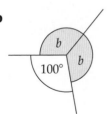

a $a + a + a = 180°$
$3a = 180°$ 3× something = 180
$3a ÷ 3 = 180° ÷ 3$
$a = 60°$

b $b + b + 100 = 360°$
$2b + 100° = 360°$ 2× something + 100 = 360
$2b + 100° - 100° = 360° - 100°$
$2b = 260°$
$2b ÷ 2 = 260° ÷ 2$
$b = 130°$

● **Vertically opposite** angles are equal.

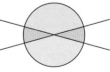

Example

Calculate the value of *x*.

$5x = 45°$
$5x ÷ 5 = 45° ÷ 5$
$x = 9°$

▲ The two red acute angles are equal. The two green obtuse angles are equal.

p.86 >

Exercise 5a

1 Use the small letters to describe.

   a angle *C*   **b** angle *D*

   c angle *ABC*   **d** angle *CBE*

   e angle *DEF*   **f** angle *DEB.*

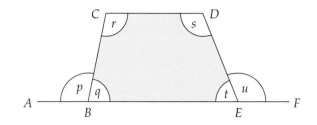

2 Calculate the value of the letters.

   a   **b**

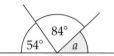

   c   **d**

3 Calculate the value of the unknown angles.

   a   **b**

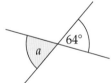

   c   **d**

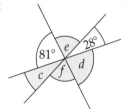
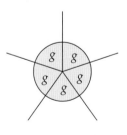

4 Calculate the value of the letters.

   a   **b**

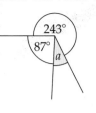
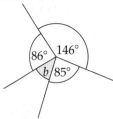

   c   **d**

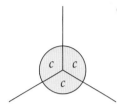
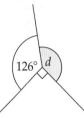

   e   **f**

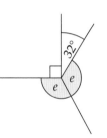
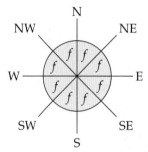

   g   **h**

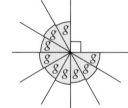
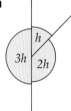

Problem solving

5 Calculate the smaller angle between the arms on the clocks at

   a three o'clock

   b one o'clock

   c half past nine.

MyMaths.co.uk   Q 1082   **SEARCH**

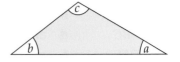

<p.32>
● The **interior** angles of a triangle add to 180°.
$a + b + c = 180°$

You should learn the mathematical names of these triangles.

<p.212 >

| Equilateral | Isosceles | Scalene | Right-angled |

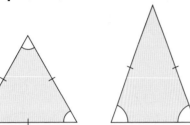

The two red lines in this right-angled triangle are **perpendicular**. This means they are at 90°.

3 equal sides
3 equal angles

2 equal sides
2 equal angles

No equal sides
No equal angles

One 90° angle

Example

Calculate the values of a and b.

a

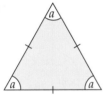

b

a $a + a + a = 180°$
$3a = 180°$ 3× something = 180
$3a ÷ 3 = 180° ÷ 3$
$a = 60°$

b $b + b + 44° = 180°$
$2b + 44° = 180°$ 2× something + 44 = 180
$2b + 44° - 44° = 180° - 44°$
$2b = 136°$
$2b ÷ 2 = 136° ÷ 2$
$b = 68°$

You find an **exterior** angle of a 2D shape by extending a side.

$a + b + c = 180°$ Angles in a triangle add to 180°
$a + d = 180°$ Angles on a straight line add to 180°
So $b + c = d$ By comparing the equations

● The exterior angle of a triangle is equal to the sum of the two interior opposite angles.

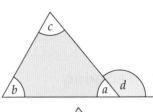

Exercise 5b

1 Calculate the value of the letters.

a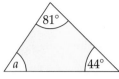

b

c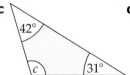

d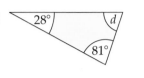

2 Two angles in a triangle are given. Calculate the third angle and state the type of triangle.

a 60°, 60°   **b** 38°, 71°

c 45°, 45°   **d** 38°, 64°

e 42°, 96°   **f** 51°, 78°

3 The base angles in an isosceles triangle are as given. Find the third angle.

a 42°   **b** 83°

c 15°   **d** 45°

4 Calculate the size of the unknown angles.

a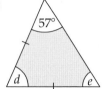

b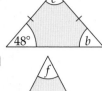

c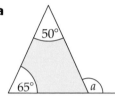

d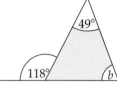

5 Calculate the size of the unknown angles.

a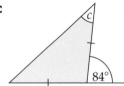

b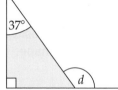

c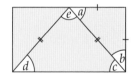

d

Problem solving

6 Some triangles are drawn in this rectangle. Calculate the value of each letter.

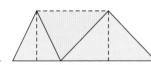

7 Draw and cut out a triangle.
Find the midpoint of two sides and fold along the dotted line.
Fold along the two further dotted lines.
Explain why this shows that the sum of the interior angles of a triangle is 180°.

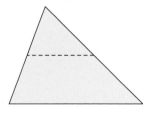

5c Angles in parallel lines

Parallel lines occur everywhere you look!

🔵 **Parallel** lines are always the same distance apart.

When a line **intersects** two parallel lines, different types of angle are formed.

Vertically opposite angles are equal.

Alternate angles are equal.

Corresponding angles are equal.

‹ p.82

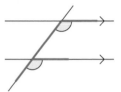

Vertically opposite angles form an **X** shape.

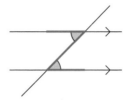

Alternate angles form a **Z** shape.

Corresponding angles form an **F** shape.

Example

Calculate the values of angles *a* and *b*.

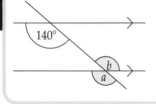

$a = 140°$ Corresponding angles are equal.

$b = 140°$ Alternate angles are equal.

or $b = 140°$ Vertically opposite angles are equal.

a and 140° form an F shape.

b and 140° form a Z shape.

a and *b* are equal.

Example

Prove that the opposite angles of a parallelogram are equal.

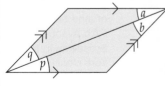

You need to prove $a + b = p + q$

$a = p$ Alternate angles are equal.

$b = q$ Alternate angles are equal.

So $a + b = p + q$ and the opposite angles of a parallelogram are equal.

a and *p* form a Z shape.

b and *q* form a Z shape.

Exercise 5c

1 Draw a line crossing two parallel lines.
  a Measure the size of *a* and *b* in your diagram.
  b Draw a Z or an F on your diagram to help you decide whether the angles *a* and *b* are alternate or corresponding.

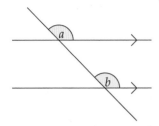

2 Copy the diagrams and label the alternate angles to the ones shown.

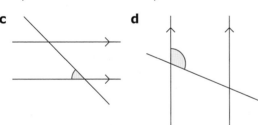

3 Copy the diagrams and label the corresponding angles to the ones shown.

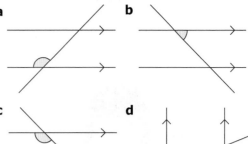

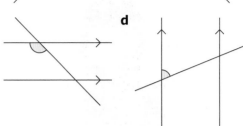

4 Calculate the angles marked by the letters. Give a reason for your answers.

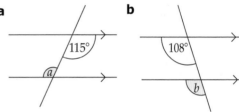

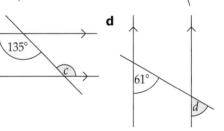

Problem solving

5 Calculate the unknown angles.

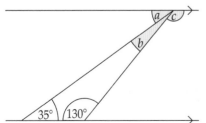

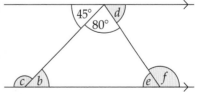

6 Give three examples of parallel lines that you see in everyday life.

5d Properties of a quadrilateral

A **quadrilateral** is a 2D shape with four sides and four angles.

The **interior** angles of a quadrilateral add to 360°.

$p + q + r + s = 360°$

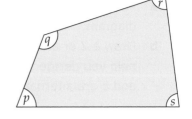

There are lots of different types of quadrilateral and you should learn their names and properties.

Square	**Rectangle**	**Rhombus**	**Parallelogram**

Square
4 equal sides
4 angles of 90°
2 sets of parallel sides

Rectangle
2 sets of equal sides
4 angles of 90°
2 sets of parallel sides

Rhombus
4 equal sides
2 pairs of equal angles
2 sets of parallel sides

Parallelogram
2 sets of equal sides
2 pairs of equal angles
2 sets of parallel sides

Trapezium	**Isosceles trapezium**	**Kite**	**Arrowhead**

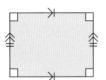
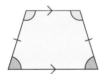

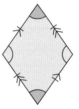
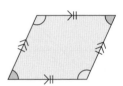

Trapezium
1 set of parallel sides

Isosceles trapezium
1 set of equal sides
2 pairs of equal angles
1 set of parallel sides

Kite
2 sets of equal sides
1 pair of equal angles
No parallel sides

Arrowhead
2 sets of equal sides
1 pair of equal angles
No parallel sides

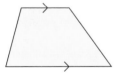

You can think of rectangles and rhombi as special types of parallelogram....

.... and a square is a special type of rectangle and a special type of rhombus.

Exercise 5d

1 Find the fourth angle in each of these quadrilaterals.

   a 92°, 57°, 123°   **b** 110°, 90°, 105°   **c** 39°, 150°, 81°   **d** 200°, 25°, 35°

2 Three angles in a quadrilateral are given. Calculate the fourth
  angle in each and suggest the type of quadrilateral.
  There could be several answers for each question.

   a 90°, 90°, 90°   **b** 60°, 120°, 120°   **c** 90°, 90°, 110°   **d** 30°, 90°, 210°

   e 63°, 87°, 110°   **f** 80°, 80°, 100°   **g** 53°, 67°, 140°   **h** 30°, 30°, 50°

3 Copy and complete the table to show the properties of the
  diagonals of these quadrilaterals. Use Yes or No for each answer.
  Here is some language you will need:

> bisect = cut in half
> perpendicular = angle of 90°

	The diagonals		
	are equal in length	**bisect each other**	**are perpendicular**
Parallelogram			
Kite			
Rhombus			
Square			
Rectangle			

Problem solving

4 Name the different types of quadrilaterals in the regular
  pentagon on the right.

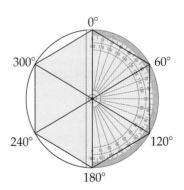

5 ▶ Draw a circle.

  ▶ Use a protractor to mark off points at 60° intervals at
    0°, 60°, 120°, 180°, 240°, 300° and 360° (same as 0°).

  ▶ Join up the points with straight lines to make a regular
    hexagon and cut out the six equilateral triangles.

  a Rearrange six triangles to make a parallelogram. Show that
    the opposite angles of this parallelogram are equal.

  b Rearrange five triangles to make an isosceles trapezium. Show
    that this isosceles trapezium has two pairs of equal angles.

  c Rearrange four triangles to make an equilateral triangle.
    Explain why you know the triangle is equilateral.

  d Rearrange three triangles to make an isosceles trapezium.
    Calculate the sum of the interior angles of a trapezium.

  e Rearrange two triangles to make a rhombus. Show that the
    opposite angles of this rhombus are equal.

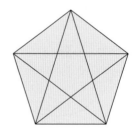

A **polygon** is a shape with three or more straight sides. You should know the names of some polygons.

If the sides and angles are equal, you call the polygon **regular**.

▲ An irregular hexagon

▲ A regular hexagon

Number of sides	Name
3	Triangle
4	Quadrilateral
5	Pentagon
6	Hexagon
7	Heptagon
8	Octagon
9	Nonagon
10	Decagon

Example

Draw a regular pentagon.

There are five equal angles at the centre.

$360° \div 5 = 72°$

Draw a circle.

Use a protractor to mark off points at 72° intervals at 0°, 72°, 144°, 216°, 288° and 360° (same as 0°).

Join up neighbouring points with straight lines.

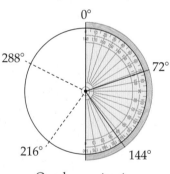

Overlay protractor

You can often fit polygons together to make a tiling pattern.
Their properties can decide how they fit together.

p.162 > ● A **tessellation** is a tiling pattern with no gaps.

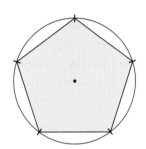

▲ Moroccan art uses some very complex tessellations.

Example

Copy this diagram and draw at least five more octagons to show the shape tessellates.

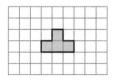
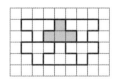

Exercise 5e

1   What is the mathematical name for
    a   a regular triangle
    b   a regular quadrilateral?

2   Calculate the value of the letters.

    a   **b**

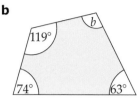

    c

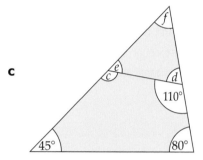

3   **a**   Use a protractor and a ruler to draw a
             regular nonagon.
             Draw a circle.
             Use a protractor to mark off points at
             40° intervals at 0°, 40°, 80° etc.
             Join up the points with straight lines.
    b   Measure one of the interior angles of
             the nonagon.
    c   Calculate the sum of the interior
             angles.

4   Tessellate each polygon on square grid
    paper.

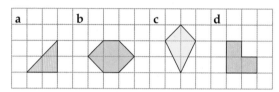

Problem solving

5   Regular octagons do not tessellate as
    squares are needed to fill the gaps.
    Calculate the size of the interior
    angle of a regular octagon.

6   Draw a circle.
    Use a protractor to mark off points
    at 60° intervals at 0°, 60°, 120° etc.
    Draw a regular hexagon and six of the
    diagonals.
    Cut out the 12 triangles and the
    smaller hexagon.
    Rearrange the pieces to make three
    congruent hexagons.

    Congruent means identical.

Did you know?

The top surface of
many of the stones at
the Giant's Causeway
in Ireland is a
hexagon.

7   Draw a tessellation made from regular
    hexagons, squares and equilateral triangles.
    All sides must be the same length.

These shapes may look different, but they are the same size and the same shape.

If you cut them out, they would all fit on top of each other.
These shapes are **congruent**.

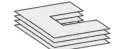

⬤ **Congruent** shapes are identical to each other.

Example

Write down the letters of the congruent shapes.

A   **B**   **C**   **D**   **E**

A, B and D are congruent as they are the same size and the same shape.
C and E are congruent as they are the same size and the same shape.

p.162, 214 ❯

⬤ If shapes are congruent, then
  – **corresponding angles** are equal
  – **corresponding sides** are equal.

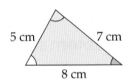

5 cm   7 cm   5 cm   7 cm
   8 cm   8 cm

Example

The pink triangle and the blue triangle are congruent.

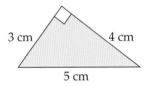

3 cm   4 cm

5 cm

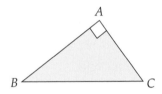

A

B   C

State the lengths of   **a** AB   **b** AC   **c** BC

a AB = 4 cm
b AC = 3 cm
c BC = 5 cm

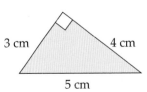

3 cm   4 cm

5 cm

A

C   B

Flip over the blue triangle so it can fit on top of the pink triangle.

Compare the triangles.

Exercise 5f

1 Draw the shape that is not congruent to the others.

a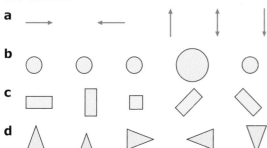

b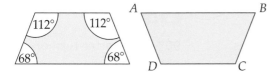

c

d

e

2 The blue isosceles trapezium and the green isosceles trapezium are congruent.

State the values of angles *A, B, C* and *D*.

3 The red triangle and the green triangle are congruent.

State the lengths of

a *AB*   **b** *AC*   **c** *BC*

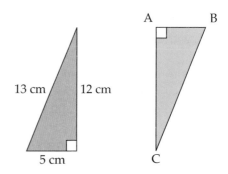

4 Identify the congruent shapes in this diagram.

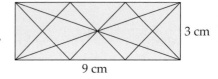

Problem solving

4 **a** Copy the diagram based on a 3cm by 9cm rectangle.

b Use different colours to identify the congruent shapes.

c How many different shapes are in the diagram?

5 The rectangular faces of each brick in a wall are congruent.
Write down three other examples of congruent shapes from real life.

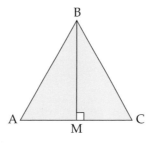

6 Triangles ABM and BCM are congruent. AMB is a straight line.

a Explain why

    i AB = BC

    ii angle BAM = angle BCM

    iii AM = MC

    iv angle AMB = angle BMC = 90°

b What kind of triangle is ABC?

Check out
You should now be able to ...

Test it ➡
Questions

✓ Work with angles at a point and on a line.	5	1
✓ Work with angles in a triangle.	5	2
✓ Work with angles on parallel and intersecting lines.	6	3
✓ Recognise quadrilaterals and know their properties.	6	4
✓ Know and use some properties of polygons.	6	5, 6
✓ Recognise congruent shapes.	6	7

Language	Meaning	Example
Angle	A measure of turn, given in degrees	90° is a quarter turn or right angle
Triangle	A 2D shape with three straight sides and three angles	Equilateral, isosceles, scalene and right-angled are special types of triangle
Perpendicular	Lines which meet at right angles	Horizontal and vertical lines are perpendicular
Parallel	Lines which are always the same distance apart	Railway tracks are parallel
Quadrilateral	A 2D shape with four straight sides and four angles	Squares, rectangles, kites and parallelograms are special types of quadrilateral
Polygon	A 2D shape with three or more straight sides	Pentagons, hexagons and octagons are examples
Tessellation	A tiling pattern with no gaps	A chess board shows tessellated squares
Congruent	Identical to	Shapes are congruent if their *corresponding* sides and angles are equal

1 Calculate the value of the letters in these diagrams.

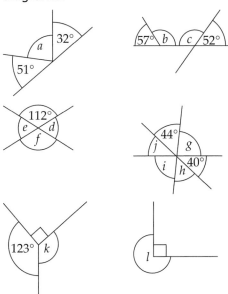

2 Calculate the value of the letters in these triangles.

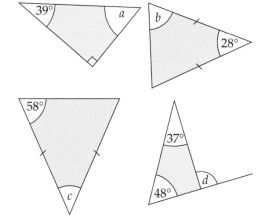

3 Calculate the angles marked by the letters in these diagrams. Give reasons for your answers.

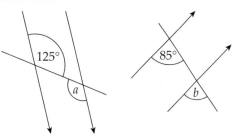

4 Which quadrilateral has
  a 4 equal sides, 2 pairs of equal angles and 2 sets of parallel sides
  b 2 sets of equal sides, 1 pair of equal angles and no parallel sides
  c exactly 1 set of parallel sides?

5 Draw a regular octagon.

6 Calculate the value of the letters in this diagram.

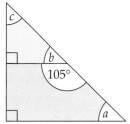

7 The two triangles below are congruent. State
  a the length of AB
  b the length of AC
  c the size of angle A.

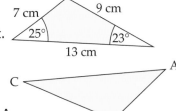

What next?

Score		
	0 – 3	Your knowledge of this topic is still developing. To improve look at Formative test: 2B-5; MyMaths: 1080, 1082, 1100, 1109 and 1320
	4 – 6	You are gaining a secure knowledge of this topic. To improve look at InvisiPen: 317, 342, 343, 344, 345 and 346
	7	You have mastered this topic. Well done, you are ready to progress!

5a

1   Calculate the value of the unknown angles.

a

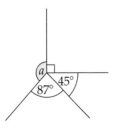

b

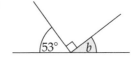

c

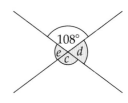

2   Arrange these six angle values so they fit on a straight
line and at a point.

14°   22°   24°   124°   142°   214°

5b

3   Two angles in a triangle are given.
Calculate the third angle and state the type of triangle.

a   30°, 75°   b   43°, 47°   c   36°, 108°

d   35°, 64°   e   45°, 90°

4   One angle in an isosceles triangle is 70°.
What is the size of the other two angles?

There are two possible
answers to this question.

5c

5   Calculate the unknown angles.
Give a reason in each case.

a

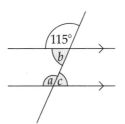

b

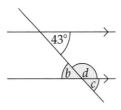

c

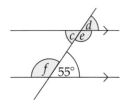

6   Calculate the unknown angles.

a

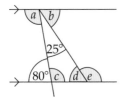

b

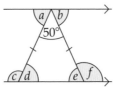

7 Calculate the unknown angles in these quadrilaterals.

a

Kite

b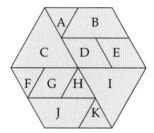

Rhombus

c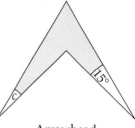

Arrowhead

8 State which shapes are the same in this regular hexagon and give the mathematical name of each shape.

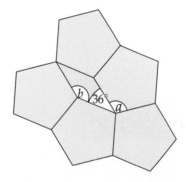

9 The diagram shows five regular pentagons and a rhombus.
One angle in the rhombus is 36°.

Calculate the values of *a* and *b*.

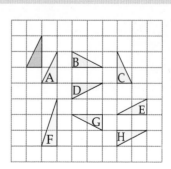

10 Identify the triangles that are congruent to the green triangle.

6 Graphs

Introduction

The world is increasingly feeling the effects of climate change on the environment, such as melting polar ice caps and severe hurricanes.

Meteorologists use complex mathematical models of the Earth's climate, from which they can create functions and draw graphs, to predict likely future weather patterns as the Earth warms up.

What's the point?

Graphs provide a clear picture of real life data, allowing us to see patterns and predict what might happen next. This is vital as the world gets hotter, so we can know what precautions to take.

Objectives

By the end of this chapter, you will have learned how to ...

- ● Draw a straight-line graph of a function.
- ● Recognise the equations of sloping lines and lines parallel to the axes.
- ● Interpret and draw real life graphs.
- ● Construct and interpret simple line graphs for time series.

Check in

1 On square grid paper draw and label a set of axes from -5 to 5.
   Plot the points (2, 4), (3, -1), (-2, 1) and (-3, 3). Comment on what you notice.

2 For **i** $x = 0$ **ii** $x = 1$ **iii** $x = 2$ **iv** $x = -1$
   find the value of y in these equations.

   a $y = x + 1$ **b** $y = 3x - 4$ **c** $y = 7 - 2x$ **d** $8 = 3x + 2y$

3 Draw a graph of your speed versus time for your journey to school in the morning
   and label the main features.

Starter problem

You need to take turns to place a counter of your colour on the grid.

To win a game of 'four-in-a-line', a player needs to have placed four of their pieces in a straight line. In this game the winning line of four is clearly marked.

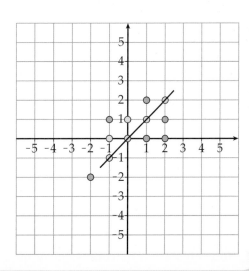

What is the connection between the x and y coordinates of the points on the winning line?

Investigate other winning lines of four that are possible on the grid.

⬤ A function is a rule that matches a given input to a unique output.
▶ Functions are often described using equations.

It's easy to draw a graph if you follow a simple step-by-step list of instructions!

Here is a **function**: $y = x - 1$.
This means for any value x you subtract 1 to get y

$$x = 5 \qquad y = 5 - 1$$
$$= 4$$

You can put some more values of x into the function, to see what values of y come out.

When $x = -1$, $y = -2$
$x = 0$, $y = -1$
$x = 1$, $y = 0$
$x = 2$, $y = 1$
$x = 3$, $y = 2$
$x = 4$, $y = 3$

1 Create a **table of values** from the pairs of x and y values.

x	-1	0	1	2	3	4
y	-2	-1	0	1	2	3

You can write **coordinates** from the table of values

(-1, -2), (0, -1), (1, 0), (2, 1), (3, 2), (4, 3)

2 Plot these coordinates as points on a **graph**.

First draw the **axes**.   Next **plot** the points.   Now join the points with a **straight line**.

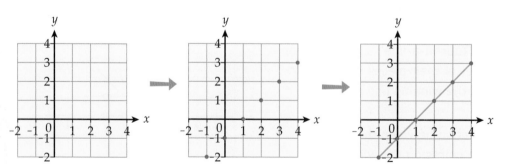

This is the graph of the function $y = x - 1$.

⬤ You can show a function visually by drawing its graph.

Exercise 6a

1 **a** For the function $y = x + 4$ find the values of y when $x = 0, 1, 2, 3, 4$ and 5. Put your results in a copy of this table

x	0	1	2	3	4	5
y						

b Copy the axes shown and plot six points at the coordinates contained in the table.

c Join the points to draw the graph of the function $y = x + 4$.

2 For each function,
   i copy and complete the table from question **1**
   ii plot points on axes labelled as in question **1**
   iii join your points to draw the graph of each function.

   a $y = x + 2$ **b** $y = x - 1$
   c $y = 2x + 1$ **d** $y = 2x - 3$
   e $y = 10 - x$ **f** $y = 5 - x$

3 For each of these functions, copy and complete this table.

x	0	2	4	6	8	10
y						

Draw the graph of each function. Label your x-axis from 0 to 10 and your y-axis from -4 to 10.

   a $x + y = 10$ **b** $x + y = 6$
   c $x + y = 8$ **d** $y = 9 - x$

Problem solving

4 Lengths of cloth can be bought over the internet.
   Their cost £C depends on their length, x metres, where $C = 4x + 2$.
   a Copy and complete this table.

x	1	2	3	4	5
C					

   b Draw a graph of C against x.
   c Use your graph to find the length of cloth which costs £12.

5 The cost £C of hiring a canoe depends on the length of time, t hours, according to the formula $C = 10 + 5t$.
   a Draw a graph of C for t values between 0 and 6.
   b How long was a canoe hired for if **i** $C = 25$ **ii** $C = 32.5$?

6 The word **function** has many meanings in the English language.
   Find different meanings of the word.
   Is the mathematical meaning in any way similar to the other meanings?
   Where does the word come from originally and what did it mean then?

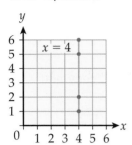

Graphs of straight lines can look quite different, depending on their equation.

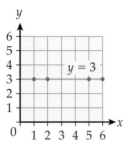

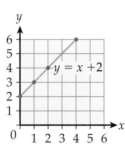

You need to be able to recognise the equations of sloping lines and lines parallel to the axes.

If x is **constant** (e.g. $x = 4$), the line is parallel to the y-axis.

If y is constant (e.g. $y = 3$), the line is parallel to the x-axis.

If the equation has both x and y, the line slopes up or down.

Example

Draw graphs of these lines.

a $x = 3$ **b** $y = 4$ **c** $y = x - 2$

a The line $x = 3$ has points $(3, 0)$, $(3, 1)$, $(3, 2)$ and is parallel to the y-axis.

b The line $y = 4$ has points $(1, 4)$, $(2, 4)$, $(3, 4)$ and is parallel to the x-axis.

c The line $y = x - 2$ has this table of values

x	0	1	2	3
y	-2	-1	0	1

giving the points $(0, -2)$, $(1, -1)$, $(2, 0)$, $(3, 1)$.

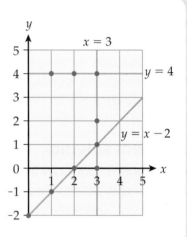

Most straight-line graphs have an equation that can be written in the form $y = mx + c$ where m and c are numbers.

Examples are:
  $y = 2x + 3$ $(m = 2,\ c = 3)$
  $y = 3x - 4$ $(m = 3,\ c = -4)$
  $y = x + 1$ $(m = 1,\ c = 1)$
  $y = -2x + 2$ $(m = -2, c = 2)$
  $y = 4x$ $(m = 4,\ c = 0)$

c tells you where the line crosses the y-axis. m tells you how steep the line is.

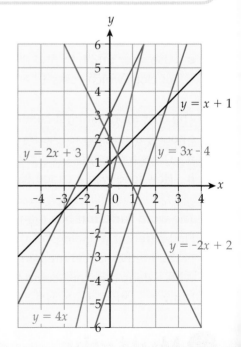

Exercise 6b

1 Here are the equations of some straight lines.

Say whether each line is

A a line parallel to the x-axis

B a line parallel to the y-axis

C a sloping line.

a $y = 3$ **b** $x = 5$

c $y = x - 4$ **d** $y = 2x + 3$

e $x = 2$ **f** $x + y = 7$

g $y = 6$ **h** $y = 4x - 1$

2 Write the equations of these five straight lines **a** to **e**.

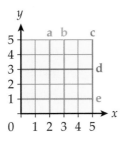

3 On axes labelled from 0 to 10, draw the lines

$x = 4$, $x = 6$, $y = 1$ and $y = 5$.

Find the area of the shape enclosed by these lines.

4 a Copy and complete the table for the equation $y = 2x + 3$.

x	0	1	2	3
y				

b Draw its graph. Label the x-axis from 0 to 4, and the y-axis from 0 to 10.

5 a Copy and complete the table for the equation $y = 3x - 2$.

x	0	1	2	3
y				

b Draw its graph. Label the x-axis from 0 to 4, and the y-axis from -3 to 8.

6 Match the equations to the graphs. Which is the odd equation out?

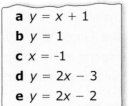

a $y = x + 1$

b $y = 1$

c $x = -1$

d $y = 2x - 3$

e $y = 2x - 2$

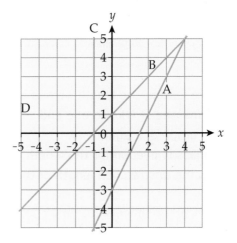

Problem solving

7 The average lifespan of a man in the UK is eighty years. A man who is x years old now might expect to live for another y years, where $y = 80 - x$.

Copy and complete this table.

x	20	30	40	50	60
y					

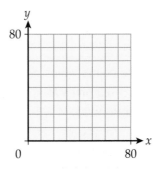

Draw a graph of y against x on axes like these.

6c Real life graphs 1

Graphs can be drawn to describe real life situations. Here are two examples.

Janina goes to the shop for her mother.
This graph describes her journey.

a How far away is the shop?

b How long did it take Janina to get there?

c How long did she spend at the shop?

d Was she faster going or coming back?

Distance from home, m

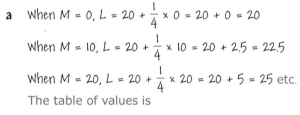

a The shop is 800 metres away.

b She took 5 minutes to get there.

c She spent 15 − 5 = 10 minutes at the shop.

d She took 25 − 15 = 10 minutes to come back. So, she was faster going to the shop.

In a Science lesson, the length L cm of a spring is increased by adding masses of M kg to one end so that $L = 20 + \frac{1}{4}M$.

a Draw a graph of L against M.

b What mass is needed for the length to be 23 cm?

c What is the *unstretched* length of the spring?

a When $M = 0$, $L = 20 + \frac{1}{4} \times 0 = 20 + 0 = 20$

When $M = 10$, $L = 20 + \frac{1}{4} \times 10 = 20 + 2.5 = 22.5$

When $M = 20$, $L = 20 + \frac{1}{4} \times 20 = 20 + 5 = 25$ etc.

The table of values is

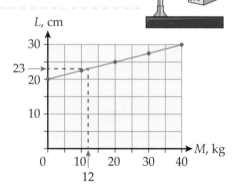

L, cm

Mass, M kg	0	10	20	30	40
Length, L cm	20	22.5	25	27.5	30

The table gives five points which are plotted to draw a graph.

b From the graph, $L = 23$ gives $M = 12$. A mass of 12 kg is needed.

c When the spring is unstretched, $M = 0$ and $L = 20$. The unstretched length is 20 cm.

Exercise 6c

1 This graph converts US dollars ($) to pounds sterling (£).

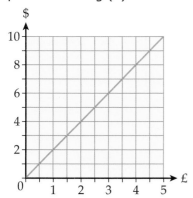

How many pounds do you get for

a $10   **b** $8   **c** $5?

How many dollars do you get for

d £3   **e** £3.50   **f** £2.50?

g Find the missing number where

dollars = □ × *pounds*.

2 An approximate equation for converting kilometres to miles is

$$kilometres = \frac{5}{8} \times miles.$$

Copy and complete this table.

Kilometres	8	16	24	40	44	48
Miles						

Use your table to draw a **conversion graph** on axes as shown here.

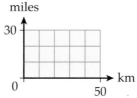

Use your graph to change

a 30 km into miles

b 20 miles into km.

Problem solving

3 This graph describes Peter's walk from his home to the fish shop and back.

  a How far is it from home to the fish shop?

  b How long does it take Peter to get there?

  c How long does Peter have to wait at the fish shop?

  d How long does it take Peter to come home?

  e Can you give a good reason why he gets home more quickly?

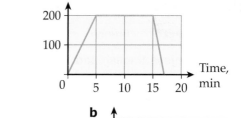

4 These two graphs have lost their labels, they describe these situations.

  a The depth of water in a bath against time.

  b The temperature of water in a kettle against time.

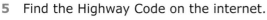

Match the graph with the situation it describes.

Explain your answer.

5 Find the Highway Code on the internet.

Research stopping distances for cars travelling at different speeds.

  a Plot a graph of stopping distance against speed.

  b How could you illustrate thinking distance and braking distance on your graph?

Sometimes real life graphs will not be straight lines. Sometimes they can be sketched rather than accurately drawn. Here are two examples of this.

Example

The level of rainwater in a barrel is monitored during one week.

Describe the level of water and suggest when it might have rained heavily.

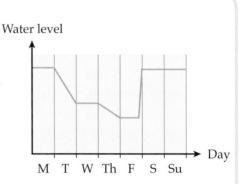

On Monday the water level is high.

On Tuesday it drops, then stays constant on Wednesday.

It drops a bit more on Thursday, then stays constant on Friday until Friday night, when it rises sharply.

The level stays constant on Saturday and Sunday.

It probably rained heavily on Friday night.

Example

Sarah enjoys school for most of the time.

Today she has these five lessons, with a short morning break and 45 minutes for lunch.

Lesson	9am–10am	10am–11am	11:15am–12:15pm	1pm–2pm	2pm–3pm
Subject	French	History	Mathematics	English	Science

She enjoys English and Science most. She quite enjoys French and Mathematics.

She enjoys History least.

She has many friends and thoroughly enjoys the two breaks in the day.

At the end of the day, she takes an hour to travel home in heavy traffic.

Sketch a graph which shows her level of enjoyment from 9am to 4pm

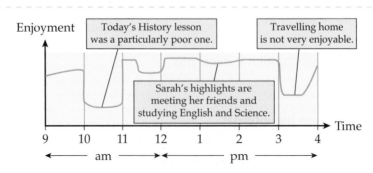

Exercise 6d

1 **a** A baby is born and her weight is measured.
This graph shows changes in her weight over eight weeks.

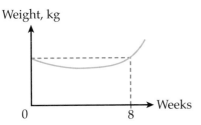

Write a few sentences to describe these changes.

b As the baby grows into an adult, her weight changes over the years.

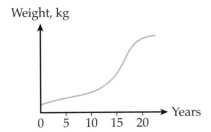

Describe the changes which take place over 20 years.

c Extend a copy of the graph in part **b** to cover the next 60 years. Explain what you have drawn.

2 Jim went on a bike ride lasting five hours. This graph shows his speed during the ride.

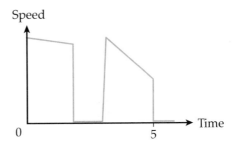

Describe his journey.

3 These two graphs, P and Q, show the brightness of
a a car's indicator when it is turning a corner
b a security light which turns on when someone walks by.

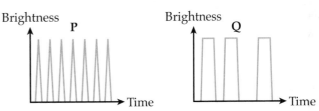

Match P and Q to **a** and **b**.
Write your reasons for deciding which is which.

Problem solving

4 Maria goes on foot to her grandma's house.
She sets off running fast but she gradually tires.
Suddenly she stops at a road and waits a short time until it is safe to cross.
She then walks steadily to reach her grandma's.
Sketch a graph of her speed against the time that she takes.

5 David records his heart rate (in beats per minute) during a race.
Sketch a graph of his heart rate over time and describe your graph in words.

Take account of
- waiting and warming-up
- changes of speed
- stopping to tie a shoe lace
- the last lap.

Some of the real life graphs you may have met already involve time, usually on the horizontal axis.

● **Time series** graphs show data changing over time.

Example

The table shows the temperature at noon each day in June for a town in Wales.
Draw a time series graph for this set of data.

Date	1	2	3	4	5	6	7	8	9	10	11	12	13	14	15
Temperature °C	9	10	9	11	10	10	8	12	14	16	17	21	20	15	13

Date	16	17	18	19	20	21	22	23	24	25	26	27	28	29	30
Temperature °C	12	14	13	14	15	13	13	12	15	18	19	20	19	18	19

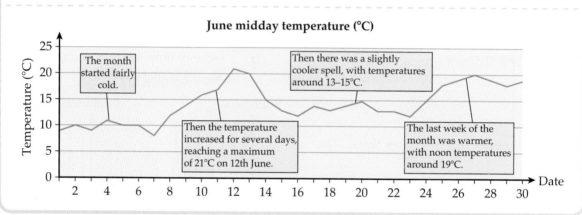

Time series graphs can show **trends** over a period of years.

Example

This graph shows the average number of children born to women in the UK from 1960 to 2010. Describe the main trends shown on the graph.

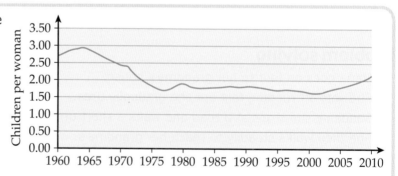

The average number of children born to each woman increased from about 2.7 in 1960 to nearly 3 in 1965.
After that, there was a fairly steady decrease to around 1.7 children per woman by about 1977.
Since then the number has remained relatively stable until 2000, varying between about 1.6 and 1.9 children per woman.
Since 2000 the number has climbed steadily to 2 children per woman.

Exercise 6e

1   A researcher used CCTV footage to estimate the number of people on a railway station platform. The table shows the data.

Time	07:00	07:30	08:00	08:30	09:00	09:30	10:00
People	48	145	113	82	45	31	17

Draw a time series graph for this set of data.

2   The table shows the approximate number of miles of track for railway in the UK. Draw a time series graph for this set of data.

Year	1830	1840	1850	1860	1870	1880	1890	1900	1910
Track Miles	0	1000	6000	9000	14000	16000	17000	19000	20000

Year	1920	1930	1940	1950	1960	1970	1980	1990	2000
Track Miles	20000	20000	20000	20000	18000	12000	10000	10000	10000

Problem solving

3   The chart shows the depth of water in a harbour.

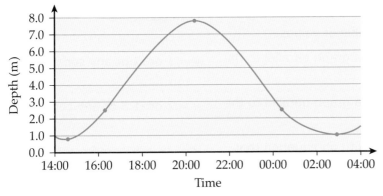

Did you know?

The depth of water in a harbour is governed by the pull of the moon, nearly 400 000 km away!

a   Describe the main features of the graph.

b   Captain Jack's boat can only enter or leave the harbour when the depth of water is above 2.5 m. What is the earliest time that he can enter the harbour? What is the latest time that he can leave?

4   This chart shows the changes in the prices of goods (the consumer price index) during the 20th century. Describe the main features of the graph.

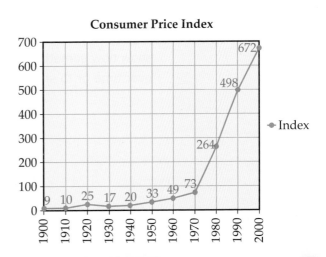

Consumer Price Index

6 MySummary

Check out

You should now be able to ...

Questions

✓ Draw a straight-line graph of a function.	1
✓ Recognise the equations of sloping lines and lines parallel to the axes.	2, 4
✓ Interpret and draw real life graphs.	3, 5
✓ Construct and interpret simple line graphs for time series.	6

Language	Meaning	Example
Function	A rule that gives a unique output for a given input. The rule is usually written as an equation	$y = 2x + 1$ gives an output value y for an input value x If $x = 2$ then $y = 5$
Equation	A function involving x and y which can be plotted on a graph using a table of values	$y = 7 - 3x$ and $y = 10x^2$ are both equations
Horizontal line	A line on a graph parallel to the x-axis	$y = 1$ or -3 or any constant
Vertical line	A line on a graph parallel to the y-axis	$x = 2$ or -1.5 or any constant
Straight line graph	A graph with an equation that can be written in the form $y = mx + c$	$y = 2x + 5$, $y = 5x$, $y = -6$ and $2x + 3y = 5$ are all straight lines
Real life graph	A graph which can be used to illustrate a real life situation	A graph of distance versus time for your journey to school
Time series graph	A graph which can be used to show how something changes over time or to show trends	A graph of your weekly pocket money versus the year

1 For the equation $y = 3x + 1$

  a copy and complete the table

x	0	1	2	3	4
y					

  b draw axes with x from 0 to 4 and y from 0 to 14 then draw the graph.

2 Write the equations of lines A, B, C and D.

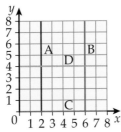

3

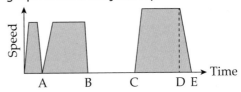

Celsius (°C)

This graph converts Celsius (°C) to Fahrenheit (°F).

  a What is 77 °F in degrees Celsius?

  b At what temperature in Fahrenheit does water freeze?

4 $y = -2$ $x = 5$ $y = 3x^2$

  $y = 4x$ $y + x = 8$

  Which of the equations above are

  a a horizontal   **b** a vertical

  c a sloping straight line

  d not a straight line?

5 Max drives to the shops and back, this graph shows his journey.

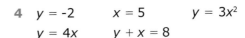

  a At what time, A, B, C, D or E, does he

    i leave the shop

    ii stop at traffic lights

    iii arrive home?

  b Does Max drive more quickly to the shop or home from the shop?

6 The number of children in an infant school is recorded over nine years.

Year	Children
2006	90
2007	95
2008	110
2009	145
2010	175
2011	180
2012	150
2013	120

Draw a time series graph for this set of data.

What next?

Score			
	0 – 3		Your knowledge of this topic is still developing. To improve look at Formative test: 2B-6; MyMaths: 1153, 1168 and 1184
	4 – 5		You are gaining a secure knowledge of this topic. To improve look at InvisiPen: 262, 265 and 275
	6		You have mastered this topic. Well done, you are ready to progress!

6a

1 **a** Copy and complete this table for the equation $y = x + 5$.
Plot points on axes labelled as shown here.
Draw the graph of the equation $y = x + 5$.

x	−1	0	1	2	3	4
y						

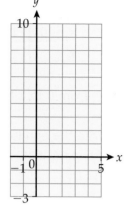

b Repeat for the equations
i $y = x + 2$
ii $y = 2x − 1$
iii $x + y = 9$

6b

2 For each of these equations, copy and complete this table.
Plot points for each equation on axes, both labelled from -2 to 8.
Draw the graph of each equation and label it.

x	0	1	2	3	4
y					

a $y = x + 1$ **b** $y = x − 1$ **c** $y = 2x − 1$ **d** $y = 8 − x$

3 Label both axes from 0 to 10. Draw the graphs of these lines
a $x = 6$ **b** $y = 5$ **c** $y = x + 1$ **d** $y = 2x$

6c

4 **a** You can convert euros € into pounds £ with this formula: $£ = \dfrac{3 \times €}{4}$.

Copy and complete this table using the formula.

€	0	8	12	20
£				

b Draw a graph to convert euros to pounds, with both axes labelled from 0 to 20.
i How many pounds will you get for €16?
ii How many euros will you get for £3?

5 Khaleda walks the 500 m to the shop in five minutes.
She spends three minutes in the shop and then returns home the same way in two minutes.
a Draw a graph to show her visit to the shop on axes as shown here.
b Was Khaleda faster going to the shop or coming back?

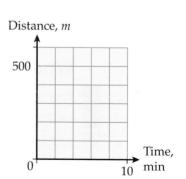

6 Sam heats some soup in the microwave for two minutes.
He takes it out and finds it is not warm enough.
He immediately reheats it for another minute
and then leaves it for a further minute before
starting to eat it.

Sketch a graph of the temperature of the soup during
this time.

7 The graph shows the number of people getting
on trains at a busy railway station.

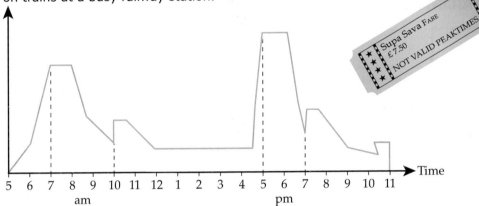

Time

5 6 7 8 9 10 11 12 1 2 3 4 5 6 7 8 9 10 11
am   pm

a Describe the main features of the graph.
b Explain the shape of the graph.

8 In an experiment, Jackie heated up a beaker of water, and then
left it to cool. She recorded the temperature every minute
(in degrees Celsius). Here are her results.
95, 79, 67, 57, 49, 43, 38, 34, 31, 28, 26, 25, 23, 22
Draw a time series graph for this set of data.

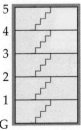

9 A department store has five floors: ground, 1, 2, 3 and 4.
There are up and down escalators between each floor.
Each escalator takes one minute to go up or down one floor, and it
takes 30 seconds to walk between escalators on each floor.
Monica starts on the ground floor, and travels up to the top floor as
quickly as possible.
Draw a time series graph for her journey.

5
4
3
2
1
G

Case study 2: Patchwork

Patchworks are made by sewing together several small pieces of fabric, often polygons that are chosen because they fit together to make the desired design. You can describe these designs as tessellations, because they fit together without leaving gaps.

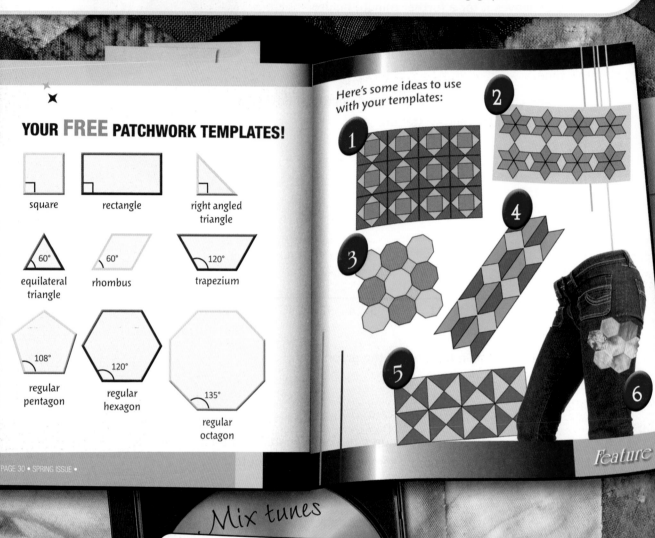

YOUR FREE PATCHWORK TEMPLATES!

square

rectangle

right angled triangle

60° equilateral triangle

60° rhombus

120° trapezium

108° regular pentagon

120° regular hexagon

135° regular octagon

Here's some ideas to use with your templates:

1 2 3 4 5 6

Feature

Mix tunes

7:33 PM
1 of 12
Patch It Up
2:42   -1:21

Task 1

Look at the patchwork templates, and the ideas 1 to 6 in the magazine above.

a   For each of the ideas 1 to 6, describe which templates have been used.

b i   Which patchworks use only one template?

ii   Which patchworks use more than one?

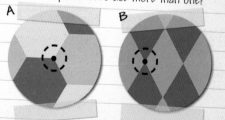

A   B

Task 2

Look at the patterns A and B. They are made up of the patchwork templates shown in the magazine.

a   For each pattern A and B, describe which template has been used.

b   (Harder) The angles at a point add up to 360°.

Can you explain why regular hexagons tessellate but regular pentagons do not?

c   What other combinations of the templates might tessellate? You can combine two or more templates.

Some patchworks do not seem to use recognisable polygons:

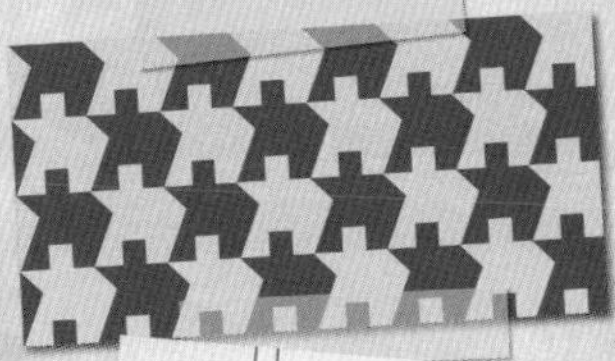

In fact, this patchwork is based on a tessellation of squares:

Remember: For your patchwork pattern to work, the shapes must be congruent (identical). 😊

8:00 PM

Task 3

a To make a template for this kind of patchwork, start with a square:

Draw a new shape inside the square:

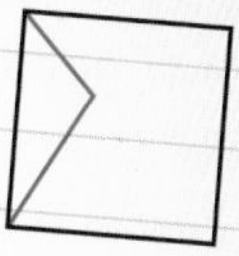

Draw exactly the same shape on the opposite side, but this time outside:

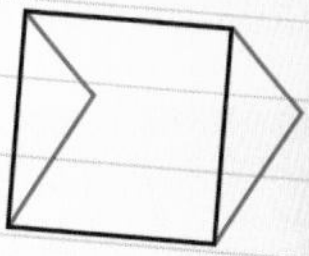

Repeat the process as much as you like, always copying the shape from one side to the outside of the opposite side:

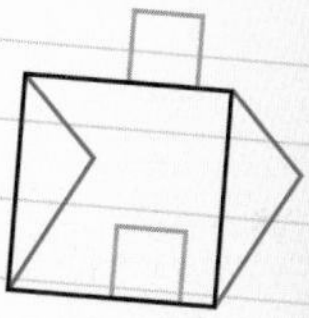

Draw around the new outline and rub out any unwanted lines. You have a template ready to cut out and use for your own patchwork design:

b Now try other ideas...

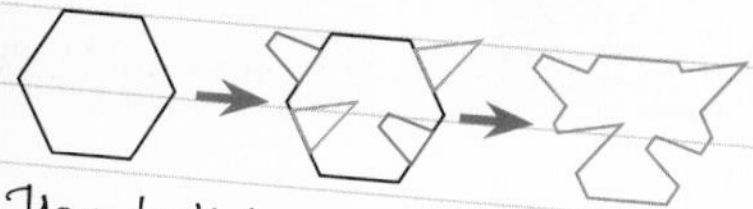

You don't have to start with a square

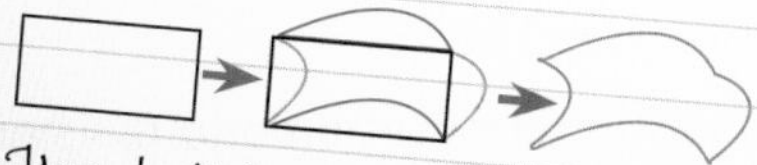

You don't have to draw straight lines (as long as you can repeat any curves accurately!)

VENICE
ART & ARCHITECTURE

As with this church floor in Venice, tessellation can be used to create 3D effects

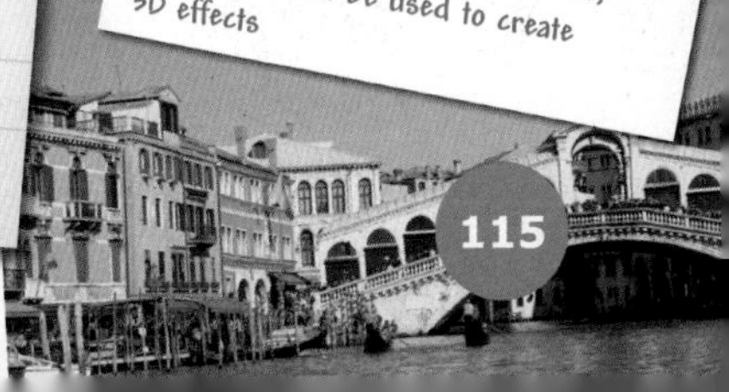

7 Mental Calculations

Introduction

Man has always tried to use technology to make all aspects of his life easier and more efficient. Mathematical calculation is no exception and the first devices invented to perform this task were called abacuses. They were mainly used to help with the buying and selling of goods.

It wasn't until 1642 (some two thousand years later) that Pascal invented the first mechanical calculator called the Pascaline.

It then took until the 1960s before Sharp produced the first battery powered calculator called the QT-8D.

What's the point?

Calculators help you perform calculations with large and awkward numbers. However you still need to understand what you're asking the calculator to work out, and check whether the answer is sensible.

Objectives

By the end of this chapter, you will have learned how to ...
- ● Round numbers.
- ● Use a range of mental strategies for addition, subtraction, multiplication and division.
- ● Multiply and divide a number by 10, 100 and 1000, and 0.1 and 0.01.
- ● Solve problems using mental strategies by breaking the problems down into smaller steps.

Check in

1   Round each of these numbers to the nearest   **i** 1000   **ii** 100   **iii** 10
   a 3462   **b** 5278   **c** 791   **d** 1072

2   Calculate these using a mental method.
   a 76 + 19   **b** 85 − 29   **c** 3.5 + 8.6   **d** 8.2 − 1.9

3   Calculate these using a written method.   **a** 34.6 + 51.5   **b** 87.5 − 19.7

4   Calculate
   a 39 × 10   **b** 4.8 × 100   **c** 58 ÷ 100   **d** 485 ÷ 10

5   Calculate these using mental methods.
   a 17 × 9   **b** 13 × 15   **c** 12 × 19   **d** 11 × 18

6   In each of these questions use an appropriate written method.
   a 32 × 15   **b** 112 ÷ 7   **c** 18 × 265   **d** 208 ÷ 16

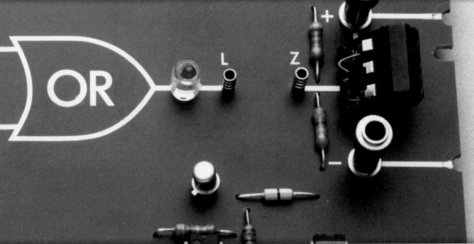

Starter problem

Here is a route of the streets a postman must
walk along for his daily route.

He starts at the sorting office which is
labelled A.

What is the shortest distance he can cover so
that he travels along every street at least once
and returns to his sorting office at A?

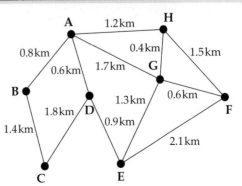

In many real life situations it is often best to **round** numbers, for example crowd attendances.

- When you round a number to the nearest whole number, nearest tenth or nearest hundredth
  - ▶ Look at the next digit.
  - ▶ If it is 5 or more, then the number is rounded up.
  - ▶ If it is less than 5, then the number is rounded down.

| 3 | 4 | 2 | . | 6 | 8 |

| 3 | 4 | 2 | . | 7 | |

Example

Round 3.6476 kg to the

a nearest whole number

b nearest tenth (1 dp)

c nearest hundredth (2 dp)

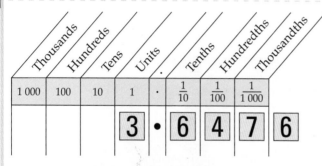

a Look at the tenths digit – this is 6.
   So round **up**.
   3.6476 kg ≈ 4 kg (nearest whole number)

b Look at the hundredths digit (4).
   So round **down**.
   3.6476 kg ≈ 3.6 kg (1 decimal place)

c Look at the thousandths digit (7).
   So round **up**.
   3.6476 kg ≈ 3.65 kg (nearest hundredth, or 2 decimal places)

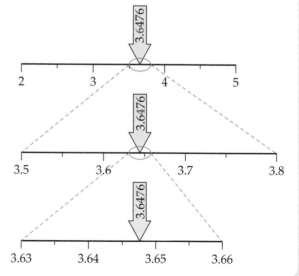

Exercise 7a

1 Round each of these numbers to the nearest

i	1000	ii	100	iii	10.
a	4072	**b**	7188	**c**	3654
d	7528	**e**	5594	**f**	6573
g	4938	**h**	13394	**i**	27593
j	31694	**k**	65959	**l**	74999

2 Round each of these numbers to the nearest
 i whole number **ii** tenth (1 dp)
 iii hundredth (2 dp).

a	3.736	**b**	4.218	**c**	7.2856
d	9.349	**e**	13.858	**f**	13.036
g	4.3061	**h**	7.9384	**i**	2.0394
j	2.6389	**k**	1.31846	**l**	3.58223

Problem solving

3 Mona runs 100 m in 17.999 seconds.
Mona decides to round her time to the nearest
whole number and also to the nearest tenth.
This is what she writes down:

17.999 ≈ 18 (nearest whole number)

17.999 ≈ 18 (nearest tenth)

Is Mona correct?

Explain your answer.

4 Work out these using a calculator and give your
answer to an appropriate degree of accuracy.
 a 13% of £25 **b** $\frac{2}{7}$ of £8
 c 4.75% of £230 **d** $\frac{1}{3}$ of 47p

5 Here is some information about a famous
event. Write a short article for a newspaper
about the event, rounding the numbers you
use to an appropriate degree of accuracy.

Date: 16 October 1987

Mini-hurricane strikes the
south east corner of England!
Duration of winds at high levels
6 hours 43 mins.
Maximum wind speed
115.0779 mph at Shoreham in
Sussex.

Average wind speed reached
86.3085 mph for 63 minutes.
14 983 000 trees lost during the
storm.

There are lots of mental strategies to help you work out additions and subtractions in your head.

● You can use the **partitioning** method to split the numbers into easier parts.

● You can use the **compensation** method by rounding one of the numbers and then adding or subtracting the extra.

Example

Calculate

a 6.6 + 8.7

b 13.4 − 8.9

a Use partitioning.

+8

+0.7

6.6   14.6 15.3

6.6 + 8.7 = 6.6 + 8 + 0.7
          = 14.6 + 0.7
          = 15.3

b Use compensation.

−9

4.4 4.5   13.4

+0.1

13.4 − 8.9 = 13.4 − 9 + 0.1
           = 4.4 + 0.1
           = 4.5

● You can find the difference between two numbers by counting up from the smaller number to the larger number.

Example

Laura attends Heswick School. In 2014 she was in Year 8. In a History lesson Laura finds out that the first Viking invasion of Britain took place in the year 793. How many years ago did this event take place?

+7   +200   +1000   +14

793 800   1000   2000 2014

2014 − 793 = 7 + 200 + 1000 + 14
           = 1221

The invasion was 1221 years ago.

Exercise 7b

1 Calculate these using a mental method.
   a 12.7 + 2.4   **b** 15.7 + 4.9
   c 17.4 − 9.6   **d** 18.8 + 6.6

2 Copy and complete each of these addition pyramids.

   a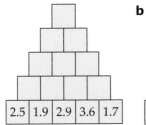

   b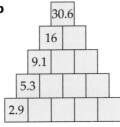

3 Calculate these using a mental method.
   a 14.6 + 9.5   **b** 3.57 + 4.9
   c 3.7 + 6.83   **d** 4.19 + 5.99

4 Find the missing numbers in each of these number sentences.
   a 6.43 + ☐ = 10
   b 8.95 + ☐ = 12.1
   c ☐ + 7.3 = 13.25
   d 6.99 + ☐ = 20
   e 30.5 − ☐ = 7.9
   f ☐ − 5.89 = 6.2

Problem solving

5 Here are some MP3 music files.
   a How much longer is track 02 compared to track 01?
   b How much bigger is the file for track 01 compared to track 03?
   c What is the total time of the four tracks?
   d Zeb can store 11 MB of MP3 music files on his mobile phone. Can he fit all four tracks onto his mobile phone? Explain your answer.

   Track 01
   Hip Hip Hop
   by the Hoppettes
   3m 28s   3.65MB

   Track 02
   Down the other side
   by Friends of the
   Fell Runners
   4m 15s   3.89MB

   Track 03
   Running up the hill
   by the Fell Runners
   3m 06s   2.9MB

   Track 04
   Hop Hop Hip
   by the Hippettes
   1m 58s   1.59MB

6 Here are some famous events in British history and the year they took place.

Battle of Hastings	1066
Magna Carta signed	1215
Battle of Bannockburn	1314
Spanish Armada defeated	1588
English Civil War	1642
Battle of Waterloo	1815

   a Work out how many years ago each event took place.
   b Imagine you live in the year 3542. How many years in the past would each event be now?
   c Imagine you lived in the year 2839 BC. How many years in the future would each event be?

MyMaths.co.uk   1345   SEARCH

121

Example

When you **multiply** a number by 10, 100 or 1000, all the **digits** move to the left.

Calculate 4.7 × 100

H	T	U	•	$\frac{1}{10}$	
		4	•	7	
4	7	0	•		

4.7 × 100 = 4.7 × 100
            = 470

When you **divide** a number by 10, 100 or 1000, all the digits move to the right.

Example

Calculate 28.9 ÷ 10

T	U	•	$\frac{1}{10}$	$\frac{1}{100}$	
2	8	•	9		
	2	•	8	9	

28.9 ÷ 10 = 28.9 ÷ 10
            = 2.89

You can also multiply and divide by 0.1 (tenths) and 0.01 (hundredths).

Multiplying by 0.1 is the same as dividing by 10.

Multiplying by 0.01 is the same as dividing by 100.

0.1 equals $\frac{1}{10}$, so multiplying by 0.1 is the same as finding a tenth.

Example

Calculate **a** 9 × 0.1   **b** 8 × 0.01

a $9 \times 0.1 = 9 \times \frac{1}{10}$
      $= 9 \div 10 = 0.9$

b $8 \times 0.01 = 8 \times \frac{1}{100}$
      $= 8 \div 100 = 0.08$

Dividing by 0.1 is the same as multiplying by 10.

Dividing by 0.01 is the same as multiplying by 100.

There are ten lots of a tenth in 1.

Example

Calculate **a** 4 ÷ 0.1   **b** 8 ÷ 0.01

a $4 \div 0.1 = 4 \div \frac{1}{10}$
      $= 4 \times 10 = 40$

b $8 \div 0.01 = 8 \div \frac{1}{100}$
      $= 8 \times 100 = 800$

Exercise 7c

1 Calculate

   a 7×10 **b** $40 \div 10$

   c 49×10 **d** $78 \div 100$

   e 0.3×1000 **f** $4.7 \div 10$

   g 0.094×10 **h** $59.3 \div 1000$

2 Calculate

   a $\frac{1}{10}$ of £300   **b** $\frac{1}{10}$ of $45\,\text{kg}$

   c $\frac{1}{100}$ of \$4000   **d** $\frac{1}{100}$ of $385\,\text{km}$

3 **a** Work out $3 \div 0.1$ by finding how many tenths there are in 3.

   b Work out $2 \div 0.01$ by finding how many hundredths there are in 2.

4 Calculate

   a 3×0.1 **b** 5×0.1

   c 9×0.01 **d** 7×0.01

   e $6 \div 0.1$ **f** $9 \div 0.1$

   g $5 \div 0.01$ **h** $3 \div 0.01$

5 Calculate

   a 25×0.1 **b** 29×0.01

   c $36 \div 0.1$ **d** $45 \div 0.01$

   e 290×0.1 **f** 370×0.01

   g $410 \div 0.1$ **h** $200 \div 0.01$

6 Calculate

   a 39×0.1 **b** $247 \div 0.1$

   c 2.9×0.1 **d** $4.1 \div 0.1$

   e $17.4 \div 0.01$ **f** $0.93 \div 0.01$

   g 34.5×0.1 **h** 2.7×0.01

   i 54.8×0.01 **j** 0.37×0.1

   k $27 \div 0.01$ **l** $0.08 \div 0.1$

7 **a** Convert $1560\,\text{ml}$ into litres.

   b Convert $36\,\text{km}$ into metres.

   c Convert $281\,\text{g}$ into kilograms.

   d Convert $5726\,\text{mm}$ into cm.

   e Convert 53.6 litres to millilitres.

   f Convert $19.23\,\text{kg}$ to grams.

Problem solving

8 Here are six number cards.

1000	100	10	1	0.1	0.01

Fill in the missing numbers in each of these statements using one of these cards.

   a $5 \times \square = 50$ **b** $0.2 \times \square = 20$

   c $470 \div \square = 47$ **d** $230 \div \square = 23$

   e $6 \div \square = 60$ **f** $0.3 \div \square = 30$

   g $520 \times \square = 52$ **h** $180 \div \square = 18$

9 Calculate

   a $57 \times 10 \times 0.01 \times 1000$

   b $11.2 \div 0.1 \div 0.1$

   c $0.57 \times 100 \div 0.1$

   d $2.6 \div 0.01 \times 0.1 \div 100$

Did you know?

The decimal system is not the only number system used in the world. The binary system is based on powers of 2 and is what computers rely on to work!

There are lots of mental strategies to help you work out multiplications and divisions in your head.

● You can re-write a number as a pair of **factors** and then do two simpler multiplications or divisions.

Dividing by 15 is the same as dividing by each of its factors in turn.

Example

Calculate   **a** 23×0.03 **b** $225 \div 15$

a $23 \times 0.03 = 23 \times 3 \times 0.01$
    $23 \times 3 = 69$
    $69 \times 0.01 = 0.69$
    $23 \times 0.03 = 0.69$

b $225 \div 15 = 225 \div 5 \div 3$
    $225 \div 5 = 45$
    $45 \div 3 = 15$
    $225 \div 15 = 15$

● You can use **partitioning** to split the numbers you are multiplying or dividing into parts that are easier to work with.

320 is an easy multiple of 16 to do in your head.

Example

Calculate   **a** 12×4.2 **b** $340 \div 16$

a $12 \times 4.2 = (10 \times 4.2) + (2 \times 4.2)$
      $= 42 + 8.4$
      $= 50.4$

b $340 \div 16 = (320 \div 16) + (20 \div 16)$
      $= 20 + 1\,R4$
      $= 21\,R4$

● You can use **compensation** when the number you are multiplying is nearly a multiple of 10 or 100. Round this number up or down and then adjust the answer accordingly.

Example

Calculate   **a** 4.1×19 **b** 7.2×21

a $4.1 \times 19 = (4.1 \times 20) - (4.1 \times 1)$
      $= 82 - 4.1$
      $= 77.9$

b $21 \times 7.2 = (20 \times 7.2) + (1 \times 7.2)$
      $= 144 + 7.2$
      $= 151.2$

Exercise 7d

1 Calculate these mentally using factors.

a	8 × 30	b	5 × 40
c	6 × 300	d	7 × 500
e	25 × 20	f	17 × 30
g	12 × 50	h	33 × 200
i	24 × 0.2	j	5 × 0.03
k	18 × 0.5	l	15 × 0.04
m	32 × 0.3	n	51 × 0.06
o	44 × 0.4	p	26 × 0.02
q	156 ÷ 6	r	140 ÷ 4
s	264 ÷ 12	t	360 ÷ 15
u	216 ÷ 8	v	126 ÷ 18
w	135 ÷ 15	x	108 ÷ 12
y	216 ÷ 8	z	504 ÷ 9

2 Calculate these using the method of partitioning.

a	3.4 × 12	b	2.1 × 15
c	13 × 1.4	d	16 × 3.5

2 | | | | |
|---|---|---|---|
| e | 2.8 × 11 | f | 4.3 × 15 |
| g | 3.9 × 12 | h | 14 × 6.2 |
| i | 150 ÷ 7 | j | 190 ÷ 8 |
| k | 220 ÷ 12 | l | 280 ÷ 13 |
| m | 310 ÷ 14 | n | 385 ÷ 15 |
| o | 410 ÷ 16 | p | 480 ÷ 22 |

3 Calculate these using the method of compensation.

a	21 × 2.9	b	19 × 4.4
c	8.1 × 21	d	3.6 × 31
e	3.5 × 19	f	4.2 × 29
g	19 × 1.9	h	21 × 5.9
i	3.8 × 19	j	2.4 × 22
k	18 × 1.6	l	49 × 2.5
m	7.9 × 39	n	64 × 0.58
o	21 × 19	p	79 × 31
q	48 × 52	r	62 × 78
s	7.1 × 19	t	6.9 × 22

Problem solving

4 Use an appropriate mental method to solve each of these problems.

a A chocolate bar contains 6.3 g of fat. In a month, Ciaron eats fifteen of the chocolate bars. How much fat does he consume each month by eating the chocolate bars?

b Kiefer drinks 2.3 litres of water a day. How much water does he drink in the month of January?

5 a Copy and complete the table, clearly showing the mental method you would use to work out each calculation.

b Compare your answers with a partner. Discuss the questions where you used different methods.

Calculation	Method I would use
8 × 19	Work out 8 × 20. Subtract 8.
7 × 21	
13 × 15	
156 ÷ 4	
16 × 19	
12 × 34	
31 × 6	
90 ÷ 7	
9 × 30	
11 × 15	

7e Mental addition and subtraction problems

You can solve real life problems using your strategies for mental addition and subtraction.

Here are the distances in kilometres between four towns.

Hanif walks from Deeport to Aton and then to Ceeley.

Jack walks from Deeport to St Bees and then to Ceeley.

Who walks the furthest distance and by how much?

Aton			
4.2 km	St Bees		
6.85 km	3.15 km	Ceeley	
2.65 km	5.4 km	7.6 km	Deeport

Hanif's journey = Deeport to Aton + Aton to Ceeley

Approximation $2.65 + 6.85 ≈ 3 + 7$

$≈ 10$ km

Exact $2.65 + 6.85 = 9.5$ km

Jack's journey = Deeport to St Bees + St Bees to Ceeley

Approximation $5.4 + 3.15 ≈ 5 + 3$

$≈ 8$ km

Exact $5.4 + 3.15 = 8.55$ km

Hanif walks further by $9.5 - 8.55 = 0.95$ km

You should start by making a good **approximation**.

Carrie has a £20 voucher for downloading films and music.

She downloads a movie for £6.89, an album for £7.95 and a music video for £1.87.

How much does she have left to spend?

Use compensation.

$£6.89 = £7 - 11p$ $£7.95 = £8 - 5p$ $£1.87 = £2 - 13p$

$£7 + £8 + £2 = £17$ $11p + 5p + 13p = 29p$

$£17 - £0.29 = £16.71$

Calculate how much is left.

$20 - 16.71 = 20 - 17 + 0.29$

$= £3.29$

Exercise 7e

Problem solving

1   A road runs from Preston to Colne. The distance between places on the road are shown in kilometres.

    a   How far is it from Preston to Burnley?

    b   Is it further from Preston to Accrington, or from Accrington to Colne? Explain your answer.

    c   Mr Mulachy is a teacher. He travels from his home in Blackburn to his school in Brierfield every day. How many kilometres does he travel in a week?

Colne
Brierfield
Burnley   7.2km
5.49km
Preston   Blackburn   Accrington   10.02km
16.4km   9.74km

2   Here are some items for sale in a shop. Work out the cost of these orders and the change they should be given.

    a   Malcolm buys a memory pen and a book. He pays with a £20 note.

    b   Jameela buys a mobile phone and a memory stick. She pays £50.

    c   Yuri buys a DVD, a computer game and a book. He pays £25.

    d   Valerie buys a DVD and a book. Natasha buys two identical memory pens. Who spends the most and by how much?

DVD   Computer game   Mobile phone

£8.95   £6.99   £36.35

Memory stick   Book

£7.20   £4.89

3   Five students at Verifast School run in the 100 m race. Here are their times.

Adam	14.3 seconds
Brett	14.08 seconds
Cris	13.9 seconds
Dominic	14.37 seconds
Eli	14.6 seconds

    a   How much longer did the slowest person take compared to the fastest person?

    b   Which two runners were 0.18 seconds apart?

4   Read this information carefully and then answer the questions.

> Bernice is 1.4 m tall.
> Shabeena is 0.18 m shorter than Bernice.
> Ingrid is 0.08 m shorter than Stephanie.
>
> Stephanie is 0.3 m taller than Bernice.
> Carla is 0.25 m shorter than Stephanie.

    a   Who is the tallest student and what is their height?

    b   How much taller than Shabeena is Ingrid?

    c   What is the difference in height between Carla and Bernice?

MyMaths.co.uk

7f Mental multiplication and division problems

You can solve real life problems involving multiplication and division using your mental strategies. Make sure you check your answer!

Example

Karen pays £7460 for printing 2000 holiday guidebooks.
These are the prices the printing firm charges for printing each holiday guidebook:

> 12p per page
> 85p for the cover

How many pages are there in Karen's guidebook?

Step 1 – Find the cost of one guidebook.
Cost of 1 guidebook = total cost ÷ number of guidebooks
= £7460 ÷ 2000
= £3.73

Step 2 – Find the cost of one guidebook without the cover.
Cost of all pages = 373p – 85p
= 288p

Look for multiples of 12 to split 288 into.

Step 3 – Find the number of pages.
Number of pages = cost of all pages ÷ cost of one page
= 288 ÷ 12
288 ÷ 12 = (240 ÷ 12) + (48 ÷ 12)
= 20 + 4
= 24 pages

> You should always check your working by performing an **inverse operation**.

Karen's guide has 24 pages + 1 cover
= 24 × 12p + 85p
= £3.73
Total cost of 2000 guides = £3.73 × 2000
= £7460

Exercise 7f

Problem solving

1 Jody is trying to improve her fitness levels. When she is cycling, Jody's heartbeat is 84 beats per minute.

When she is running, Jody's heartbeat is 92 beats per minute.

Jody cycles for 21 minutes per day and runs for 19 minutes per day.

Does Jody's heart beat more in total when she cycles or when she runs?

Explain and justify your answer.

2 Debbie pays £56 300 for printing 10 000 holiday guidebooks.

> 13p per page
> 95p for the cover

These are the prices the printing firm charges for printing each holiday guidebook.

How many pages are there in Debbie's guidebook?

3 Here are some items for sale on the 'Nut-e-nuts' website.

Type of nut	Cost per kg
Almonds	£8.85
Peanuts	£3.75
Walnuts	£6.95
Pecans	£11.69

3 Use an approximation to decide if each person has enough money for the cost of their orders. Explain and justify your answers.

a Maurice orders 5 kg of almonds and 4 kg of peanuts. He has £65.

b Jenna orders 11 kg of walnuts and 12 kg of pecans. She has £215.

c Callum orders 2 kg of almonds, 3 kg of peanuts and 5 kg of pecans. He has £95.

d Asha orders 6 kg each of almonds, peanuts, walnuts and pecans. She has £95.

4 Every person is recommended to consume five portions of fruit and vegetables every day. A 150 ml glass of orange juice counts as one daily portion. A carton of orange juice contains 1000 ml (= 1 litre).

a How many recommended daily portions of orange juice are there in one carton?

b A family of four decide to each drink 150 ml of orange juice every day. How much orange juice will they drink in one week? How many cartons of orange juice will they need to buy?

Check out

You should now be able to ...

✓ Round numbers.	5	1, 2
✓ Use a range of mental strategies for addition and subtraction.	5	3
✓ Multiply and divide by 10, 100 and 1000, and 0.1 and 0.01.	6	4, 5
✓ Use a range of mental strategies for multiplication and division.	5	6–8
✓ Solve problems using mental strategies by breaking the problems down into smaller steps.	5	9–11

Language	Meaning	Example
Round	To write a number as a near approximation	$153 = 150$ to the nearest 10 and $= 200$ to the nearest 100
Factors	Writing a number as a product of smaller numbers to make multiplication and division easier	$17 \times 0.3 = 17 \times 3 \times 0.1$ $= 51 \times 0.1$ $= 5.1$ $171 \div 9 = 171 \div 3 \div 3$ $= 57 \div 3$ $= 19$
Partitioning	To split a number into easier parts to make adding, subtracting or multiplying easier to do in your head	$27 + 18 = 27 + 10 + 8$ $= 37 + 8$ $= 45$
Compensation	A mental strategy that involves rounding one of the numbers and then adjusting the final answer to your sum	$27 + 18 = 27 + 20 - 2$ $= 47 - 2$ $= 45$
Inverse operation	A second operation that undoes the effect of a first operation	-5 is the inverse of $+5$ $\div 4$ is the inverse of $\times 4$

1 Round 29.507 to the nearest
  a whole number
  b tenth (1dp)
  c hundredth (2dp).

2 Work out these using a calculator and give your answers to an appropriate degree of accuracy.
  a 22.5% of £45   **b** $\frac{2}{3}$ of £25

3 Calculate these using a mental method.
  a 24.7 + 8.2   **b** 35.7 − 14.8
  c 27.8 − 9.9   **d** 5.34 + 7.82
  e 4.7 + 5.82   **f** 12 − 8.45
  g 6.23 − 5.81   **h** 14.45 + 9.67

4 Calculate
  a 56 ÷ 10   **b** 103 ÷ 100
  c 7 × 0.1   **d** 4 × 0.01
  e 25 × 0.001   **f** 0.4 ÷ 0.01
  g 99 × 0.001   **h** 350 × 0.01
  i 87 ÷ 0.1   **j** 0.9 × 0.01

5 Calculate
  a $\frac{1}{10}$ of £650   **b** $\frac{1}{100}$ of 29 kg

6 Calculate these using factors.
  a 35 × 0.2   **b** 61 × 15
  c 468 ÷ 6   **d** 585 ÷ 50

7 Calculate these using the method of partitioning.
  a 5.4 × 15   **b** 18 × 5.2
  c 176 ÷ 16   **d** 492 ÷ 12

8 Calculate these using the method of compensation.
  a 12 × 19   **b** 32 × 31
  c 5.6 × 39   **d** 18 × 1.9

9 At the newsagents, fizzy drinks cost 89p each and magazines cost £3.99
Jamie buys two fizzy drinks and a magazine. Use mental methods to calculate how much change he gets from a £10 note.

10 Milk costs 78p per litre.
  a Suzy buys 19 litres. How much does it cost?
  Suzy fills 200 ml cups with the milk.
  b How many cups can she fill with her 19 litres?
  c What is the cost of a 200 ml cup of milk?

11 Richard buys a 3 kg jar of sweets for £22. He plans to divide the sweets into 125 g packets and sell them for 99p each.
  a How many packets can he make?
  b How much profit will Richard make?

What next?

Score		
	0 – 4	Your knowledge of this topic is still developing. To improve look at Formative test: 2B-7; MyMaths: 1004, 1013, 1345
	5 – 8	You are gaining a secure knowledge of this topic. To improve look at InvisiPen: 112, 114, 121, 122 and 123
	10 – 11	You have mastered this topic. Well done, you are ready to progress!

7a

1 Round each of these numbers to the nearest
   i   1000   ii   100   iii   10
   a   3182   b   6273   c   4765   d   8632   e   6713   f   7682
   g   5049   h   24505   i   38 604   j   42783   k   76060   l   39494

2 Round each of these numbers to the nearest
   i   whole number   ii   tenth (1 dp)   iii   hundredth (2 dp).
   a   4.847   b   3.107   c   8.3967   d   8.238   e   24.969   f   22.623
   g   3.4172   h   8.0495   i   3.1405   j   3.0078   k   2.429 57   l   4.545 45

7b

3 Calculate these using a mental method.
   a   492 − 187   b   799 − 203   c   2615 − 616   d   3639 − 1009
   e   2215 − 1797 f   3011 − 1688 g   4383 − 3985   h   7473 − 4749
   i   5629 − 730   j   1057 − 862   k   9087 − 8123   l   2536 − 1985

4 Calculate these using a mental method.
   a   11.8 + 7.4   b   2.68 + 8.9   c   4.8 + 5.92   d   3.07 + 2.98
   e   13.7 − 8.88 f   6.99 − 3.49 g   8.71 − 4.8   h   9.67 − 3.85
   i   0.867 − 0.577 j   1.006 − 0.756 k   8.349 − 2.022 l   19.73 − 7.605

7c

5 Calculate
   a   3 × 10   b   6 × 100   c   90 ÷ 10   d   400 ÷ 100
   e   38 × 10   f   1.7 × 10   g   67 ÷ 100   h   497 ÷ 10
   i   0.075 × 10   j   6.1 ÷ 100   k   48.2 ÷ 1000   l   0.0032 × 100

6 Calculate
   a   4 × 0.1   b   6 × 0.1   c   7 × 0.01   d   2 × 0.01
   e   34 × 0.1   f   65 × 0.1   g   30 × 0.01   h   58 × 0.01
   i   85.4 × 0.01 j   0.73 × 0.1   k   68 ÷ 0.01   l   0.03 ÷ 0.1

7d

7 Calculate these using a mental method.
   a   7.3 × 11   b   6.4 × 9   c   14 × 5.2   d   13 × 31
   e   4.7 × 21   f   406 ÷ 7   g   3.4 × 13   h   300 ÷ 9
   i   235 ÷ 4   j   16 × 1.9   k   576 ÷ 8   l   3.7 × 15

8 Ali, Mary, Ben and Jules are planning a picnic. The prices of various item are shown below. For each possible order find

i the cost   **ii** the change that would be given.

a Ali buys some fruit and lemonade, paid for with £10

b Mary buys a salad pack and cheese, paid for with £20

c Ben buys a small loaf and cheese, paid for with £5

d Jules buys a cake and a bottle of lemonade, paid for with £10

e How much would the most expensive three items cost?

f How much more expensive is the lemonade than the loaf?

Fruit, 99 p   Loaf, £1.55   Salad, £2.05

Lemonade, £2.37   Cake, £3.95   Cheese, £1.67

9 Estimate these.

a The number of seconds in a week

b **i** The number of hours you sleep in a year

     ii The equivalent number of days

     iii The equivalent number of weeks

c The weight of a man in kilograms who weighs 12 stones
(1 kg is roughly 2.2 pounds, and there are 14 pounds in a stone)

d The number of adults that would weigh as much as 170 tonne blue whale

10 The cost of hiring a car for a week was £235. This was made up of a £140 fixed charge and a 20p per mile mileage charge for distances over 200 miles. How far did the car travel in the week?

8 Collecting and representing data

Introduction

A census has taken place every ten years in the United Kingdom since 1801. A census is a huge survey carried out by the government. It gathers information about every member of the population.

The first census was undertaken by the Babylonians in about 3800 BC. In this census the government counted the number of people, their livestock and quantities of food and useful materials. Another very famous historical census was the Domesday Book, commissioned by William the Conqueror in December 1085. This was a full audit of the land and resources held in England at the time, so that he could work out how much tax to charge.

What's the point?

Statistical information is used to help governments and businesses make important decisions based on understanding the attitudes, behaviours and needs of real people. Without this information, they would more often make the wrong decisions.

Objectives

By the end of this chapter, you will have learned how to …
- Identify and collect data.
- Construct pie charts.
- Construct bar charts and frequency diagrams.
- Calculate statistics for sets of discrete and continuous data.
- Construct scatter diagrams and understand correlation.
- Draw and interpret stem-and-leaf diagrams.

Check in

1   Karla asked people in her class how many books they had read in the last month.

    a   Draw a pictogram for this set of data.

    b   Draw a bar chart for the same set of data.

Number of books	Frequency
0	2
1	8
2	12
3 or more	9

2   Joe tests a dice by rolling it sixty times. He gets these results.

6, 4, 3, 6, 6, 5, 1, 2, 3, 4, 5, 4, 1, 1, 2, 4, 5, 1, 6, 3, 3, 2, 4, 4, 3, 3, 5, 1, 2, 4, 4, 6, 3, 3, 2, 4, 1, 5, 5, 2, 1, 4, 3, 3, 3, 2, 5, 6, 1, 5, 4, 4, 4, 3, 4, 1, 5, 2, 6, 1

Draw a table to represent this set of data.

Starter problem

How do students travel to your school?

What is the average time taken to travel to school?

Do boys take less time than the girls?

Do the students who live nearer the school take less time than the students who live further away?

Investigate and write a short report on your results.

Julie is carrying out a **survey** on the use of the internet.
She needs to think carefully about the data that she will need.

I could use primary data ...or secondary data.

- **Primary data** is data that you collect yourself from a survey or experiment.

- **Secondary data** is data that you look up, perhaps in a book or on the internet.

Julie decides to collect primary data. She asks a sample of 16 girls in her class to complete a short questionnaire. She gives them a range of options.

How much time did you spend on the internet last night?
Please tick one box.

Less than 15 minutes	15 minutes or more, but less than 30	30 minutes or more, but less than 1 hour	One hour or more

Julie wants to make conclusions when she has completed her survey.

If Julie is looking at internet use by girls of her age, her survey should be fairly reliable.

If she wants to make general conclusions about internet use, Julie should ask a wider range of people.

Julie's sample size of 16 is small, and she should consider increasing it because large samples generally give more reliable results.

Exercise 8a

1 Explain whether each source of data is primary or secondary data.

   a A chart published in a newspaper

   b The results of a science experiment

   c Data from a class survey

   d A table of data you find on the internet

   e Data you collect about the lengths of words in a book.

   f A set of data your teacher gives you.

2 Explain whether each of the following topics could be investigated using primary or secondary data. If secondary, suggest where you might find it. If primary, explain how you would collect it.

   a Life expectancy in different countries

   b Favourite lessons of students in Year 8

   c Best deals on mobile phone contracts

   d The most likely scores in football

   e Do teenagers watch too much television?

Problem solving

3 This is Pete, and he has something to say about the internet.
Explain why Pete might not be correct. Give examples of questions that would not be sensible to investigate in this way.

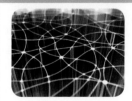

The internet is the best place to find data. You can find everything you need without having to leave your seat!

4 This is Krysia and she has something to say about collecting data.
Write a response to Krysia's statement. Include examples of questions that you could not investigate in this way.

There is no substitute for collecting your own data. It might take a little time, but you can never really trust data collected by somebody else.

5 Roisin is investigating the weight of students' school bags. She decides that she will pick up people's bags, and decide whether each one is light or heavy.
What are the problems with this approach, and how could it be improved?

6 Comment on how good the questions are in this questionnaire, and suggest improvements. Is there anything missing?

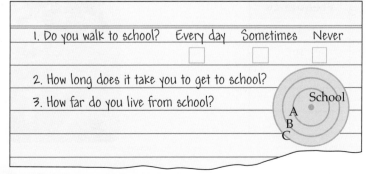

Did you know?

No one person invented the internet, but its development began in the early 1960s. Today it is estimated that almost one and a half billion people use the internet.

MyMaths.co.uk

There are different types of data that you can collect.

▲ The number of pets someone owns is discrete data

🔵 **Discrete** data is data obtained by counting.

A **two-way table** can be a useful way of displaying discrete data.

Example

The table shows information about the cats entered in a show.

How many

a   short-haired black cats

b   long-haired cats

c   tortoiseshell cats were there altogether?

	Black	Tabby	Tortoiseshell
Long-haired	2	2	3
Short-haired	3	8	2

a   3

b   2 + 2 + 3 = 7

c   3 + 2 = 5

🔵 **Continuous** data is data obtained by measuring.

You can group continuous data in a **frequency table**.

◀ The length of a hand is continuous data

Example

A scientist measured the lengths of some fish. Their lengths (in cm) were

11.7   12.7   9.8   10.1   12.5   11.7   11.5   10.7   11.5   11.5   11.8   10.6   10.4

12.9   11.6   11.9   12.8   10.5   10.8   10.9   13.7   10.5   11.8

Construct a frequency table for this set of continuous data.

Length, x cm	Tally	Frequency
$9.0 \leq x < 10.0$	I	1
$10.0 \leq x < 11.0$	I̶H̶I III	8
$11.0 \leq x < 12.0$	I̶H̶I IIII	9
$12.0 \leq x < 13.0$	IIII	4
$13.0 \leq x < 14.0$	I	1

❮ p.62

Exercise 8b

1 Here are some examples of data.
Explain whether each one is an example
of discrete or continuous data.
a Number of children in a family
b Weight of a piglet
c Length of a river
d Number of people in a car.
e Number of hairs on your head.

2 Jake counted the number of people in
cars arriving at his school for an evening
meeting. The data for 50 cars are shown.

```
2 4 2 3 3 4 1 1 2 1 1 1 1
2 2 1 1 3 1 1 1 3 2 1 1 4
2 2 1 4 4 3 3 1 2 1 1 2 2
1 3 1 1 2 3 4 3 2 4 1
```

Occupants	Tally	Frequency
1		
2		
3		
4		

Copy the table and complete it to find the
frequencies for each number of occupants.

3 Here are the heights (in metres) of
30 people.

```
1.69  1.64  1.25  1.37  1.48  1.67
1.37  1.43  1.50  1.59  1.78  1.33
1.45  1.11  1.56  1.52  1.69  1.57
1.87  1.51  1.58  1.44  1.46  1.43
1.37  1.42  1.26  1.76  1.78  1.44
```

Height, h metres	Tally	Frequency
$1.00 \leq h < 1.20$		
$1.20 \leq h < 1.40$		
$1.40 \leq h < 1.60$		
$1.60 \leq h < 1.80$		
$1.80 \leq h < 2.00$		

Copy and complete the table.

4 The lifetime, in hours, of 40 batteries was
recorded as follows:

```
34  61  48  78  76  65  56  43  57  47
62  57  31  43  72  64  64  59  58  51
75  78  53  32  70  43  67  44  59  64
67  39  78  49  64  32  55  39  45  54
```

Construct a frequency table for this data.

Problem solving

5 The diagram represents a set of plates.
There are large and small plates, and
three different colours.
Draw a two-way table to show the number
of plates of each size and colour.

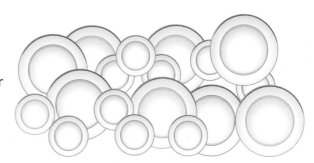

6 You have been asked to collect data
on how many seconds the students in
your class can hold their breath for.
a Decide on suitable time intervals and
create a frequency table to record your results.
b Collect and record data from your class.
c What type of graph would you draw to display your results and why?
d Suggest one way in which you could improve how you collected and recorded the data.

○ Categorical data is data obtained by describing.

You can show categorical data in a pie chart. You need to find the angle for each sector.

Eye colour is categorical data

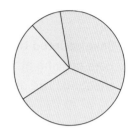

◑ A pie chart allows you to show amounts of data as portions of a circle.

▶ The whole circle represents the total amount.

Example

This table shows how a group of students travelled to school.
Draw a pie chart for this set of data.

Transport	Frequency
Walk	16
Bus	8
Car	8

Half the students walked to school, so the sector for 'Walk' has an angle of 180° (half of 360°). The angles for 'Bus' and 'Car' should both be 90° because they are a quarter each.

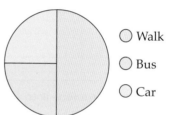

○ Walk
○ Bus
○ Car

Example

This table shows the eye colours of a group of people.

Eye colour	Frequency
Brown	6
Green	8
Blue	3

Draw a pie chart for this set of data.

Total number of people
$= 6 + 8 + 3 = 17$
Angle for Brown
$= \frac{6}{17} \times 360° = 127°$
Angle for Green
$= \frac{8}{17} \times 360° = 169°$
Angle for Blue
$= \frac{3}{17} \times 360° = 64°$

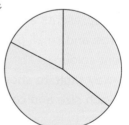

○ Brown
○ Green
○ Blue

Always include a key to say what each sector represents.

Exercise 8c

1   Sketch a pie chart for the data in each of these tables.
    You do not need to calculate angles or draw these accurately.

a

Animal	Frequency
Dogs	12
Cats	11
Birds	13

b

Country	Medals won
Spain	19
Cuba	10
USA	11
Japan	41

c

Service	Calls received
Fire	16
Police	14
Ambulance	15
Coast Guard	4

2   Draw the pie charts from question **1** accurately.
    You will need to
    • calculate the angles (mentally, with a written method or using a calculator), and
    • draw the diagram using a protractor, ruler and compasses.

Problem solving

3   Marcus used a spreadsheet to produce this pie chart for the data in the table.

	A	B
1	Genre	Number
2	Fiction	8
3	History	12
4	Reference	9
5	Biography	7

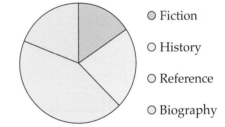

○ Fiction

○ History

○ Reference

○ Biography

a   Explain why this pie chart cannot be correct.
b   Draw a correct version of the pie chart.

4   The pie chart shows the attendance at four different films shown at a cinema one evening.
    Use the pie chart to estimate the percentage of the total cinema audience who attended each film.

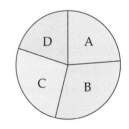

5   These two pie charts show the types of housing in two towns.

   ○ Terraces   ○ Semi   ○ Detached   ○ Flat

a   Make a list of some conclusions that you can draw from these pie charts.
b   What misconceptions might cause someone to draw incorrect conclusions from these pie charts?

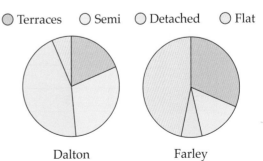

Dalton   Farley

Bar charts and frequency diagrams provide good ways to represent data.

Example

The tables show two sets of data for the students in a class.

Draw bar charts to represent the data.

a

Number of siblings	Frequency
0	6
1	4
2	5
3	2
4	1

b

Eye colour	Frequency
Green	4
Blue	11
Brown	3

a

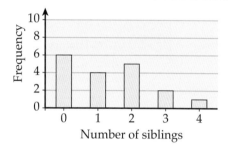

b

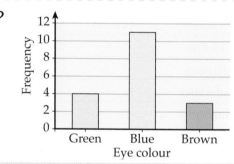

Example

The table shows the heights of students in a class.

Draw a frequency diagram for this data.

Height, h cm	Frequency
$130 \leq h < 140$	2
$140 \leq h < 150$	8
$150 \leq h < 160$	9
$160 \leq h < 170$	3
$170 \leq h < 180$	5

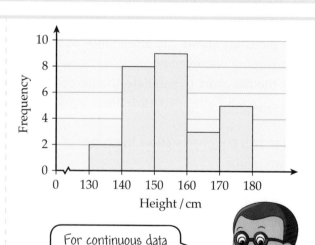

For continuous data you should have no gaps between the bars.

Exercise 8d

1   This data shows the colours of thirty cars
    in a survey.

Green	Grey	Yellow	Grey	Red
Red	Blue	Grey	Grey	White
Black	Grey	White	Red	Grey
Black	Grey	Green	Red	Blue
Green	Grey	Grey	Red	Grey
Grey	Blue	Black	Yellow	Green

Draw a bar chart for this set of
categorical data.

2   This data shows the shoe sizes of thirty
    adults in a survey.

6	3	6	6	5
7	5	7	7	4
6	7	4	6	10
8	7	6	9	8
5	8	5	5	6
8	4	9	6	8

Draw a bar chart for this set of discrete
numerical data.

Problem solving

3   This data shows the weights of thirty adults in a survey.
    a   Fill in the blanks.
    b   Draw a frequency diagram for this set of continuous
        numerical data.

Weight, w kg	Frequency
$50 \leq w < 60$	☐
☐ $\leq w < 70$	7
$70 \leq w < 80$	15
$80 \leq w < 90$	5

4   The bar chart shows the results of a survey about pet ownership.
    a   What was the modal number of pets owned by people who
        took part in the survey?
    b   How many people took part in the survey?
    c   What was the total number of pets owned by people who
        took part in the survey?
    d   What was the mean number of pets owned by people who
        took part in the survey?

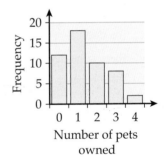

5   These diagrams show the same two sets of data in different ways.
    The data relates to the number of sightings of wildcats in two different regions.
    What are the advantages and disadvantages of each type of diagram?

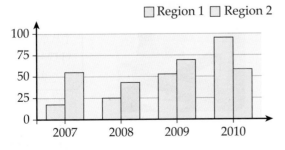

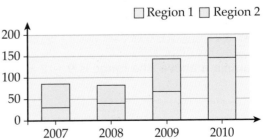

8e Averages

You can use one of three different **averages** to help you make sense of the data.

> ● The **mode** is the most common value in a set of data.

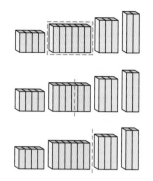

> ● The **median** is the middle value when the data is put in order.

> ● To find the **mean**, add up all the values, and then divide by the number of items.

Find the mode, the median and the mean of these sets of data.

a The number of pets owned by seven students:
2, 4, 4, 4, 5, 7, 9

b The ages of six members of a family: 3, 7, 12, 13, 16, 21

c The number of flowers on nine different plants:
6, 3, 5, 5, 9, 2, 6, 4, 1

---

a The mode is 4 pets.
The median is 4 pets.
$2 + 4 + 4 + 4 + 5 + 7 + 9 = 35$.
The mean is $\frac{31}{7}$ = 5 pets.

To find the mean, first add the values.

b There is no mode.
The median is 12.5 years old.
The mean is $\frac{72}{6}$ = 12 years old.

There are no repeated values.

There is an even number of values;
the median is halfway between the two 'middle' values.

c There are two modes: 5 and 6 flowers.
1, 2, 3, 4, 5, 5, 6, 6, 9.
The median is 5 flowers.
The mean is $\frac{41}{9}$ = 4.56 flowers.

To find the median, first put the data in order.

Another important **statistic** is the **range**.

> ● Range = maximum value − minimum value

In example **a** above, the range is 9 − 2 = 7 pets.

The range tells you about the **spread** of the data.

Exercise 8e

1 Four students in class 8A who used the 'MyFace' website recorded the number of messages they received each day.

Amy   3, 5, 5, 5, 6, 6, 2
Jen   4, 4, 8, 9, 9, 11
Selma   5, 6, 1, 2, 5, 7, 8, 4, 6, 2, 6, 6
Jo   2, 1, 7, 8, 5, 3

a How many days did each person keep records for?

b Find the *mode* of each of these sets of data.

2 Mrs Morgan asked students in class 8B to find out about mobile phone use. Five students asked people how many text messages they had sent the previous day.

Kalid   3, 5, 9
Emily   4, 5, 4, 7, 1
Dan   2, 6, 7, 9
Steph   5, 0, 8, 7, 3, 9
James   2, 3, 6, 8, 8, 9, 11

a Who asked most people?

b Calculate the **median** of each person's data.

3 Five basketball players recorded the number of points they scored in each game that they played in a tournament.

Sandra   5, 5, 5, 5
Abbie   3, 6, 7, 9, 15
Lizzie   3, 4, 5, 6
Jill   3, 6, 9, 19, 13, 7
Maya   2, 9, 7, 2

a How many games did each person play?

b Calculate the *mean* score for each player.

c Calculate the *mean* score for all five players.

4 Work out the *range* of each of these sets of data.

a Number of people living in five houses:
1, 1, 4, 6, 9

b Number of absences for five students:
5, 4, 3, 9, 6

c Number of books borrowed from the school library by six students:
9, 5, 0, 6, 4, 8

d Mass (in kilograms) of 5 cats:
4.8, 6.3, 2.1, 5.8, 2.2

Problem solving

5 Can you make up examples of sets of numbers where:

a The mean, median and mode are all equal

b The mean and median are the same, but the mode is smaller

c The mode is bigger than the median, and the median is bigger than the mean

d The mode is 1, the median is 2 and the mean is 3?

Did you know?

During the 5th century BC siege of Platea the Athenians estimated the height of the city walls by multiplying the height of a brick by the mode number of bricks counted by soldiers.

You can calculate statistics for data given in a frequency table.

Example

The **frequency table** shows the number of goals scored during a season by members of a football club.

Number of goals	Frequency
0	12
1	7
2	3
3	4
4	1

a How many players are included in the table?

b Find the **mean**, **median**, **mode** and **range** of the number of goals scored.

a The total number of players is
12 + 7 + 3 + 4 + 1 = 27.

b The mode is 0 goals.
The median is the 14th value, that is, 1 goal.
The mean is the total number of goals divided by the total number of players.

 Add up the frequencies, in order, to find the class containing the 14th value.

 The mode is the class with the highest frequency.

Number of goals	Frequency	Totals
0	12	$0 \times 12 = 0$
1	7	$1 \times 7 = 7$
2	3	$2 \times 3 = 6$
3	4	$3 \times 4 = 12$
4	1	$4 \times 1 = 4$

 Add an extra column to the table to help you calculate the total number of goals.

The total number of goals scored is
0 + 7 + 6 + 12 + 4 = 29.
The mean is $\frac{29}{27}$ = 1.07 goals per player.
The range is 4 − 0 = 4 goals.

The range is the difference between the maximum and minimum numbers of goals scored.

Exercise 8f

1 This frequency table shows the number of pets owned by the students in class 8C5.

a How many students' data are shown in the table?

b What is the **modal** number of pets owned by the students in 8C5? (This is the mode.)

c What is the range of the number of pets owned by people in 8C5?

Number of pets	Frequency
0	10
1	12
2	7
3	2

2 Students in class 8P were asked to record the number of portions of fruit and vegetables that they ate one day.

a How many students' data are shown in the table?

b What is the modal number of portions eaten?

c What was the median of the number of portions eaten?

Portions of fruit and vegetables	Frequency
0	1
1	2
2	5
3	4
4	9
5	6
6	4
7	1

3 The table shows the number of absences for the students in class 8K during one term.

a Find the total number of students whose data are shown in the table.

b Redraw the table with an extra column to show the total number of absences.

c Find the overall total number of absences for the whole class.

d Use your answers to parts **a** and **c** to calculate the mean number of absences per student.

Number of absences	Frequency
0	10
1	5
2	4
3	2
4	3
5	3
6	2
7	0
8	1

Problem solving

4 The table shows the heights of students in class 8KT.

Height, h cm	Frequency
$140 \leqslant h < 150$	5
$150 \leqslant h < 160$	14
$160 \leqslant h < 170$	9
$170 \leqslant h < 180$	3

a What is the **modal class** for this set of data? (This is just the class that has the highest frequency.)

b Why is the modal class the only average that can be worked out easily?

Did you know?

In terms of the amount grown the most popular fruit in the world is the tomato, followed by bananas, apples and oranges. In terms of what people say the most popular fruit in the world is probably the mango.

 **MyMaths**.co.uk   Q 1254   **SEARCH**

Scatter diagrams are used to show patterns in pairs of data.

Example

The table shows the number of pages and weights of ten books.

Show this data in a **scatter diagram**, and describe any patterns.

Book	A	B	C	D	E	F	G	H	I	J
Number of pages	245	136	128	410	338	237	317	92	602	320
Weight (g)	504	258	855	795	692	451	655	211	1350	700

In general, the scatter diagram shows that books with more pages are heavier.

There is one book that does not fit this pattern – this could be a large-format book with few pages.

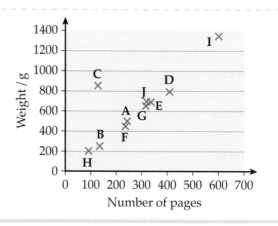

● **Correlation** describes the connection between two sets of data.

Correlation measures how close the points are to a straight line, not how steep the line is.

This is **positive correlation**.

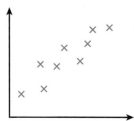

As one quantity increases, so does the other.

This is **negative correlation**.

As one quantity increases, the other decreases.

This is **no correlation**.

There is no connection between the two quantities.

Exercise 8g

1 Matt collected the scores for ten people in a Maths test
and a Science test, and started to draw a scatter diagram.

Maths	10	16	15	8	18	11	9	4	19	20
Science	12	14	12	5	16	9	6	7	16	18

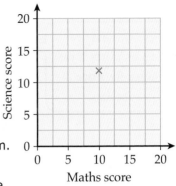

  a Copy the diagram, and complete it using the data
     from the table.
  b Describe and explain any correlation in your scatter diagram.

2 Pat gathered data about the height and arm-span of ten people.

Height (cm)	165	162	148	149	151	153	139	149	134	140
Arm-span (cm)	163	163	145	147	149	155	142	153	137	138

  a Use the data in the table to plot a scatter diagram.
  b Comment on the pattern shown in your diagram.

3 Josh wanted to see if there was any correlation between the numbers of emails and text
messages that people received in one day. The table shows the results for twelve people.

Emails	12	14	9	2	0	8	15	14	11	6	4	5
Texts	4	3	8	2	6	1	8	5	3	1	2	14

  a Draw a scatter diagram for Josh's data.
  b Explain whether or not there is a correlation between the numbers of emails and text
     messages received by the people surveyed.

Problem solving

4 The table shows the ages and weights of a group of cats.
Simon drew a scatter graph to show this set of data.

Age (years)	8	3	11	7	1	14	2	6
Weight (kg)	2.8	3.5	2.3	4.2	3.7	2.1	3.5	4.2

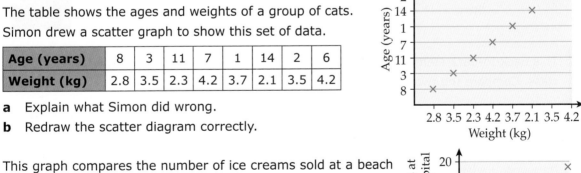

  a Explain what Simon did wrong.
  b Redraw the scatter diagram correctly.

5 This graph compares the number of ice creams sold at a beach
cafe with the number of people treated for sunburn at the local
hospital, for ten days during the summer.
Jason says, 'When more ice creams are
sold, more people get sunburnt. So, ice
cream causes sunburn.'
Is this a reasonable interpretation of the
graph?

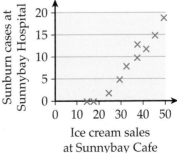

A stem-and-leaf diagram makes it easy to see the shape of the data.

Example

The table shows the heights in centimetres of twenty people in a class.

| 159 | 173 | 170 | 154 | 181 | 163 | 165 | 180 | 178 | 150 |
| 160 | 163 | 164 | 177 | 157 | 181 | 177 | 159 | 168 | 151 |

a Draw a **stem-and-leaf diagram**.

b Find the median and range.

a

```
18 │ 0  1  1
17 │ 0  3  7  7  8
16 │ 0  3  3  4  5  8
15 │ 0  1  4  7  9  9        Key  15 │ 4 = 154 cm
```

The multiples of   The units are the 'leaves'.
10 are the 'stem'.

You must always include a key.

b Median = (163 + 163) ÷ 2

= 163 cm   There are 20 values so the median is halfway between the 10th and 11th values.

Range = 181 – 150

= 31 cm.

Example

This back-to-back stem-and-leaf diagram shows the heights of the boys and the girls in a class. Compare the two sets of data.

The diagram shows two sets of data.
On the left are the girls' heights: 135, 135, ..., 163
On the right are the boys' heights: 142, 148, ..., 172
On average, the boys are taller than the girls:
    The modal class of the boys' heights is 160–170 cm
    The modal class of the girls' heights is 150–160 cm.
The boys' heights are more spread out than the girls':
    The range of the boys' heights is 172 cm – 142 cm = 30 cm
    The range of the girls' heights is 163 cm – 135 cm = 28 cm.

```
        Girls                      Boys
              │ 17 │ 1  1  2
         3  0 │ 16 │ 3  4  7  8
    8  6  5  1 │ 15 │ 1  5  8
       9  5  2 │ 14 │ 2  8
       7  5  5 │ 13 │

            Key  0 │ 16 │ 3
            Girls 160 cm
            Boys  163 cm
```

Exercise 8h

1 This stem-and-leaf diagram shows the numbers of tickets sold for twenty one different performances of a play.

```
25 | 0  0  0  0  0
24 | 2  8
23 | 0  3              Key    21 | 7
22 | 3  5  6              = 217 tickets
21 | 2  4  7  7
20 | 1  2  4  9
19 | 4
```

a Find the median number of tickets sold.
b Find the modal class of the number of tickets sold.
c Find the range of the number of tickets sold.

2 Here are the heights of 21 people in centimetres. They have been put into order.

101	113	119	121	124	124	126
130	131	134	137	138	140	145
145	147	150	155	156	162	171

Use the data to copy and complete the stem-and-leaf diagram.
The first three values have been entered.

```
100 | 1
110 | 3        9
120 |
130 |                  Key  100 | 1
140 |                    represents
150 |                    101 cm
160 |
170 |
```

3 A teacher compared the scores of one of her classes on two tests.

Test 1 scores

18, 21, 24, 24, 27,
30, 31, 32, 32, 34,
35, 35, 36, 37, 39,
42, 44, 46, 48, 48

Test 2 scores

24, 25, 25, 26, 29,
30, 32, 35, 36, 38,
38, 41, 41, 43, 44,
48, 49, 50, 50, 50

a Construct a back-to-back stem-and-leaf diagram for this set of data.
b Describe the distribution of the scores on the two tests, using your diagram to help calculate suitable statistics.

4 This table shows the weights of 27 people in kilograms.
The weights have **not** been put into order.

48	81	53	51	64	58	41	42	63
55	60	74	63	57	44	36	52	68
72	45	37	57	34	59	40	65	52

a Draw a stem-and-leaf diagram for this set of data.
Use multiples of 10 as the 'stem' and units as the 'leaves'.
Include a key to explain how the diagram works.
b Use the diagram to find the median.

Problem solving

5 You could have used bar charts or frequency diagrams to represent the data in the questions above.
What are the advantages and disadvantages of using stem-and-leaf diagrams instead of bar charts or frequency diagrams?

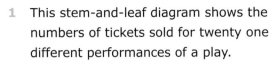 **MyMaths**.co.uk

Check out

You should now be able to ...

Test it ➡

Questions

✓ Identify and collect data.	6	1
✓ Construct pie charts.	6	2
✓ Construct bar charts and frequency diagrams.	6	3
✓ Calculate statistics for sets of discrete and continuous data.	6	4, 5
✓ Construct scatter diagrams and understand correlation.	6	6
✓ Draw and interpret stem-and-leaf diagrams.	6	7

Language	Meaning	Example
Primary data	Data which you collect yourself	The results of a survey or experiment that you carried out
Secondary data	Data which you did not collect yourself	Information from a book or the internet
Discrete data	Data which is obtained by counting	The number of pets or brothers and sisters that you have
Continuous data	Data which is obtained by measuring	Your height, weight or age
Categorical data	Data which is obtained by describing	The colour of your eyes
Bar chart	Used to represent categorical or discrete data	Examples of bar charts are on page 142.
Frequency diagram	Used to show continuous data	There is a frequency diagram on page 142.
Average	A measure of the 'typical value' of data	The mode, median and mean are averages
Range	A measure of the spread of data	The range of -5, -1, 2, 4 and 9 is $9 - (-5) = 14$
Scatter diagram	A graph which allows you to see patterns in pairs of data	A graph of height versus weight for students in your class
Stem-and-leaf diagram	A diagram which allows you to see the shape of the distribution of data while retaining the actual numerical values of the data	See page 150

1 Explain whether the data below is
   i   primary or secondary
   ii discrete or continuous.
   a Lengths you measure in a science class.
   b Days spent in hospital taken from patient records.
   c Number of house points won at your school's sports day.

2 Draw a pie chart to show peoples' favourite type of film.

Action	10	Comedy	7
Romance	5	Musical	2
Horror	4	Other	2

3 The table shows the weights of 12 mice (g).

Weight (g)	Frequency
15 ≤ w < 20	1
20 ≤ w < 25	4
25 ≤ w < 30	4
30 ≤ w < 35	2
35 ≤ w < 40	1

Draw a frequency diagram for this data.

4 Here are the shoe sizes of 12 women.
   5, 7, 6, 4, 3, 3, 5, 6, 5, 7, 6, 4
   Find
   a the mode   b the mean (1dp)
   c the median   d the range.

5 The table shows how many packets of crisps students ate in one week.

Packs of crisps	0	1	2	3	4	5	6	7
Frequency	6	4	9	10	5	3	2	1

   a Find the modal number of packs eaten.
   b Calculate the mean number of packs of crisps per student.

6 The number of hot drinks and of fizzy drinks sold at a cafe on seven different days is shown in the table.

Hot	65	40	50	30	20	15	60
Fizzy	25	35	30	40	50	45	25

   a Draw a scatter diagram for this data.
   b Describe the correlation.

7 The stem-and-leaf diagram shows the age of the first 20 people to arrive at a theme park.

```
0 | 5   9
1 | 0   0   1   3   5   6
2 | 1   6   8   9
3 | 5   7   8
4 | 3   5   5
5 | 8
6 | 1                3 | 5  = 35 years old
```

Find   a the range   b the median.

What next?

Score	0 – 2		Your knowledge of this topic is still developing. To improve look at Formative test: 2B-8; MyMaths: 1200, 1203, 1206, 1213, 1215 and 1254
	3 – 6		You are gaining a secure knowledge of this topic. To improve look at InvisiPen: 411, 414, 422, 423, 242, 427, 431, 441 and 442
	7		You have mastered this topic. Well done, you are ready to progress!

MyMaths.co.uk

1   Give some examples of primary and secondary data that you
    could use to investigate these topics.
    a   Recycling
    b   Mobile phone use
    c   Exercise and sport

2   Tom asked 30 people in his class how many books they currently
    had out on loan from the school library. Here are his results.
    3   2   2   2   1   0   3   0   1   4
    4   3   1   0   0   1   2   3   3   4
    1   3   2   2   2   3   3   4   0   1
    Organise this data into a frequency table.

3   Sara recorded the size and colour of crayons in a box.
    There are three colours of crayon – red, blue and green.
    There are two sizes of crayon – large and small.
    Sara used upper and lower case letters to represent the crayons.
    She used G for a large green, and b for a small blue, and so on.
    R   r   r   G   r   b   B   r   G   g
    B   B   G   g   r   R   r   r   b   b
    g   g   g   R   B   R   G   r   G   B
    Draw a two-way table for this set of data.

4   Here are one season's results for two football teams.

United	Wanderers
Won 14	Won 10
Drew 8	Drew 6
Lost 8	Lost 14

    Draw a pie chart for each team's results.

5   This set of data shows the number of phone calls received by a shop each day for
    20 days.
    4   5   5   3   0   2   7   4   6   5
    4   4   1   0   3   2   1   5   5   4
    Draw a bar chart to show the data.

6   This set of data shows the length (in minutes and seconds) of 20 phone calls
    received by a shop.
    0:35   1:22   2:47   1:26   3:55   2:50   0:15   1:03   3:35   4:09
    3:10   0:59   3:09   2:26   3:11   3:28   2:05   3:54   2:12   1:08
    Draw a frequency diagram to show the data.

7   Find the mean, median and range of each of these sets of numbers.
    a   4, 8, 16, 19, 25
    b   34, 67, 92, 108
    c   3.5, 9.2, 7.3, 8.3, 4.1
    d   106.3, 88.9, 71.4, 58.7, 91.9

8   The students in a class were asked how many people live in their house. The table
    shows the result.

Number of occupants	2	3	4	5	6	7	8
Frequency	3	5	11	6	4	0	1

For this set of data, find
    a   the mode   b   the median   c   the mean   d   the range.

9   John recorded the length and weight of 10 earthworms.
    Length (cm):   7   8   7   9   11   6   10   5   6   5
    Weight (g):   22   24   21   28   30   16   28   17   18   16
    Draw a scatter diagram for this set of data.

10 The ages (in years) of 20 customers in a shop were
    15   61   42   33   38   29   53   17   44   32
    39   45   41   26   22   44   43   49   55   60
    Draw a stem-and-leaf diagram for this set of data.

These questions will test you on your knowledge of the topics in chapters 5 to 8.
They give you practice in the types of questions that you may eventually be given in your
GCSE exams. There are 75 marks in total.

1   **a**   Calculate the unknown angles *a*, *b*, *c* and *d*. (3 marks)

    b   Show that the angle
      (*b* + *c*) is identical to angle *d*. (1 mark)

    c   What name do we give to
      these types of angles? (1 mark)

    d   What is the mathematical name
      for the triangle enclosed
      between the parallel lines? (1 mark)

2   What is the name given to quadrilaterals that have the following properties?

    a   One set of equal sides, two pairs of equal angles and one set of parallel sides. (1 mark)

    b   Four equal sides, two pairs of equal angles and two sets of parallel sides. (1 mark)

3   **a**   Calculate the interior angle of a regular pentagon. (1 mark)

    b   Use this knowledge to determine
      the missing angles *a*, *b* and *c*. (3 marks)

    c   What is the name given to this triangle? (1 mark)

    d   Use a protractor and a ruler to
      accurately construct a regular
      pentagon with side length 5 cm. (3 marks)

4   **a**   State whether any two of these
      triangles are congruent. (1 marks)

    b   Give your reasons. (3 marks)

5   **a**   Draw *x* and *y*-axes from -5 to +5. (2 marks)

    b   Copy and complete the table for the equation $y = x - 2$. (2 marks)

x	-2	-1	0	1	2	3	4
y							

    c   Plot these points on the graph and draw a straight line connecting them. (3 marks)

    d   Draw on the same graph the lines $x = -2$ and $y = 1$. (2 marks)

    e   Give the coordinates of the points where all of these lines cross. (3 marks)

6   This graph shows the potential difference
(volts) versus current (amps) for a resistor.

    a   What is the potential difference when the
      current is 3.0 amps? (1 mark)

    b   What is the potential difference when
      the current is 2.0 amps? (2 marks)

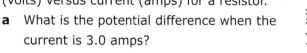

7 Round each of these numbers to the accuracy stated.
   a 2859 (nearest 10)   **b** 7.392 (1 dp)
   c 25.9855 (to 2 dp)   **d** 37 798 (nearest 10)   (4 marks)

8 Calculate
   a 54 × 0.01   **b** 0.56 ÷ 0.1
   c 621 ÷ 0.01   **d** 12.5 × 0.1   (4 marks)

9 Calculate these either mentally using factors or by the methods of
   partitioning or compensation.
   a 43 × 20   **b** 276 ÷ 12
   c 8.3 × 12   **d** 7.2 × 19   (4 marks)

10 An 8-person expedition camps for one night at a camp site.
   The costs are £6.50 per tent plus an additional cost per person
   per night. If the total cost was £49.50, and three tents were
   used, find the cost per person per night.   (3 marks)

11 The temperature in °C is recorded in twenty cities and major towns
   in one day across the UK.

   24   18   23   19   20   20   24   23   22   8
   17   18   19   23   21   19   22   9   20   18

   a Draw a stem-and-leaf diagram for this data.   (3 marks)
   b Find the median temperature.   (2 marks)
   c Find the range of temperatures and the mode.   (2 marks)
   d Find the mean temperature across all twenty cities and towns. (2 marks)

12 In a science experiment one end of a metal rod was heated and
   the temperatures, at equal distances along the rod, were recorded.

Position (cm)	1	2	3	4	5	6	7	8	9
Temperature (°C)	14.5	18.2	29.6	38.4	47.9	60.2	71.2	82.3	94.8

   a Draw a scatter graph to show this data using the x-axis
        from 0 to 10 cm to represent position and the y-axis from
        0 to 100 °C to represent temperature.   (4 marks)
   b Draw the line of best fit.   (1 mark)
   c Comment on the correlation shown.   (2 marks)

13 A packet of breakfast cereal showed its nutritional information
   per 100 g amount as
   Protein 18 g, Carbohydrate 64 g, Fat 4 g, Fibre 14 g.
   a If 360° represents 100 g of cereal, what angle represents 1 g? (2 marks)
   b Calculate the angles of the sectors for each ingredient.   (4 marks)
   c Draw a pie chart to show this information.   (3 marks)

9 Transformations

Introduction

Buddhist sand mandalas are made of coloured sand, often taking months to produce by skilled monks. A mandala symbolises the universe and is usually destroyed ritually after it is finished, as a symbol of impermanence. There are many other examples of complex geometric patterns in art, from designs in Islamic architecture, to Hindu Rangoli designs, and the work of more contemporary artists such as M C Escher.

What's the point?

Symmetry is a key feature of the natural world, often associated with beauty and simplicity. Understanding different types of symmetry allows you to create beautiful artistic compositions.

Objectives

By the end of this chapter, you will have learned how to …

- Reflect, rotate and translate 2D shapes.
- Transform 2D shapes using combinations of transformations.
- Recognise reflection and rotation symmetry.
- Enlarge a 2D shape.

Check in

1 Give the coordinates of the point A after a movement of
   a 2 units to the right and 1 unit down
   b 4 units to the left and 3 units down
   c 2 units to the left and 4 units down.

2 This photograph is rotated. Which photograph shows a rotation of
   a 90° clockwise   b 180°
   c 90° anticlockwise   d 360°?

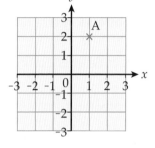

A   B   C   D

Starter problem

An orange rectangle is reflected in the line $y = x$. The image is a pink rectangle. Investigate rules for finding the image coordinates for reflections in this line.

What about reflection in the line $y = -x$?

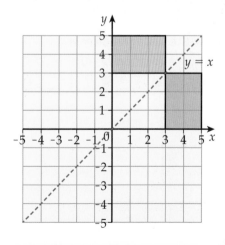

A **transformation** moves a shape to a new position. Here are some different transformations.

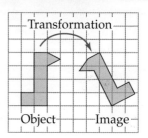

Transformation

Object   Image

⬤ A **reflection** flips an object over a **mirror line**.

You describe a reflection by giving the mirror line.

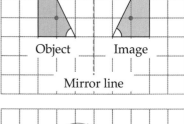

Object   Image

Mirror line

⬤ A **rotation** turns an object about a point, called the **centre of rotation**.

You describe a rotation by giving
- the centre of rotation
- the angle of rotation
- the direction of turn (clockwise or anticlockwise).

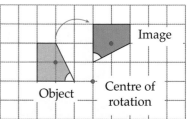

Image

Object   Centre of rotation

⬤ A **translation** slides an object.

You describe a translation by giving the distance moved left or right, *then* the distance moved up or down.

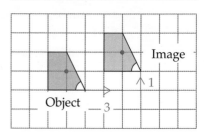

Image

Object   3   1

Example

Draw the hexagon after a clockwise rotation of 90° about (0, 1).

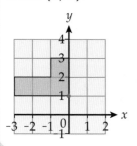

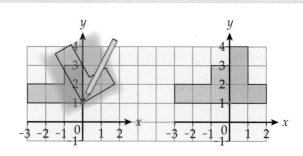

Use tracing paper to rotate the shape.

Exercise 9a

1 Copy each diagram on square grid paper. Reflect the shape in the mirror line. Give the name of the completed shape and state if it is **regular** (equal sides and equal angles).

 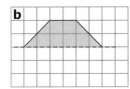

2 Copy this diagram.

a Rotate the isosceles right-angled triangle through 180° about the midpoint of the longest side.

b Mark the equal angles and the equal sides on the completed quadrilateral.

c State the mathematical name of the quadrilateral.

3 On square grid paper, draw the x-axis from 0 to 15 and the y-axis from 0 to 10.

a Plot each shape on the same grid.
Shape A (3, 7), (4, 8), (2, 10), (1, 9) and (3, 7)
Shape B (0, 5), (1, 4), (3, 6), (2, 7) and (0, 5)
Shape C (5, 6), (4, 7), (3, 6) and (5, 6)
Shape D (5, 1), (4, 3), (2, 3), (1, 1) and (5, 1)
Shape E (4, 3), (6, 5), (5, 6), (3, 4) and (4, 3)
Shape F (6, 7), (7, 8), (5, 10), (4, 9) and (6, 7)

b Give the mathematical name of each shape.

c Translate each shape on the same grid.
Shape A, 6 units to the right and 0 units up
Shape B, 10 units to the right and 3 units up
Shape C, 6 units to the right and 3 units up
Shape D, 7 units to the right and 2 units up
Shape E, 4 units to the right and 1 unit up
Shape F, 6 units to the right and 3 units down.

Problem solving

4 Draw a rhombus like this on isometric paper. Use a mirror to form these shapes. Draw diagrams to illustrate the position of the mirror in each case.

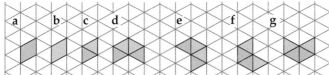

9b Combinations of transformations

You can transform 2D shapes using repeated reflections, rotations and translations.

Example

a Reflect the pink flag in mirror line 1. Call the image I_1.
b Reflect the image in mirror line 2. Call the image I_2.
c Describe a single transformation that moves the pink flag to I_2.

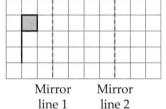

Mirror   Mirror
line 1   line 2

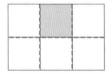

Mirror   Mirror
line 1   line 2

When the mirror lines are parallel, two reflections are **equivalent** to one translation.

c A translation of 8 units to the right.

⬤ A **tessellation** is a tiling pattern with no gaps or overlaps.

< p.90

You can tessellate shapes by repeating the same transformation.

This tessellation uses
repeated reflections.

This tessellation uses
repeated rotations.

▲ This tessellation uses
repeated translations.

Example

Use repeated rotations of 180° to tessellate
this trapezium.

You rotate the trapezium
about the midpoint of a side.

Exercise 9b

1 This tile design is drawn on a 4 by 4 square. Copy the design and use reflections in vertical and horizontal mirror lines to tessellate the tile shape.

2 a Tessellate a scalene right-angled triangle using repeated rotations of 180° about the midpoint of the sides.

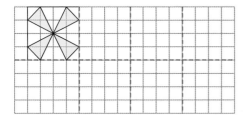

b Colour the equal angles in your tessellation.

3 Repeat question **2** for an irregular quadrilateral.

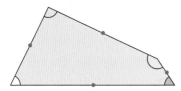

4 This pink hexagon is translated 2 units to the right and 1 unit down.

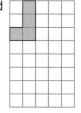

a On a copy of the diagram, draw the image and label it I_1.

b The hexagon I_1 is translated 1 unit to the left and 3 units down. Draw the new image and call it I_2.

c Describe the single transformation that moves the pink hexagon to I_2.

5 This green triangle is rotated clockwise through 90° about the black dot.

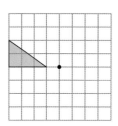

a On a copy of the diagram, draw the image and label it I_1.

b The triangle I_1 is rotated clockwise through 180° about the black dot. Draw the new image and call it I_2.

c Describe the single transformation that moves the green triangle to I_2.

Problem solving

6 Draw a 2 by 2 square.   Remove a triangle and rotate it through 180°.   Show that this shape tessellates using repeated rotations.

Colour your tessellation.

7 Investigate creating your own tessellations using repeated translations, reflections and rotations of the same simple shape.

- A **line of symmetry** divides a shape into two identical halves.
- A shape has **reflection symmetry** if it has at least one line of symmetry.

You can find the line of symmetry by using a mirror or by folding the shape.

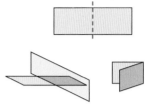

- A shape has **rotation symmetry** if it rotates onto itself more than once in a full turn.
  ▶ The **order of rotation symmetry** is the number of times a shape looks exactly like itself in a complete turn.

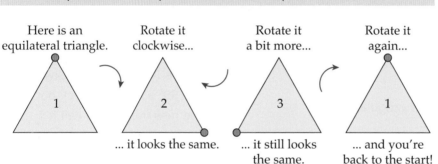

Here is an equilateral triangle.	Rotate it clockwise...	Rotate it a bit more...	Rotate it again...
1	2	3	1
	... it looks the same.	... it still looks the same.	... and you're back to the start!

▲ This starfish has order of rotation symmetry 5.

This triangle has rotation symmetry of order 3.

You can use tracing paper to find the order of rotation symmetry.

- A shape with rotation symmetry of order 1 is said to have no rotation symmetry.

Example

A regular hexagon is shown.
a   Draw the lines of reflection symmetry.
b   State the order of rotation symmetry.

a

b   order 6

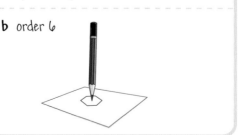

Exercise 9c

1 These symbols can often be found inside a lift.
Draw each symbol and draw any lines of symmetry.
State the order of rotation symmetry in each case.

a   **b**   **c**

d   **e**   **f**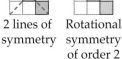

2 This shape has two lines of reflection symmetry and rotation symmetry of order 2.
Draw these shapes and describe the symmetry in a similar way.

2 lines of symmetry   Rotational symmetry of order 2

a   **b**

c   **d**

3 The lines of reflection symmetry of a rhombus are along the diagonals.
The angle shown is 50°.
Calculate the four **interior angles** of the rhombus.

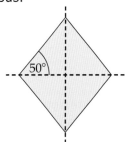

4 Draw each quadrilateral and give its mathematical name.
On each diagram, draw any lines of symmetry and state the order of rotation symmetry.

a   **b**   **c**

d   **e**   **f**

g   **h**   **i**

Problem solving

5 a Place a mirror on a copy of these two squares to form these shapes.

b Draw these shapes and describe what they all have in common.

6 Can you draw a shape that has:
a rotation symmetry but no reflection symmetry
b reflection symmetry but no rotation symmetry?
Give examples of each case.

An enlargement alters the size of a shape. You enlarge a shape by multiplying its lengths by a **scale factor**.

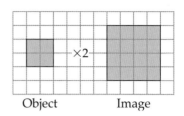

Object   Image

● The object and the image in an **enlargement** are **similar**. They are the same shape, but a different size.

Example

Calculate the scale factor of the enlargement.

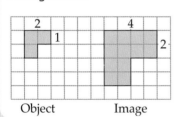

Object   Image

2 × scale factor = 4 and
1 × scale factor = 2
Scale factor = 2.

Example

Draw the enlargement of the pink triangle using a scale factor of 3.

Object

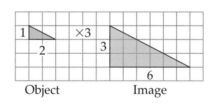

Object   Image

1 × 3 = 3   Each length is multiplied by 3.
2 × 3 = 6
The green triangle is an enlargement by scale factor 3 of the pink triangle.

● The scale factor in an enlargement is the amount you multiply lengths by in the object to get corresponding lengths in the image.

Exercise 9d

1 Decide whether these diagrams show similar shapes.
Explain your reasoning.

a   b

c

2 The pink shapes are enlarged to give the green shapes.
Calculate the scale factor of each enlargement.

a 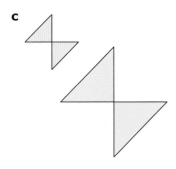 b

c

3 Copy the shapes on square grid paper and enlarge each shape by the given scale factor.

a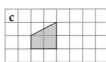
scale factor 2

b
scale factor 4

c
scale factor 3

d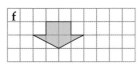
scale factor 2

e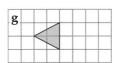
scale factor 3

f
scale factor 2

g
scale factor 2

h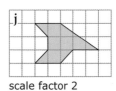
scale factor 3

i
scale factor 3

j
scale factor 2

Problem solving

4 a Draw a scalene triangle ABC.
 b Mark a point O inside the triangle.
 c Draw lines from O to and beyond the vertices.
 d Measure the distance OA. Multiply this length by 2.
   Use this answer to mark a new point measured from O on the extended line OA.
 e Repeat for OB and OC to form a new triangle.
 f Measure the three angles and the three lengths of each triangle.
 g Are the triangles similar and what is the scale factor of the enlargement?
 h Investigate with other shapes.

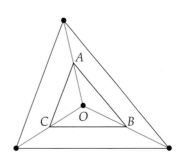

When you enlarge a shape, the position of the image is fixed if you use a centre of enlargement.

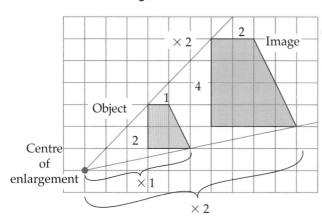

If you moved the centre of enlargement 3 squares up, what would happen to the image?

This enlargement is scale factor 2.

> ● You can describe an enlargement by giving
> – the scale factor
> – the centre of enlargement.

Example

Draw the enlargement of this flag using a scale factor of 3 and the marked centre of enlargement.

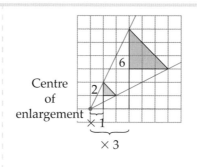

Example

Shape B is an enlargement of shape A. Mark the centre of enlargement and find the scale factor.

Join corresponding points on A and B by straight lines and mark their common intersection point.
Compare corresponding lengths or distances.

Scale factor is $\frac{6}{2} = 3$

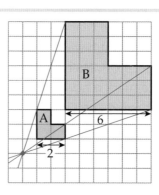

Exercise 9e

1 The pink triangle *ABC* is enlarged to give the green triangle $A_1B_1C_1$.
Copy the diagram on square grid paper.

a Draw and extend the lines from A_1 to *A* from B_1 to *B* and from C_1 to *C*.

b At the intersection of the lines, mark the centre of enlargement as *O*.

c Measure the lines *BC*, B_1C_1 and *AC*, A_1C_1.

d State the scale factor of the enlargement.

e Measure the lines *OA*, OA_1 and *OB*, OB_1 to check the scale factor.

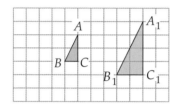

2 Copy these shapes on square grid paper. Draw the enlargement of each shape using the dot as the centre of enlargement and the given scale factor.

a

scale factor 2

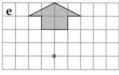

b

scale factor 3

c

scale factor 4

d

scale factor 2

e

scale factor 3

f

scale factor 4

Problem solving

3 The pink triangle is enlarged by scale factor 3 to give the green triangle, which is not all shown here.
The point (1, 4) moves to (3, 0).
Find the other two coordinates of the green triangle.

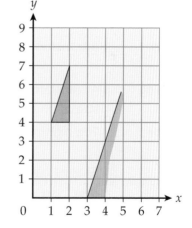

4 a i Draw a large rectangle.

ii Mark a point *O* inside the rectangle.

iii Draw lines from *O* to the vertices.

iv Find the midpoints of each line and join these four points to form a rectangle.

This rectangle is similar to the first rectangle.

b Use this method to draw other similar shapes.

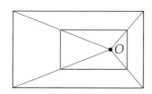

Check out

You should now be able to ...

Test it ➡

Questions

✓ Reflect, rotate and translate 2D shapes.	⑤	1–2
✓ Transform 2D shapes using combinations of transformations.	⑤	3
✓ Recognise reflection and rotation symmetry.	⑤	4
✓ Enlarge a 2D shape.	⑥	5–7

Language	Meaning	Example
Transformation	A procedure for changing the position, orientation or shape of an object	Rotations, reflections, translations and enlargements are all transformations
Rotation	A transformation that turns an object through a given angle about a given centre of rotation	Turning this book through 90° clockwise about its bottom right corner is a rotation
Reflection	A transformation which flips an object over a mirror line	Looking at this book in a mirror is a reflection
Translation	A transformation which slides an object	Sliding this book across your desk is a translation
Enlargement	A transformation which changes the size of an object	If you enlarged this book by a scale factor of two about its centre its lengths would grow to twice their size
Scale factor	The multiplier in an enlargement	
Reflective symmetry	Shapes have reflective symmetry if they have a mirror line of symmetry	A rectangle has reflective symmetry in both the horizontal and vertical lines through its centre
Rotational symmetry	A shape has rotational symmetry if it fits exactly over its original position more than once in a full turn	A rectangle has rotational symmetry of order 2 about its centre

1 Copy the diagram and translate the rhombus 4 units to the right and 2 units down.

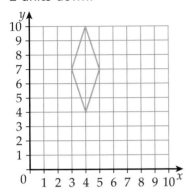

2 Copy the quadrilaterals on square grid paper.
  i Reflect the shapes in the mirror lines.
  ii Rotate the shapes 90° clockwise about the red dots.

a 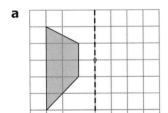   b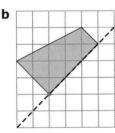

3 Copy the pentagon on square grid paper.

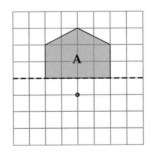

3 a Rotate shape A 180° about the red dot and label the image B.
  b Reflect shape B in the dotted line and label the image C.
  c Describe the single transformation that moves A to C.

4 Describe
  a the reflective symmetry
  b the rotational symmetry
  of this shape.

5 Are these triangles similar?

6 Copy the arrow shape on square grid paper and enlarge it by scale factor 3.

7 Copy the trapezium on square grid paper and enlarge it by scale factor 2 using the red dot as the centre of enlargement.

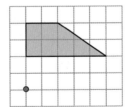

What next?

<table>
<tr><td rowspan="3">Score</td><td>0 – 2</td><td></td><td>Your knowledge of this topic is still developing. To improve look at Formative test: 2B-9; MyMaths: 1099, 1113–1116, 1125 and 1127</td></tr>
<tr><td>3 – 5</td><td></td><td>You are gaining a secure knowledge of this topic. To improve look at InvisiPen: 361, 362, 363, 364, 366 and 368</td></tr>
<tr><td>6 – 7</td><td></td><td>You have mastered this topic. Well done, you are ready to progress!</td></tr>
</table>

9a

1 Copy the diagram on square grid paper.

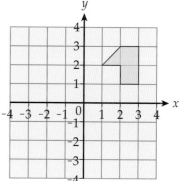

a Reflect the blue hexagon using the *x*-axis as the mirror line.

Label the shape A and give the coordinates of the vertices.

b Rotate the blue hexagon through 180° about the point (0, 0).

Label the shape B and give the coordinates of the vertices.

c Translate the blue hexagon by 4 units to the left.

Label the shape C and give the coordinates of the vertices.

9b

2 a Tessellate a parallelogram using repeated translations.

b Colour the equal angles in your tessellation.

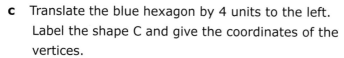

3 Copy the diagram on square grid paper.

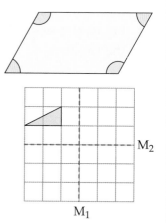

a Reflect the green triangle in the mirror line M$_1$.

Call the image I$_1$.

b Reflect I$_1$ in the mirror line M$_2$.

Call the image I$_2$.

c Describe the single transformation that moves the green triangle to I$_2$.

9c

4 Draw these symbols from Steph's calculator.

Draw any lines of reflection symmetry and state the order of rotation symmetry for each symbol.

a   **b**   **c** 4   **d** 8   **e** 0

5 a Draw a polygon with three lines of symmetry and rotational symmetry of order 3.

b Give the mathematical name of this shape.

6

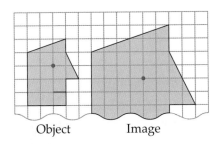

Object   Image

Part of an enlargement of the face is shown.

a Calculate the scale factor of the enlargement.

b Copy and complete the table of measurements.

	Object	**Image**
Length of the forehead	1 cm	
Slanting length of the nose		
Slanting length of the top of the head		
Thickness of the neck		
Width of the mouth		

c Draw the completed image on square grid paper.

7 a Draw the rectangle on a coordinate grid.

b Enlarge the rectangle by scale factor 2 using (0, 0) as the centre of enlargement.

c Write down the coordinates of the vertices of the object and the image.

d Explain the relationship between these coordinates.

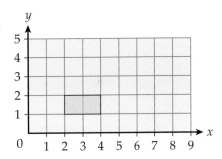

8 Chelsea began to enlarge the pink shape to give the green shape but she was distracted.

a Find the coordinates of the centre of enlargement and the scale factor.

b Complete the green shape.

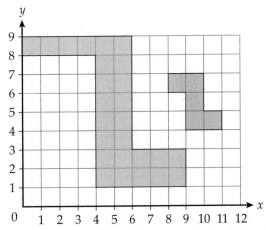

Case study 3: Food crops

Wheat has been cultivated for around 10 000 years, originating from an area that is now part of Iran. It is still vitally important to us today, and keeping the world fed is a delicate balance between production and consumption.

Task 1

The table shows world wheat production between the years 2002 and 2008. The row labelled 'stocks' shows how much wheat is left in reserve.

1	World wheat production, consumption and stocks (million tonnes)						
2		02/03	03/04	04/05	05/06	06/07	07/08
3	produced	566	556	628	620		608
4	consumed	601	596	616		611	612
5	stocks	169	129		137	123	

a Find the figure '129' in the spreadsheet. Can you work out how it was calculated? Show your workings.

b Complete the missing entries in the spreadsheet.

c In how many years does consumption of wheat exceed production?

d What is happening to the stocks of wheat that are held in reserve?

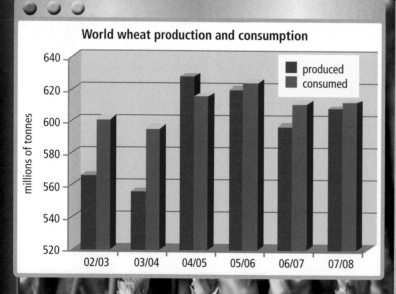

World wheat production and consumption

millions of tonnes

produced
consumed

02/03 03/04 04/05 05/06 06/07 07/08

Task 2

Here is a bar chart generated from the spreadsheet.

For the first two years, the 'produced' bar is roughly half the height of the 'consumed' bar.

a How does that compare with the figures in the spreadsheet for those years?

b Do you think that the chart is a good representation of the actual figures? Explain your reasoning. Suggest improvements if appropriate.

The graph shows the price of wheat between 2003 and 2008.
A 'bushel' is an agricultural unit, usually of weight.

Wheat prices continue to rise

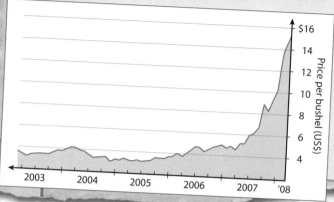

Task 3

a Roughly what is the lowest price a bushel of wheat has cost since 2003?

b When was the price at its lowest?

c How long did the price take to double from its lowest value?

d How long did it take to double again?

Crops are not only used for food.
Some crops, such as rapeseed, are used to make
biodiesel, which is an alternative source of fuel.
The bar chart shows the trend in production of biodiesel
in the EU between 2002 and 2007.

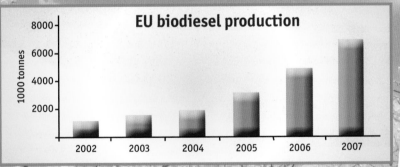

Task 4

a Write down estimated values for the biodiesel production for each year from 2002 to 2007.

b Roughly how many times bigger is the production of biodiesel in 2007 than it was in 2002?

c (Harder) Looking at the trend, what do you think the EU biodiesel production would have been in 2012? See if you can find the real value on the Internet and compare with your estimate. How close are you?

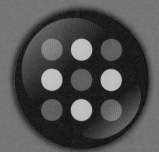

10 Equations

Introduction

Biologists use equations to predict the likely growth or decline of populations of endangered animals, such as the red kite which was saved from virtual extinction in the UK. Re-introduced into England in the Chilterns, the red kite is now thriving again with around 2000 breeding pairs.

What's the point?

Population growth is complex and involves a multitude of factors. By solving equations that include as many of these factors as possible, people can predict how populations can change.

Objectives

By the end of this chapter, you will have learned how to ...

- Solve simple, one-step equations.
- Solve multi-step equations including with the unknown on both sides.
- Solve equations including with brackets.
- Solve real life equations.

Check in

1 What numbers should be placed in these boxes to make the statements correct?

    a $12 + \square = 21$ **b** $15 - \square = 9$ **c** $3 \times \square = 21$ **d** $\dfrac{\square}{4} = 5$

2 The same number can be written in these pairs of boxes. What is the number?

    a $6 \times \square = 42$ and $\dfrac{42}{6} = \square$ **b** $7 \times \square = 56$ and $\dfrac{56}{7} = \square$

3 I think of a number, add 6 to it, and get an answer of 14. What number am I thinking of?

Starter problem

In this diagram the equation $3x + 2 = 17$ has been changed in different ways, but all of these ways still give the same solution of $x = 5$.

Describe each change to the equation.

Continue each change for at least one more step.

Invent some changes of your own.

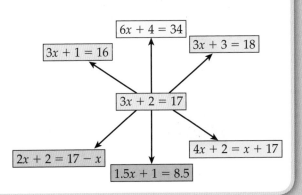

Here is a balance containing an unknown weight x.

It can be written as an **equation**.

To find x, you need to get it on its own on one side of the equation.

If you subtract 2 from the left, you must also subtract 2 from the right, to keep the balance.

The **solution** of the equation is $x = 6$.

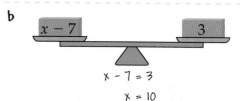

$$x + 2 \qquad = \qquad 8$$

$$x \qquad = \qquad 6$$

Example

Solve these equations.

a $x + 5 = 9$ **b** $x - 7 = 3$ **c** $3x = 12$ **d** $\frac{1}{2}x = 5$

a

$x + 5 = 9$
$x = 4$

b

$x - 7 = 3$
$x = 10$

The **inverse** of $+5$ is -5, so subtract 5 from both sides.

The inverse of -7 is $+7$, so add 7 to both sides.

c

$3x = 12$
$x = 4$

d

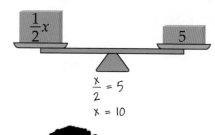

$\frac{x}{2} = 5$
$x = 10$

The inverse of $\times 3$ is $\div 3$, so divide both sides by 3.

The inverse of $\div 2$ is $\times 2$, so multiply both sides by 2.

Exercise 10a

1 Find the value of x in each of these balances.

a
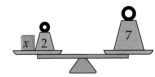

b
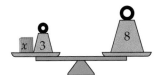

c
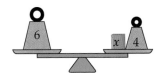

d
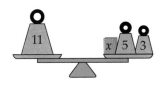

2 Solve these equations by using inverse operations.

a i $x + 6 = 8$ ii $x + 3 = 12$
iii $x + 4 = 5$ iv $x + 7 = 9$
v $x + 8 = 12$ vi $x + 1 = 10$
vii $3 + x = 4$ viii $5 + x = 7$

2 b i $x - 8 = 1$ ii $x - 2 = 7$
iii $x - 4 = 3$ iv $x - 1 = 9$
v $x - 3 = 11$ vi $x - \frac{1}{2} = 3$
vii $9 = x - 2$ viii $6 = x - 8$

c i $2x = 10$ ii $3x = 12$
iii $4x = 8$ iv $2x = 18$
v $5x = 20$ vi $7x = 14$
vii $33 = 3x$ viii $20 = 4x$

d i $\frac{x}{2} = 5$ ii $\frac{x}{3} = 4$
iii $\frac{x}{4} = 2$ iv $\frac{x}{3} = 6$
v $\frac{x}{2} = 7$ vi $\frac{x}{5} = 4$
vii $\frac{x}{10} = 6$ viii $\frac{x}{6} = 3$

3 Solve these equations. They need various different operations.

a $x + 7 = 8$ b $x - 7 = 8$
c $x + 1 = 5$ d $x - 1 = 5$
e $2x = 20$ f $3x = 12$
g $\frac{x}{2} = 9$ h $\frac{x}{3} = 6$
i $x + 6 = 17$ j $x - 5 = 1$
k $\frac{x}{5} = 12$ l $6x = 30$

Problem solving

4 Find the value of x in each of these balances.

a
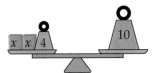

b
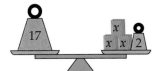

c
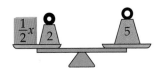

5 Each person gives their age as a riddle.
Write an equation for each riddle and solve it to find the person's age.

a In 12 years' time Zach will be 40.

b Seven years ago Yvonne was 25.

c If Xavier was four times as old he would be 28.

d Half a lifetime ago Wendy was 21.

e Three years after Valentin is three times as old he will be 39.

f If Ursula was a quarter of her age then two years before that she would have been two.

10b Solving multi-step equations

Solving some **equations** involves more than one step.

Solve $2x + 5 = 17$

You can think of this equation as a balance.

$2x + 5 = 17$

The inverse of $+5$ is -5.
Subtract 5 from both sides.

$2x = 12$

The inverse of $\times 2$ is $\div 2$.
Divide both sides by 2.

$x = 6$

The **solution** of the equation is $x = 6$.

This balance has the **unknown** in both scale pans.

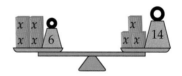

The balance shows the equation
Subtract $3x$ from both sides.
Subtract 6 from both sides.

$$4x + 6 = 3x + 14$$
$$x + 6 = 14$$
$$x = 8$$

The solution $x = 8$ can be checked by **substitution**.

$$4x + 6 = 3x + 14$$

$4 \times 8 + 6 = 38$ $3 \times 8 + 14 = 38$
The check works.   Both sides are equal.

Invent your own problem with the unknown on both sides and try to solve it. Does your answer work when you check it by substitution?

Start by rewriting the equation so that there are only unknowns on one side.

Solve the equation $3z + 4 = 9z - 8$

$9z - 8 = 3z + 4$ Subtract $3z$ from both sides.
$6z - 8 = 4$ Add 8 to both sides.
$6z = 12$ Divide both sides by 6.
$z = 2$

The solution is $z = 2$.

Algebra Equations

Exercise 10b

1 Solve these equations. Each of them needs two steps.

a $2x + 4 = 10$ **b** $2x + 3 = 13$

c $3x + 1 = 13$ **d** $3x + 5 = 11$

e $4x + 3 = 19$ **f** $10x + 7 = 57$

g $2x - 4 = 8$ **h** $2x - 1 = 8$

i $3x - 2 = 10$ **j** $3x - 5 = 4$

k $10x - 7 = 33$ **l** $2x + 3 = 10$

2 Find the value of x in each of these balances.

a
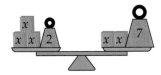

b
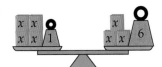

c
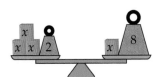

3 Solve these equations.

a $4x + 5 = 3x + 8$

b $8x + 4 = 7x + 6$

c $5x + 3 = 4x + 7$

d $3x + 1 = 2x + 10$

e $7x + 3 = 5x + 9$

f $10x + 4 = 8x + 8$

g $14x + 6 = 7x + 13$

h $9x + 4 = x + 24$

3 **i** $3\frac{1}{2}x + 1 = \frac{1}{2}x + 7$

j $6x + 1 = 3x + 13$

k $12x + 7 = 2x + 27$

l $x + 7 = 3x + 1$

4 Solve these equations.

a $4x - 5 = 3x + 1$

b $6x - 2 = 5x + 4$

c $7x - 4 = 5x + 2$

d $9x - 1 = 7x + 7$

e $8x - 4 = 5x + 8$

f $6x - 7 = x + 3$

g $10x - 3 = 7x + 3$

h $5x - 2 = x + 10$

i $4\frac{1}{2}x - 8 = \frac{1}{2}x$

j $5x - 3 = x + 5$

k $3x + 1 = 4x - 6$

l $6x = 8x - 4$

5 Solve these equations. They need a mixture of methods.

a $4x + 3 = 2x + 11$

b $4x - 3 = 2x + 11$

c $8x + 2 = x + 30$

d $6x - 7 = x + 3$

e $2x + 20 = 8x + 2$

f $3x + 1 = 5x - 13$

g $6x - 8 = 2x$

h $7x - 3 = 5x - 3$

i $2x = 9x - 28$

j $8x = 5x + 18$

k $2x = 9 - x$

l $3x = 21 - 4x$

Problem solving

6 A joiner has seven boxes of screws and four extra screws. His workmate has five similar boxes and twenty eight extra screws. They have the same total number of screws. If there are n screws in each box

a form an equation involving n **b** find the value of n.

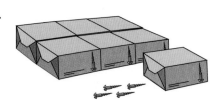

This balance shows two identical bags, each holding an unknown mass x and 4 grams.

They are balanced by 18 grams.

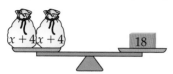

Think $2 \times x = 2x$
and $2 \times 4 = 8$

Don't forget to check the answer
$2(5 + 4) = 2 \times 9 = 18$ ✓

The equation is $\qquad$ $2(x + 4) = 18$

< p.48 **Expand** the **brackets**. $\qquad$ $2x + 8 = 18$

Subtract 8 from both sides. $\qquad\qquad$ $2x = 10$

Divide both sides by 2. $\qquad\qquad\quad$ $x = 5$

The unknown mass is 5 g

Equations can have brackets containing unknowns on both sides.

Example

Solve the equation $3(2x - 1) = 5(x + 2)$

$3(2x - 1) = 5(x + 2)$

$6x - 3 = 5x + 10$ $\qquad$ Expand the brackets.

$6x = 5x + 13$ $\qquad$ Add 3 to both sides.

$x = 13$ $\qquad$ Subtract $5x$ from both sides.

Remember to expand the brackets first!

You can solve real life problems using equations.

Example

Katrina is three times older than her sister Siobhan.

In four years' time, Siobhan will be half Katrina's age.

How old are they both now?

Call Siobhan's age n, Katrina's age $= 3n$.

$3n + 4 = 2(n + 4)$ $\qquad$ In four years time...

$3n + 4 = 2n + 8$ $\qquad$ Expand the brackets.

$3n = 2n + 4$

$n = 4$

Siobhan is 4, and Katrina is 12.

Exercise 10c

1 Solve these equations by expanding
  the brackets.
  a $2(x + 3) = 16$ b $3(x + 3) = 15$
  c $2(4x + 5) = 26$ d $3(2x + 1) = 21$
  e $3(2x − 1) = 21$ f $2(2x − 7) = 4$
  g $2(x − 4) = 1$ h $6(2x − 1) = 18$

2 Solve these equations.
  a $3(3x + 2) = 2(3x + 6)$
  b $2(5x + 1) = 4(2x + 3)$
  c $7(x + 2) = 4(x + 5)$
  d $5(2x + 1) = 3(3x + 4)$
  e $3(6x + 5) = 4(4x + 7)$
  f $5(2x − 1) = 3(3x + 2)$
  g $4(3x − 1) = 2(5x + 7)$
  h $3(5x − 2) = 4(3x + 6)$
  i $9x − 1 = 2(1 + 4x)$

3 Solve these equations.
  You will have to collect 'like terms' after
  expanding the brackets.
  a $3(2x + 1) + 2(4x + 2) = 21$
  b $2(x + 2) + 3(x + 4) = 31$
  c $5(2x + 1) + 2(5x + 3) = 91$
  d $2(4x + 3) + 3(2x + 1) = 23$
  e $4(3x + 2) + 8(x + 1) = 56$

3 f $5(2x + 1) + 2(x + 4) = 13$
  g $6(x + 2) + 4(x − 3) = 50$
  h $4(2x + 2) + 2(x − 3) = 12$
  i $3(4x + 1) + 2(6x − 1) = 13$
  j $2(3x − 5) + 3(3x + 4) = 17$
  k $4(2x + 1) + 2(3x − 1) = 30$
  l $5(3x − 1) + 4(2x + 7) = 69$

4 Solve these equations. Use a number line
  to help with the negatives.
  a $x + 2 = 2$ b $x + 2 = 1$
  c $x + 2 = -1$ d $x + 2 = -4$
  e $2x + 5 = 1$ f $2x + 9 = 3$
  g $3x + 4 = 1$ h $3x + 2 = -4$
  i $4x + 7 = -1$ j $6x + 8 = 8$
  k $2x + 9 = 5$ l $7x + 4 = -10$
  m $y − 2 = 3$ n $y − 2 = -2$
  o $y − 2 = -3$ p $y − 4 = -2$

5 Solve these equations.
  The answers have fractions in them.
  a $2x + 3 = 10$ b $2x + 8 = 13$
  c $4x + 3 = 8$ d $8x − 2 = 23$
  e $2(x − 4) = 1$ f $4(x − 3) = 5$
  g $5(2x + 3) = 40$ h $4(2x + 5) = 29$
  i $2(2x − 1) = 11$ j $4(8x + 3) = 36$

Problem solving

6 This year, a man is three times older than his daughter.
  In ten years' time, the man will be twice his daughter's age.
  If the daughter is x years old now, find the value of x.

7 You can convert temperatures in °F to °C using the formula
  $C = \dfrac{5(F − 32)}{9}$.
  There is a temperature $T°$ that is the same in both Fahrenheit and Celsius.
  Use the formula above to find the value of T.
  Where on Earth might you experience this temperature?

You meet equations in real life all the time.

The equation for converting between temperatures given in Celsius, C, and Fahrenheit, F, is

$F = 1.8C + 32$

If £1 buys you $1.50 than the equation for the exchange rate between x pounds and y dollars is

$y = 1.5x$

> An equation connecting real life quantities is often called a **formula**.

Example

The equation for converting Celsius, C, to Fahrenheit, F, is

$F = 1.8C + 32$

a 10 °C to °F   **b** 25 °C to °F

c 86 °F to °C   **d** 302 °F to °C

- - - - -

a $F = 1.8 \times 10 + 32$ **b** $F = 1.8 \times 25 + 32$

$\quad = 18 + 32$ $\quad = 45 + 32$

$\quad = 50$ $\quad = 77$

c $86 = 1.8C + 32$ **d** $302 = 1.8C + 32$

$\quad 54 = 1.8C$ $\quad 1.8C = 270$

$\quad C = 54 \div 1.8$ $\quad C = 270 \div 1.8$

$\quad\quad = 30$ $\quad\quad = 150$

Example

A taxi company charges £2.00 per journey plus 30 pence per mile.

a Write down an equation for £T, the total cost of a journey of m miles.

b How much would it cost to travel 5 miles?

c If I am charged £4.70 for my journey, how far did I travel?

> If the cost is written in pence the equation is
> $T = 200 + 30m$

- - - - -

a Total cost is £2 $+$ £0.30 per mile

$T = 2 + 0.3m$

b $T = 2 + 0.3 \times 5 = 2 + 1.5 = 3.5$

My journey cost £3.50

c $4.7 = 2 + 0.3m$ Subtract 2

$\quad 2.7 = 0.3m$ Divide by 0.3

$\quad\quad 9 = m$

The journey was 9 miles.

Exercise 10d

1 Use the equation $F = 1.8C + 32$ to convert
   a 100 °C to °F
   b -40 °C to °F
   c 140 °F to °C
   d 0 °F to °C

2 Write down equations connecting the number of miles, m, and the total cost of the journey, T, for these taxi companies.
   a A fixed charge of £3.00 plus 25 pence per mile
   b A fixed charge of £2.50 plus 35 pence per mile
   c A fixed charge of £2.00 plus 40 pence per mile
   d No fixed charge plus 48 pence per mile

3 For each of the taxi companies, **a – d**, in question **2**
   i What is the cost of a 12 mile journey?
   ii If the cost of a journey was £6 how far did you travel?

4 An equation connecting the number of dollars, y, you get per pound, x, at the bank is given as $y = 1.532x$. Use this equation to convert
   a £100 into dollars
   b £250 into dollars
   c £820 into dollars
   d $750 into pounds
   e $1532 into pounds
   f $10500 into pounds

Problem solving

5 Two mobile phone companies, CheapTalk and BargainPhone, are advertising their newest tariffs to customers.
   a Write down an equation for the total cost per month, £y, in terms of the number of minutes used, x, of a phone purchased from i CheapTalk.
       ii BargainPhone.
   b Which of the phone companies will be cheaper if you want to talk for
       i 20 minutes per month
       ii 50 minutes per month
       iii 150 minutes per month?
   c i Write an equation for the number of minutes used if the cost using a CheapTalk phone equals the cost of using a BargainPhone phone.
       ii Solve the equation for the number of minutes.
   d Explain how you should choose the best phone company based on how many minutes you expect to use your phone a month.

CheapTalk
FANTASTIC NEW DEAL
£5 per month and then only **15 pence** per minute!!

Bargain Phone
NEW TARIFF
Only £10 per month plus 10 pence per minute

Check out

You should now be able to ...

Test it ➡

Questions

✓	Solve simple, one-step equations.	5	1
✓	Solve multi-step equations including with the unknown on both sides.	6	2
✓	Solve equations including with brackets.	6	3–5
✓	Solve real life equations.	6	6–8

Language	Meaning	Example
Equation	A mathematical statement, written in algebra and including an equal sign, which is true for one or more values of the unknown	$2x + 1 = 7$ is an equation
Solution	The value(s) of the unknown that the equation is true for	$x = 3$ is the only solution of the equation above
Inverse	A second operation that undoes the effect of a first operation	The inverse of -6 is $+6$ and the inverse of $\times 2$ is $\div 2$
Expand	To multiply out all brackets and then collect like terms	Expanding $2(3x + 5) - 7 + 4x$ gives $10x + 3$
Substitution	A method for checking if your solution to an equation is correct by replacing the unknown with the solution	Substituting $x = 3$ into $2x + 1$ gives $2 \times 3 + 1 = 6 + 1 = 7$

1 Solve these equations.

   a $x - 9 = 24$ **b** $x - 7 = 14$

   c $6 + x = 35$ **d** $x + 12 = 20$

   e $5x = 55$ **f** $3x = 27$

   g $\frac{x}{3} = 12$ **h** $\frac{x}{4} = 4$

2 Solve these multi-step equations.

   a $2x + 5 = 23$

   b $3x + 7 = 25$

   c $4x - 8 = 60$

   d $5x - 2 = 43$

   e $2x - 14 = x - 8$

   f $6x - 17 = 4x + 1$

   g $5x - 9 = 3x + 15$

   h $4x + 3 = x + 18$

3 Solve these equations.

   a $3(4x - 5) = 33$

   b $2(6x - 8) = 5(x + 8)$

   c $3(x + 7) - 4(2x + 1) = 12$

   d $5(2x - 3) - 4(x - 2) = 71$

4 Solve these equations.

   a $x + 8 = 5$

   b $x - 7 = -5$

   c $3x + 11 = 8$

   d $2(x + 4) = 0$

   e $5x + 7 = 7$

   f $6x - 9 = -33$

5 Solve these equations, using fractions in your answers.

   a $4x + 10 = 12$

   b $5(6x - 7) = 10$

   c $6x + 3 = 2x + 8$

   d $2(4x - 6) - 5(x - 7) = 24$

6 I think of a number x.

If I subtract the number 7 from it, I get the same answer as if I double it and add 3. Find the value of x.

7 Rope is sold for 85p per metre.

   a Write an equation for the cost, £y, of x metres of rope.

   b What are the cost of the following lengths of rope?

     i 12 m   **ii** 22.5 m   **iii** 1500 m

   c How much rope was bought if these were the prices paid?

     i £4.25   **ii** £68   **iii** £6.38

8 EasiBuild sells and delivers bricks in bulk. The fixed delivery charge is £75 plus £200 per pallet of bricks ordered.

   a Write an equation for the cost, £y, of ordering x pallets.

   b If the cost of an order was £1675, how many pallets were ordered?

   c Ted complains that his bill for £1900 cannot be correct. Explain how he knows this.

What next?

Score	0 – 2	Your knowledge of this topic is still developing. To improve look at Formative test: 2B-10; MyMaths: 1154, 1182 and 1247
	3 – 6	You are gaining a secure knowledge of this topic. To improve look at InvisiPen: 233, 234, 235, 236 and 237
	7 – 8	You have mastered this topic. Well done, you are ready to progress!

MyMaths.co.uk

1 Find the value of x in each of these balances.

a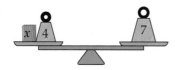

b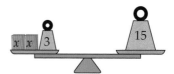

2 Solve these equations by using inverse operations.

a $x + 3 = 7$ **b** $x - 3 = 7$ **c** $2x = 8$ **d** $\dfrac{x}{2} = 5$

e $4 + x = 6$ **f** $x - 4 = 1$ **g** $3x = 18$ **h** $\dfrac{x}{4} = 2$

3 Solve these equations. Each of them needs two steps.

a $2x + 4 = 14$ **b** $3x + 2 = 23$ **c** $2x - 1 = 11$

d $5x - 6 = 9$ **e** $\dfrac{x}{2} + 1 = 6$ **f** $\dfrac{x}{3} - 3 = 3$

4 Find the value of x in each of these balances.

a $3x + 4$ $2x + 9$ **b** $3x + 5$ $x + 13$

5 Solve these equations. There are unknowns on both sides.

a $4x + 2 = 3x + 7$ **b** $6x + 1 = 5x + 13$ **c** $3x + 6 = x + 10$

d $7x + 2 = 4x + 8$ **e** $6x + 9 = x + 24$ **f** $7x = 3x + 20$

6 Solve these equations. Take care with the negative signs.

a $3x - 1 = 2x + 4$ **b** $7x - 2 = 5x + 6$ **c** $5x - 5 = 3x - 1$

d $8x - 11 = 5x - 2$ **e** $9x + 8 = 7x + 4$ **f** $6x + 14 = 3x + 5$

7 Sarah has six packets of Christmas cards and two loose cards. Her sister, Jane, has three similar packets of cards and seventeen loose cards. Each packet has x cards in it. When the sisters open all their boxes and count their cards, they find that they have the same total.

Write an equation and find the value of x.

8 a Think of a number, multiply it by 5 and then subtract 3. If you double the same number and add 15, you get the same answer. Find the number.

   b This mobile is made from different shapes. It can hang from the ceiling. If the square shape has a mass of 60 grams, find the masses of all the other shapes.

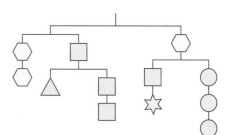

9 Solve these equations.

  a $2(3x + 4) = 20$ **b** $3(2x - 1) = 21$ **c** $5(x - 2) = 20$

  d $3(4x + 1) = 123$ **e** $4(2x + 1) = 6(x + 2)$ **f** $5(3x + 2) = 4(3x + 4)$

10 Solve these equations by expanding the brackets and collecting like terms.

  a $3(2x + 4) + 2(3x + 1) = 38$ **b** $5(2x + 1) + 2(x + 3) = 35$

  c $4(x + 3) + 6(x + 1) = 28$ **d** $2(2x + 3) + 4(2x + 1) = 18$

  e $3(5x + 1) + 2(1 - 6x) = 9$ **f** $5(x + 5) + 2(2x - 3) = 31$

11 I think of a number. I subtract it from 2 and then treble what is left.
My final answer is 18. Find the number.

12 I think of a number x.
If I subtract the number from 16, I get the number itself.
Find the value of x.

13 I think of a number n.
If I double it and add 12, I get the same answer as if I treble it and add 2.
Find the value of n.

14 In this triangle, the number in each square is found
by adding the two numbers in the corner circles on
either side of it.

  a Find expressions to write in the two empty circles.

  b Write an equation in x and find the value of x.

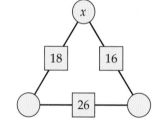

15 A taxi company charges £2.30 per journey plus 25 pence per mile.

  a Write down an equation for the total cost, C, of the journey in terms of the
number of miles, m.

  b Work out the cost of my journey if I travel a total of 12 miles.

  c How many miles will I have travelled if I am charged £6.05?

16 The equation used to convert pounds, x, into Euros, y, is $y = 1.162x$.

  a Convert £400 into Euros.

  b Convert £1500 into Euros.

  c Convert €1000 into pounds.

  d Convert €740 into pounds.

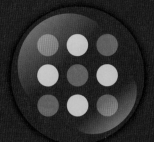

11 Written and calculator methods

Introduction

When you write down a mathematical calculation it might seem obvious to work through it from left to right across the page, in the same way that you read a book. But languages don't all work in the same way. Arabic and Hebrew read from right to left across the page, whereas traditional Chinese and Japanese are read from top to bottom in vertical columns! Mathematics is an international language, so mathematicians around the world agreed a convention for clarifying which operations should be performed first in a written calculation.

What's the point?

Scientists and mathematicians across the world write down all their calculations using the same order of operations – this allows them to understand each other's work and to exchange their ideas without confusion.

Objectives

By the end of this chapter, you will have learned how to …

- Develop standard written methods for addition, subtraction, multiplication and division.
- Use the order of operations.
- Solve problems using standard methods for addition, subtraction, multiplication and division.

Check in

Calculate these using a mental method.

1 a 13.6 + 7.5 **b** 2.57 + 3.9 **c** 13.4 − 8.59 **d** 7.65 − 4.29 **e** -2.81 + 7.98

2 a 21 × 0.3 **b** 252 ÷ 12 **c** 12 × 1.4 **d** 340 ÷ 15 **e** 7.1 × 21

Calculate these using a written method.

3 a 43.72 + 514.2 + 3.47 **b** 23.8 + 147.3 + 61.97

4 a 9 × 3.73 **b** 6 × 3.34 **c** 23 × 1.7 **d** 18 × 2.4 **e** 3.4 × 6.7

5 Give your answers as decimals to 1 dp where appropriate.

 a 55 ÷ 7 **b** 40 ÷ 9 **c** 336 ÷ 12 **d** 720 ÷ 16 **e** 567 ÷ 17

Starter problem

Make up an amazing story using this information.

Weight of a blue whale: 120 tonnes

Weight of an elephant: 7500 kg

Weight of a mouse: 22 g

Average weight of 1 mouthful for a person: 9 g

Average time for eating 1 mouthful: 19.3 seconds

Average number of mouthfuls in a meal: 62

When numbers are too difficult to add or subtract in your head, you can use a written method. Look at these two examples to see how ...

Example

Craig travels on the motorway from Woking to Bristol.
What is the total distance he has travelled?

Bristol — Swindon — Reading — Bracknell — Woking

64 km   65.05 km   18.76 km   21.4 km

Need to calculate 21.4 km + 18.76 km + 65.05 km + 64 km

```
  21.40          Set out the calculation in columns.
  18.76          Line up the decimal points.
  65.05          Fill in with zeros.
+ 64.00
 169.21
  1 1 1
```

Total distance travelled = 169.21 km

Example

A gritter lorry puts rock salt on roads to stop ice forming on the surface.
At the start of its journey the lorry is loaded with 593.68 kg of rock salt.
After 15 minutes it has released 75.7 kg of rock salt.
How much rock salt is left in the lorry?

Need to calculate 593.68 kg – 75.7 kg

```
  8 12 1
  593.68          Set out the calculation in columns.
 – 75.70
  517.98
```

You don't need to write the red zero in, but it might help.

Total rock salt remaining = 517.98 kg

Exercise 11a

1 Calculate these using a written or mental method.

a	54.6 + 41.5	**b**	27.9 + 16.4
c	28.3 + 55.4	**d**	47.6 + 75.7
e	45.9 + 8.3	**f**	84.4 + 19.7
g	14.7 − 3.2	**h**	18.6 − 12.1
i	7.84 − 5.29	**j**	8.36 − 4.7
k	0.871 − 0.658	**l**	0.473 − 0.082

2 Calculate these using a written method.

a	5.45 + 9.4	**b**	35.7 − 9.76
c	36.42 + 7.7	**d**	38.4 + 19.74
e	8.7 + 34.96	**f**	38.79 + 34.5
g	94.5 − 89.79	**h**	36.7 − 8.68
i	8.63 + 99.2	**j**	12.5 − 0.704
k	16.32 − 7.08	**l**	83.09 − 0.721

3 Calculate these using a written method.

a	534.9 − 51.2	**b**	659.76 + 46.9
c	34.68 + 862.9	**d**	1161.7 − 49.36
e	652.61 − 74.3	**f**	265.73 − 38.9
g	673.4 + 9.18	**h**	1357.2 − 89.73
i	52 173 + 4961	**j**	83.157 − 7.068
k	628.74 − 89.671	**l**	9.6805 + 892.14

4 Calculate these using a written method.

a 63.52 + 344.1 + 6.17

b 33.6 + 185.8 + 71.47

c 5.23 + 6.5 + 8 + 0.37

d 15.6 + 19.7 + 5.07

e 54.6 + 265.3 + 177.9

f 348.6 + 137.25 + 18.8

g 15 709 + 18.621 + 589.06

Problem solving

5 Use a mental or written method to solve each of these problems.

a Betty uses a route finder to travel from Gorley to Poole. On the way she stops for a coffee at Iredale and does some shopping at Darby.
What is the total distance she travels?

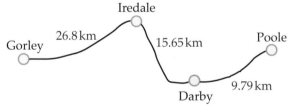

b In an iron works, Michel mixes metals together to make alloys with special properties. He makes a batch of wear-resistant alloy using 3.2 kg of carbon, 0.95 kg of manganese, 16.8 kg of chromium, 2.783 kg of molybdenum and 76.5 kg of iron. What is the total weight of the alloy?

5 c In the school discus competition, Titus throws the discus 52.86 m. He beats the school record by 9.375 m. What was the old school discus record?

6 Find the missing amount in each of these number sentences.

a ☐ + 3.78 kg = 12.5 kg

b 16.78 km + 3.8 km + ☐ = 25.27 km

c 89.3 litres + ☐ + 14.06 litres = 164.14 litres

d 3.86 tonnes + 12.7 tonnes + 49.1 tonnes + ☐ = 70.05 tonnes

11b Written methods of multiplication

It's best to use a standard method for written multiplication.

You should start by making an **estimate**

Calculate

a 239 × 94

b 31 × 1.9

Estimate

a 239 × 94 ≈ 200 × 100

≈ 20 000

Exact calculation

$$
\begin{array}{r}
239 \\
\times\ 94 \\
\hline
21\,5\,10 \\
+\ 95\,6 \\
\hline
22466 \\
\hline
\end{array}
$$

= 90 × 239
= 4 × 239

Answer 22 466

Estimate

b 31 × 1.9 ≈ 30 × 2

≈ 60

Change to an **equivalent** whole number calculation.

31 × 1.9 → 31 × 19

$$
\begin{array}{r}
31 \\
\times\ 19 \\
\hline
310 \\
+\ 279 \\
\hline
589 \\
\hline
\end{array}
$$

= 10 × 31
= 9 × 31

Answer 31 × 1.9 = 58.9

This method is often called 'long multiplication'.

You can solve real life problems using the standard written method of multiplication.

Siobhan downloads a 1.87 MB file from the internet. Unfortunately her computer has a virus and downloads the same file a total of fourteen times. What is the total size of files that her computer has downloaded?

Estimate

14 × 1.87 MB ≈ 10 × 2

≈ 20 MB

Whole number calculation

14 × 1.87 → 14 × 187

14 × 1.87 = 26.18

The total size of the files downloaded = 26.18 MB

Exact

$$
\begin{array}{r}
187 \\
\times\ 14 \\
\hline
1870 \\
+\ 748 \\
\hline
2618 \\
\hline
\end{array}
$$

= 10 × 187
= 4 × 187

Exercise 11b

Use the standard method to calculate these multiplications. Remember to do a mental approximation first.

1
a 12 × 15   b 19 × 24
c 18 × 26   d 21 × 34
e 43 × 25   f 4 × 122
g 136 × 3   h 6 × 331
i 59 × 278   j 26 × 658
k 395 × 627   l 841 × 234

2
a 7 × 4.6   b 5 × 3.5
c 8 × 7.9   d 8 × 6.8
e 9 × 5.3   f 8 × 4.6
g 31 × 0.9   h 26 × 5.4
i 729 × 2.8   j 426 × 9.8
k 634 × 17.3   l 806 × 40.3

3
a 5 × 2.16   b 4 × 2.45
c 7 × 6.99   d 8 × 9.28
e 9 × 5.43   f 8 × 3.84
g 6 × 4.17   h 5 × 9.09

4
a 13 × 5.4   b 24 × 1.6
c 19 × 2.1   d 37 × 7.6
e 29 × 7.4   f 48 × 5.5
g 49 × 8.9   h 35 × 3.2

5
a 12 × 2.54   b 16 × 3.36
c 13 × 4.71   d 27 × 3.86
e 39 × 6.74   f 42 × 7.25
g 68 × 5.49   h 95 × 7.99
i 572 × 4.13   j 461 × 2.36
k 4951 × 7.5   l 6421 × 9.8

Problem solving

6
a Kayleigh buys 25 boxes of apples. Each box costs £4.24. What is the total cost of the boxes of apples?
b Petrol costs £1.30 per litre. On a journey Danielle uses 31 litres of petrol. What is the total cost of the petrol for her journey?
c Megan runs for 55 seconds at 6.8 metres per second.
Hayden runs for 43 seconds at 7.7 metres per second.
Who has run the furthest? Explain your answer.

7
a At Modeschool there are 37 students who are each 1.56 m tall. If the students lie on the floor in a straight line, from head to toe, how long will the line of students be?

7
b At Medianschool the average student's thumb in Jane's class is 5.73 cm long. There are 29 students in Jane's class. Estimate the total length of the students' thumbs in Jane's class.

8 Hanif works out 15 × 4.7 = 70.5.
Use Hanif's answer to work out these calculations. In each case explain clearly the method you have used.
a 15 × 47   b 15 × 0.47   c 15 × 470
d What other multiplications can you work out using Hanif's calculations? Represent your answers on a copy of this spider diagram.
e Can you use Hanif's calculations to work out any divisions?

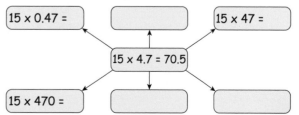

15 x 0.47 =

15 x 47 =

15 x 4.7 = 70.5

15 x 470 =

11c Written methods of division

You can do written division sums by either long division or by short division.

Short division works best when dividing by a single digit number. Otherwise long division is usually best.

Here is an example of long division.

Calculate 88.3 ÷ 15 giving your answer to 1 decimal place.

Estimate

$88.3 ÷ 15 ≈ 90 ÷ 15$

$≈ 6$

Exact calculation

```
        5.88
  15)88.30      5 × 15 = 75
     -75
      133
     -120       8 × 15 = 120
      130
     -120
       10
```

Make sure you do an estimate first and keep the digits lined up in columns.

You will have to work out your 15 times table as you go along.

Stop calculating after 2 decimal places as the answer is only needed to 1 dp.

$88.3 ÷ 15 = 5.88...$

$= 5.9$ (1 dp)

Here is an example of short division.

Calculate 15 ÷ 8 giving your answer to 2 decimal places.

Estimate

$15 ÷ 8 ≈ 16 ÷ 8$

$≈ 2$

Exact calculation

```
      1.875
       764
  8)15.000
```

$15 ÷ 8 = 1.875$

$= 1.88$ (2 dp)

Think:

$15 ÷ 8 = 1$ remainder 7

$70 ÷ 8 = 8$ remainder 6

$60 ÷ 8 = 7$ remainder 4

$40 ÷ 8 = 5$ and no remainder.

Exercise 11c

1 Calculate these divisions using an appropriate method. Give your answer with a remainder where appropriate.

a $161 \div 7$ b $156 \div 6$

c $279 \div 9$ d $272 \div 8$

e $195 \div 13$ f $225 \div 14$

g $360 \div 15$ h $360 \div 17$

2 a What is $729 \div 27$?

b What is the remainder when 750 is divided by 27?

c What is the remainder when 720 is divided by 27?

3 Calculate these divisions using an appropriate method.

a $45.6 \div 6$ b $63.2 \div 8$

c $64.8 \div 9$ d $39.2 \div 7$

e $64.8 \div 12$ f $81.9 \div 13$

g $99.4 \div 14$ h $99 \div 15$

4 Calculate these divisions using an appropriate method. Give your answer as a decimal rounded to 1 decimal place where appropriate.

a $55 \div 8$ b $20 \div 7$

c $35 \div 6$ d $46 \div 9$

e $120 \div 11$ f $137 \div 12$

g $150 \div 16$ h $223 \div 18$

i $4921 \div 15$ j $6482 \div 14$

5 Calculate these divisions using an appropriate method. Give your answer as a decimal rounded to 1 decimal place where appropriate.

a $25.6 \div 8$ b $32.5 \div 7$

c $14.5 \div 6$ d $24.6 \div 9$

e $34.8 \div 14$ f $37.5 \div 15$

g $46.3 \div 18$ h $55.4 \div 21$

i $351.6 \div 16$ j $999.9 \div 12$

k $409.3 \div 11$ l $620.7 \div 13$

Problem solving

6 In each calculation, decide whether to give your answer either as a remainder or as a decimal to 1 decimal place.

a Devvon's car uses 27 litres of petrol to travel 400 km. Alec's car uses 25 litres of petrol to travel 365 km. Which car travels further for each litre of petrol? Explain your answer.

b Farah has been alive for 765 hours. Is she more or less than a month old? Explain and justify your answer.

c Xan downloads a file at 28 kB per second. The file is 95.2 kB in size. How many seconds does it take to download the file?

d A train company expects 14000 extra passengers due to a cricket match. Its trains have six coaches and each coach can safely carry 84 passengers. How many extra trains should the company put into service?

7 'Purfect' cat biscuits come in three different sizes:

     100 g   costs 16 p

     150 g   costs 22 p

     250 g   costs 39 p

a Which size of biscuits is the best value for money?

b Explain and justify your answer.

MyMaths.co.uk

⊙ When a calculation contains more than one **operation**, you must do the operations in the correct order.

| Brackets | Work out the contents of any **brackets** first. |

| Powers | Then work out any **powers**. |

Then work out any **multiplications** and

| Multiply | Divide | **divisions**. |

Then work out any **additions** and

| Add | Subtract | **subtractions**. |

A useful acronym is:

B **B**rackets
I **I**ndices (or powers)
D **D**ivision
M **M**ultiplication
A **A**ddition
S **S**ubtraction

Example

Calculate

a $3 + 5 \times 2^2$

b $3 + (5 \times 2)^2$

a $3 + 5 \times 2^2$

There are no **brackets** | Bracket |

Work out the **power** | Powers |
$= 3 + 5 \times 4$

Work out the
multiplication | Multiply | Divide |
$= 3 + 20$

Work out the **addition** | Add | Subtract |
$= 23$

b $3 + (5 \times 2)^2$

Work out the **brackets** $5 \times 2 = 10$
$= 3 + (10)^2$

Work out the **power**
$= 3 + 100$

Work out the **addition**
$= 103$

A fraction can act like a **pair of brackets**.
This is useful to know when you are using a calculator.

Example

Calculate $\dfrac{8 + 3^2}{32 - 8}$ Give your answer to 2 decimal places.

Re-write using brackets as
$\dfrac{(8 + 3^2)}{(32 - 8)} = (8 + 3^2) \div (32 - 8)$

```
(8+3²)÷(32−8)
0.708333333
```

Answer = 0.71 (2 dp)

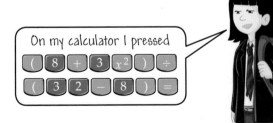

On my calculator I pressed

(8 + 3 x^2) ÷
(3 2 − 8) =

Exercise 11d

1 Work out these calculations using the order of operations.

a $5 + 4 \times 6$ **b** $15 - 3 \times 2$

c $12 + 2 \times 5$ **d** $24 - 16 \div 4$

e $5 \times 3 - 2 \times 3$ **f** $4 \times 7 + 6 \times 3$

g $18 \div 9 + 15 \div 5$ **h** $7 + 5 \times 3 - 2$

2 Match each calculation with the correct answer.

Calculation

a $3 + 4^2 \times 5$

b $20 - 3^2 \times 2$

c $(19 - 4^2) \times 2$

d $5 \times (3 + 7)^2$

e $25 - 3 \times (2^2 - 1)$

f $3 \times 5^2 + 12 \div 3$

g $6 \times 7 - 3^2 \times 4$

Answer X	Answer Y
83	245
578	2
250	6
245	31
87	16
79	29
132	6

Explain your method and reasoning for each answer.

3 Calculate these giving your answer to 1 decimal place where appropriate. You may wish to use a calculator.

a $\dfrac{8 + 4}{5 - 2}$ **b** $\dfrac{5^2 - 1}{3^2 + 4}$

c $\dfrac{(28 - 3)}{10 - 3^2}$ **d** $\dfrac{(4 + 3)^2}{4^2 - 1}$

4 Copy and complete each of these calculations by putting brackets in the correct place.

a $8 + 5 \times 4 - 3 = 49$

b $8 + 5 \times 4 - 3 = 13$

c $8 + 5 \times 4 - 3 = 25$

d $7 + 3^2 \div 4 = 4$

e $7 + 3^2 \div 4 = 25$

f $7 + 3^2 \div 4 = 10\dfrac{1}{4}$

5 Use a calculator to work out these calculations. Give your answers to 2 decimal places where appropriate.

a $(5 + 2.8) \div 7$

b $34 - 1.7^2 \times 4$

c $6 \times (3.5 - 1.6)^2$

d $(4 + 2.5) \times 7$

e $\dfrac{7 + 3^2}{19 - 4^2}$ **f** $\dfrac{13^2 + 6^2}{13^2 - 6^2}$

g $\dfrac{48}{6 \times 8}$ **h** $\dfrac{5 + 2^2}{(18 - 9)}$

i $\dfrac{1.9^2 + 2.1}{53.2 - 7^2}$ **j** $\dfrac{3(7^2 - 8)}{5 + 9}$

k $\dfrac{(12 - 7)(5 - 3)}{7^2 + 4}$

l $\dfrac{2(3.4^2 - 5.6) + 8.1}{3(6 + 2.2)}$

Problem solving

6 John and Vernon are working out this calculation: $\dfrac{60}{3 \times 4}$

John works out $3 \times 4 = 12$, and then $60 \div 12 = 5$
Vernon works out $60 \div 3 = 20$, and then $20 \div 4 = 5$
Explain how and why both methods work.

7 Enter the numbers from 1 to 9 into the empty boxes to make the calculations in each row and column work. You must not use a number more than once.

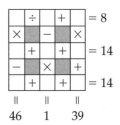

You can solve problems by breaking them down into smaller steps...

...and you can check your answers using inverse operations.

Example

Tom records the weights of all the parts of a space shuttle before it launches.

2 booster rockets	= 1.18 million kg
separate fuel tank	= 0.75 million kg
payload	= 0.0249 million kg
crew + other	= 0.0015 million kg
shuttle body	= ?
Total weight	= 1.998 million kg

Use this information to calculate the weight of the shuttle body.

First find the weight of all the parts using addition.

```
  1 . 1 8
  0 . 7 5
  0 . 0 2 4 9
+ 0 . 0 0 1 5
  1 . 9 5 6 4
    1   1
```

Second subtract the weight of all the parts from the total weight.

```
  1 . 9 9 8⁷0¹
- 1 . 9 5 6 4
  0   0 4 1 6
```

Weight of shuttle body = 0.0416 million kg

Example

Lorna and Gina run the 200 m race at the school sports day.

Lorna's time is 27.8 secs   Gina's time is 30.07 secs

Sam works out the difference between Lorna's time and Gina's time as 2.73 seconds.

a How do you know Sam's answer is wrong?

b What is the correct answer?

a Check Sam's answer using addition.

Lorna's time + Difference = Gina's time

```
 27.80
+2.73
 30.53
  1
```

This is not Gina's time, so Sam has made a mistake.

b Do the subtraction using a written method.

```
 ²30.⁹07¹
-27.80
  2.27
```

Lorna is 2.27 seconds faster than Gina.

Exercise 11e

Problem solving

1 Tron is a robot chef. He measures all his ingredients very precisely. Work out the total weight of each of his recipes.

Risotto	
24.7 g	Butter
605 g	Onions
245.4 g	Rice
520 g	Water
2.036 g	Salt
224.8 g	Mushrooms

Spiced Rice	
14.34 g	Ghee
212.7 g	Rice
520 g	Water
3.207 g	Salt
1.08 g	Pepper
6.2 g	Turmeric

2 Veronica has measured the perimeter of the main school building. Here is a plan showing the measurements she has made.

a What is the length of the side marked X?

b What is the perimeter of the school building?

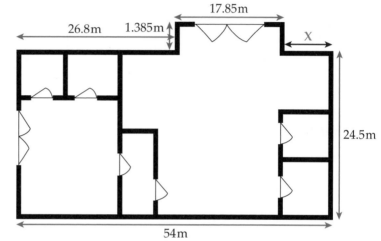

3 A satellite navigation system is trying to calculate the shortest route from Ayton to Gewizzle. All distances are in km.

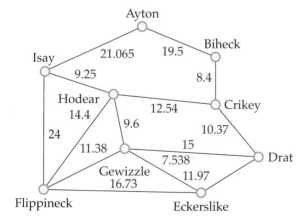

a Find the shortest route from Ayton to Eckerslike. Clearly show the towns visited and the total distance travelled.

b Will the shortest route by distance be the quickest? Explain your answer.

c Investigate finding the shortest route between other places.

d Can you find the shortest route which visits all the towns and starts and finishes at Ayton?

When you are solving a complex problem, you should write down the information you know and what you are trying to find out.

Example

Here are the prices of buying some calculators.

Number ordered	DAZIO CX 283	DAZIO CX 283P	SHIP TQ 83S	SHIP TQ 83SE
1–5	£3.45	£3.85	£4.85	£5.15
6–14	£3.30	£3.70	£4.49	£4.99
15–30	£3.19	£3.55	£4.30	£4.89
Over 30	£3.09	£3.40	£4.19	£4.79

Gina buys 35 DAZIO CX 283P calculators.

Nadia buys 23 SHIP TQ 83SE calculators.

Who spends the most money on calculators and how much more does she spend?

First identify the prices of the calculators and write down the calculations for the total costs.

Gina spends 35 × £3.40   Nadia spends 23 × £4.89

Use a standard method to do the equivalent whole number calculations.

```
    340                          489
  ×  35                        ×  23
  ------                       ------
  1 0200                        9780
  1 700                       + 1467
  ------                       ------
  11900                        11247
```

Convert back to the original calculations.

Gina spends £119.00   Nadia spends £112.47

119.00 > 112.47

Gina spends more than Nadia.

Calculate the exact difference.

Difference = 119.00 − 112.47   You can use a mental method here.

           = 6.53

Gina spends £6.53 more than Nadia.

Exercise 11f

Problem solving

1 Here are the offers from three phone companies for text messages.

a Klaus buys 35 text messages from Four. How much money would he save if he switched to Yello to buy his text messages?

Number of texts	CO2	Yello	Four	Skyte
1 – 9	4.5p	3.8p	4.3p	4.1p
10–49	4.2p	3.7p	4.1p	4.0p
50–99	3.9p	3.6p	3.9p	3.9p
Over 100	3.6p	3.5p	3.7p	3.8p

b Xuan buys 180 text messages a week from Skyte. How much money would he save each week if he switched to Yello to buy his text messages?

c How much money would Xuan save in a year if he switched?

2 a Hector saves £8.40 a week for his holiday for 12 weeks. If he is on holiday for 14 days, how much money does he have to spend each day?

b Anna takes 8 days to complete a long distance walk. Each day she walks the same distance of 9.25 miles. Louise completes the same walk in 5 days. How far does Louise walk each day? What assumption do you need to make about Louise's journey?

3 Calculate the rate of pay for 1 hour for each of these workers.

a Anton works in an office for 8 hours a day, for 5 days a week, and gets paid £251.20 a week.

b Habib works for an emergency service. He works 4 shifts each lasting 12 hours in 1 week. His weekly pay is £393.60.

c Hannah works in advertising. She works 7 hours a day. In the month of May she works 23 days. Her monthly pay for May is £2125.20.

4 A Manx shearwater flew 6520 miles from its summer home on the Welsh coast to its winter home in Argentina in two weeks. What was its average speed in miles per hour?

You should write down all the steps in your working, choose an appropriate method and check your answer is correct at the end.

Example

Flour comes in three different-sized packets.
Work out which packet is the best value for money.

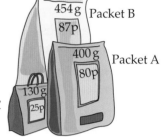

454 g Packet B
87p

400 g Packet A
80p

130 g Packet C
25p

Calculate the amount you get for 1p in each packet.

Packet A   1p will buy you   400 ÷ 80 grams of flour

> This is a **mental calculation**, using factors (÷ 10 and then ÷ 8).

= 400 ÷ 10 ÷ 8
= 40 ÷ 8
= 5g

Packet B   1p will buy you   454 ÷ 87 grams of flour

> This is best done with a **calculator**.

454 ÷ 87
5.218390805

= 5.22 g (2 dp)

Packet C   1p will buy you   130 ÷ 25 grams of flour

> This could be done using a **written method**.

= 5.2 g

$$\begin{array}{r} 5.2 \\ 25\overline{)130.0} \\ -125 \quad 5 \times 25 = 125 \\ \hline 50 \\ -50 \quad 2 \times 25 = 50 \\ \hline 0 \end{array}$$

Packet B is the best value for money.

There are several ways to check your answer.

Compare with your **approximation**.
Is it close?

Ensure an appropriate degree of **accuracy**.

Answer

Check your answer is sensible.

How many decimal places?

Check using **inverse operations**.

Is it the right sort of size?
Have you found what the question asked for?

Check subtraction with addition, check division using multiplication.

Exercise 11g

Problem solving

Choose the most appropriate method (mental, written or calculator) for solving each of these calculations. In each case, explain your choice and then use that method to solve the problem.

1   ChocChoc biscuits come in three different-sized packets.
    Work out which packet is the best value for money by
    calculating the cost of one biscuit for each packet.

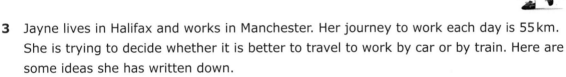

Packet B

24 biscuits
120p

15 biscuits
165p
Packet C

30 biscuits

Packet A

2   Oliver goes on a sponsored charity walk from
    Maryport to Liverpool, dressed as a giant leek.
    He takes 17 days to walk from Maryport to Liverpool.
    Each day he walks the same distance.
    He returns by car along the same route in
    3 hours at an average speed of 47.6 mph.
    He raises £28.63 for charity for each mile he walks.
    i   How far did Oliver travel each day on his charity walk?
    ii How much money did Oliver raise for charity by completing
        his walk?

3   Jayne lives in Halifax and works in Manchester. Her journey to work each day is 55 km.
    She is trying to decide whether it is better to travel to work by car or by train. Here are
    some ideas she has written down.

Travelling by car...		Travelling by train...	
Car insurance	= £280.45 (each year)	Monthly season ticket	= £285.29
Road tax	= £180 (yearly)	Daily return ticket	= £13.75
Servicing	= £195 (twice a year)	Travelling time...	
MOT	= £50.63 (each year)	Home to station	= 19 mins walk
Fuel costs...		Journey on train	= 38 mins
Petrol	= 113.9 p per litre	Station to work	= 13 mins walk
Consumption	= 12.3 km per litre		
Travelling time...			
Each journey lasts about 55 mins			

Jayne works for 46 weeks a year. She has a 4-week holiday in August.
Write a short report recommending which form of transport Jayne should take. Explain and
justify your answer.

Check out

You should now be able to ...

✓ Use standard written methods for addition, subtraction, multiplication and division.	5	1–5
✓ Use the order of operations.	5	6, 7
✓ Solve problems using standard methods for addition, subtraction, multiplication and division.	6	8–12

Language	Meaning	Example
Estimate	Simplify a calculation, by rounding the numbers, in order to have a value to check the full calculation against	$2 \times 3 = 6$ is an estimate for 1.87×3.251
Short division	A way of setting out workings when dividing by a single digit number	$\begin{array}{r} 1\ 8\ 9\ r\ 1 \\ 7\overline{)13^62^64} \end{array}$
Long division	A way of setting out workings when dividing by a multi-digit number	$\begin{array}{r} 110\ r\ 4 \\ 12\overline{)1324} \\ 12 \\ \hline 12 \\ 12 \\ \hline 04 \end{array}$
BIDMAS	A word which helps you to remember the order in which to carry out operations: **B**rackets, **I**ndices, **D**ivision and **M**ultiplication, **A**ddition and **S**ubtraction	$(9 \times 3 - 3) \div (2^2 + 2) - 4$ $= (27 - 3) \div (4 + 2) - 4$ $= 24 \div 6 - 4$ $= 4 - 4$ $= 0$
Long multiplication	A way of setting out workings when multiplying	$\begin{array}{r} 317 \\ \times\ \ 51 \\ \hline 15850 \\ +\ \overset{3}{3}17 \\ \hline 16167 \\ \hline {}_1 \end{array}$

1 Calculate these using a written method.
  a 54.3 + 16.9 **b** 235.87 + 14.075
  c 45.34 − 27.97 **d** 821.4 − 67.09

2 Calculate these using the standard written method.
  a 24 × 78 **b** 8 × 3.9
  c 39 × 4.7 **d** 72 × 3.81

3 Calculate these using an appropriate written method.
  a 243 ÷ 9 **b** 322 ÷ 14

4 What is the remainder when 515 is divided by 19?

5 Calculate these using an appropriate method. Give your answer as a decimal rounded to 1 decimal place.
  a 87 ÷ 9 **b** 150 ÷ 8
  c 47.6 ÷ 7 **d** 205.38 ÷ 8

6 Calculate these using the correct order of operations.
  a 13 + 2 × 7
  b 12 − 6 ÷ 2
  c (15 + 9) × 4
  d 34 − 2 × (3 + 7)
  e 4 × 3² + 8 ÷ 2
  f $\dfrac{(5 + 1)^2}{15 - 2 \times 3}$

7 Add brackets to these calculations to make them correct.
  a 4 + 8 ÷ 4 − 1 = 2
  b 4 + 8 ÷ 4 − 1 = 4
  c 6 − 3 × 12 − 8 = 12
  d 6 − 3 × 12 − 8 = -6

8 A family have the following weights
  Dad: 85.6 kg
  Mum: 58.4 kg
  Daughter: 37 kg
  Baby: 5.47 kg
  What is the total weight of the family?

9 Dillon buys 36 reams of paper.
  Each ream costs £3.82.
  What is the total cost of the paper?

10 Josh buys 18 burgers at a total cost of £22.32. What is the cost of one burger?

11 A family of 3 people budget £7.89 per person per day for food.
  What is their weekly budget for food?

12 A doctor works 6 hours a day for 5 days a week seeing patients. During this time she must see 99 patients. On average, how long can she spend with each patient? Give your answer to the nearest minute.

What next?

Score		
	0 – 4	Your knowledge of this topic is still developing. To improve look at Formative test: 2B–11; MyMaths: 1007, 1026 and 1167
	5 – 10	You are gaining a secure knowledge of this topic. To improve look at InvisiPen: 124, 126, 127, 129, 131, 133 and 134
	11 – 12	You have mastered this topic. Well done, you are ready to progress!

MyMaths.co.uk

1 Calculate these using a written method.

    a 257.3 − 67.9   **b** 540.87 + 55.9   **c** 45.79 + 753.4

    d 1252.6 − 38.79   **e** 763.72 − 85.4   **f** 376.62 − 49.8

    g 582.5 + 10.36   **h** 2476.2 − 78.67   **i** 1468.4 − 72.56

    j 816.3 − 95.9   **k** 923.28 + 359   **l** 43.5 + 2186.39

2 Calculate these using the standard method.

    a 15 × 6.5   **b** 35 × 2.7   **c** 16 × 4.8   **d** 43 × 8.5

    e 39 × 9.2   **f** 57 × 6.7   **g** 38 × 7.6   **h** 88 × 7.7

3 Calculate these using the standard method.

    a 19 × 3.68   **b** 27 × 4.18   **c** 46 × 5.53   **d** 62 × 7.26

    e 49 × 5.69   **f** 74 × 8.57   **g** 79 × 8.37   **h** 99 × 9.99

4 Calculate these using an appropriate method. Give your answer as a decimal rounded to 1 decimal place where appropriate.

    a 76 ÷ 8   **b** 40 ÷ 9   **c** 85 ÷ 6   **d** 99 ÷ 9

    e 252 ÷ 18   **f** 314 ÷ 19   **g** 388 ÷ 21   **h** 404 ÷ 25

5 Calculate these using an appropriate method. Give your answer as a decimal rounded to 1 decimal place where appropriate.

    a 36.7 ÷ 8   **b** 43.6 ÷ 7   **c** 25.6 ÷ 6   **d** 35.7 ÷ 9

    e 50.4 ÷ 24   **f** 52.7 ÷ 39   **g** 91.6 ÷ 24   **h** 41.8 ÷ 17

6 Calculate

    a 2 × 8 ÷ 4   **b** 40 ÷ 2 ÷ 2   **c** 3 × 16 − (7 − 3)

    d 216 ÷ 18 − (3² + 1)   **e** 9 × 19 − (14 − 5)   **f** 90 ÷ 50 − (5² − 4²)

7 Use a calculator to work out these calculations. Give your answers to 2 decimal places where appropriate.

    a (7 + 3.9) ÷ 5   **b** 48 − 2.3² × 5   **c** 9 × (7.2 − 1.9)²   **d** (3 + 6.7) × 4

    e $\dfrac{8 + 5^2}{39 - 5^2}$ **f** 12² − 8²   **g** $\dfrac{256}{2^2 \times 2^3}$ **h** $\dfrac{11 + 5^2}{(7^2 - 13)}$

8 An airline baggage handler has 1.35 tonnes of capacity left on a plane. Can she load all of the following packages?

| car parts, 560 kg | cut flowers, 34.6 kg | a sack of letters 76 kg |
| two sacks of parcels 98 kg each | a crate of mangoes 425 kg | |

9 Darren is having trouble with his arithmetic. For each problem

i work out the correct answer   **ii** explain Darren's probable mistake.

a 346.95 + 564.32   Darren's answer, 811.27

b 1.0046 − 0.045   Darren's answer, 1.0001

c 627.43 − 451.62   Darren's answer, 275.81

d 126.6 + 59.3 + 384.13   Darren's answer, 4027.2

10 Fiona and Alison have part-time jobs

a Fiona gets paid £5.66 an hour and works for 12 hours. How much does she get paid?

b Alison works for 15.5 hours and earns £93.78. What is her hourly rate?

c Fiona is saving for a holiday and needs £500. How many more hours will she need to work?

d Tom works 7 hours a day for 5 days and gets paid £201.25. Is his hourly rate higher or lower than Fiona's hourly rate?

11 Depak is driving the 249 miles home from holiday.

a His average speed is 45 miles per hour. How long will it take him?

b His fuel consumption is 33 miles per gallon. How much fuel will he need?

c When full his petrol tank holds 14 gallons but at the start of this journey it is only five-eighths full. Can he make it home without having to fill up?

d Depak doesn't know it but his car has a leak, and it is losing 0.15 gallons of petrol every hour. Will he still make it home?

12 a Elliot is cooking an 8.5 kg turkey for his family. The instructions say cook at a high heat for 5 min per kg, then turn the heat down and cook for 25 min per kg and finally cook for 30 min at the high heat again.
How long will it take to cook the turkey?

b After cooking the turkey must rest for 45 min. It will take Elliot a further 20 min to carve and serve. If Elliot wants to serve dinner at 4 o'clock in the afternoon, when should he put the turkey in the oven?

MyMaths.co.uk

12 Constructions

Introduction

As supermarket companies get bigger they open new branches in different towns. The warehouses that supply to each branch need to be positioned carefully. In order to save costs, the supermarket companies try to choose a site that has good transport links and is close to an equal distance from each branch that it services.

This problem can be solved using mathematical constructions by finding the regions on a map that are approximately an equal distance from each branch.

What's the point?

Accurate geometrical constructions allow you to solve real life problems involving scale drawings and maps.

Objectives

By the end of this chapter, you will have learned how to ...

- Construct triangles and quadrilaterals accurately.
- Construct angle bisectors, perpendicular bisectors and perpendicular lines.
- Describe the locus of a point and draw it accurately.
- Use bearings to specify directions.
- Use scale drawings to represent real life objects.

Check in

1 **a** Draw a circle of radius 5 cm and copy this diagram.

   b What is the length of the triangle's side?

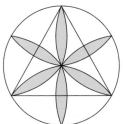

2 Measure these angles with a protractor.

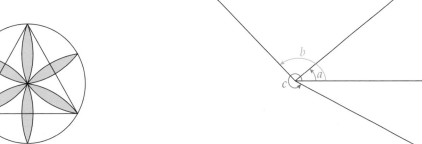

Starter problem

Construct an equilateral triangle of side 8 cm.

Construct the perpendicular bisector of each side and you should notice that all three bisectors meet at a point.

Using this point as the centre, draw a new circle.

Investigate other types of triangles.

You can construct a unique triangle using a ruler and a protractor given the right information.

You can have two angles and the included side (ASA)...

...or you can have two sides and the included angle (SAS).

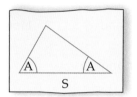

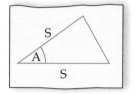

Example

Construct the triangle *ABC*

C 110° 20° 3.5 cm B

———————————
C   3.5 cm   B

Draw the base line of 3.5 cm using a ruler.

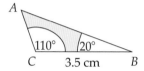

Draw an angle of 110° at C using a protractor.

Draw an angle of 20° at B using a protractor to complete the triangle.

Example

Construct the triangle *DEF*

D
4 cm
F 70° E
4.5 cm

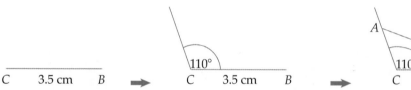

F ——— E
  4.5 cm

Draw the base line of 4.5 cm using a ruler.

Draw an angle of 70° at E using a protractor.

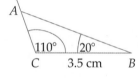

Mark D at 4 cm from E and draw FD to complete the triangle.

Exercise 12a

1 Construct these triangles.
State the mathematical name of each
triangle.

a

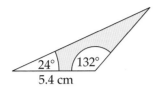

24° 132°
5.4 cm

b

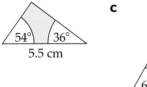

54° 36°
5.5 cm

c

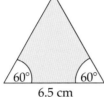

60° 60°
6.5 cm

2 Construct these triangles.
Measure the unknown length in each
triangle.

a

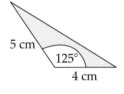

5 cm
125°
4 cm

c

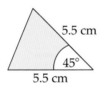

5.5 cm
45°
5.5 cm

b

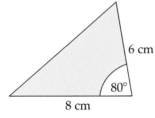

6 cm
80°
8 cm

3 Calculate the missing angles and then
construct each triangle.

a

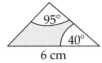

95°
40°
6 cm

b

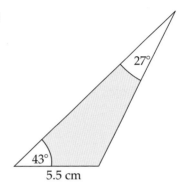

27°

43°
5.5 cm

c

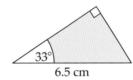

33°
6.5 cm

d

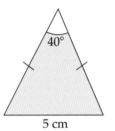

40°

5 cm

Problem solving

4 A field is in the shape of a triangle.
   a Using a scale of 1 millimetre to represent 1 metre, construct an
   accurate scale drawing of the field.
   b Calculate the smallest length of fencing that is needed to enclose
   the field.

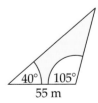

40° 105°
55 m

5 **a** Construct this parallelogram.
   b Measure the lengths of the diagonals.

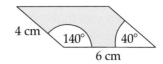

4 cm
140° 40°
6 cm

You can construct a triangle using a ruler and a pair of compasses if you know the lengths of the sides of the triangle.

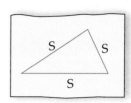

Example

a Construct the triangle *ABC*.
b Measure the angles *A*, *B* and *C*.

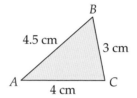

a

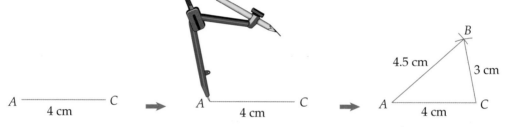

Draw the base line of 4 cm using a ruler.

Draw an arc 4.5 cm from *A* using compasses.

Draw an arc 3 cm from *C*. Draw *AB* and *CB* to complete the triangle.

b Use a protractor to measure the angles.

angle *A* = 41°, angle *B* = 60.5° and angle *C* = 78.5°.

You can construct some quadrilaterals by constructing two triangles.

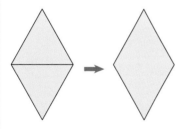

Two equilateral triangles can combine to make a rhombus.

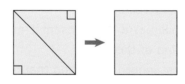

Two right-angled triangles can combine to make a square.

What other quadrilaterals can you make by constructing different types of triangles?

Exercise 12b

1 Construct these triangles using ruler and compasses.
Measure the angles in each triangle and check that the total is 180°.

a

55 mm 55 mm
55 mm

b

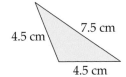

4.5 cm 7.5 cm
4.5 cm

c

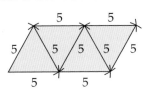

7 cm 5 cm
6 cm

2 Construct these quadrilaterals using ruler and compasses.
Write down the mathematical name of each quadrilateral.

a

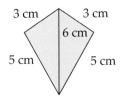

3 cm 3 cm
6 cm
5 cm 5 cm

b

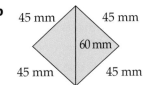

45 mm 45 mm
60 mm
45 mm 45 mm

c

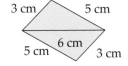

3 cm 5 cm
6 cm
5 cm 3 cm

Problem solving

3 A teacher asks the students to construct a triangle ABC so that angle A = 55°, angle B = 80° and angle C = 45°.
Each child constructs their triangle correctly and all the angles are drawn accurately. However all the triangles are not identical. Explain why this is possible.

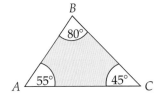

B
80°
A 55° 45° C

4 **a** Using compasses, construct this triangle.
b State the type of the triangle.

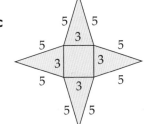

3 cm 4 cm
5 cm

5 Using compasses, construct these nets of solids.
All the dimensions are in centimetres.
Cut out each net and make the solid.
What is the mathematical name of each solid?

a

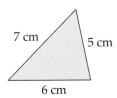

5 5
5 5 5 5 5
5 5

b

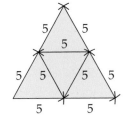

5 5
5
5 5 5 5
5 5

c

5 5
3
5 3 3 5
5 3 5
5 5

An **angle bisector** cuts an angle exactly in half.

A **perpendicular bisector** cuts a line exactly in half.

You can construct both of these bisectors using **compasses**.

Example

Draw two lines at 45° and use compasses to construct the angle bisector.

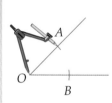 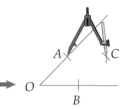 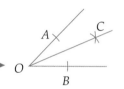

Use compasses to draw equal **arcs** on each line.

Draw equal arcs from *A* and *B* that intersect at *C*.

Draw a line from *O* to *C* and beyond.
angle *AOC* = angle *COB*

Example

Draw a straight line and use compasses to construct the perpendicular bisector.

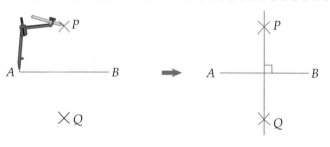

Draw equal arcs from *A* and *B* above and below the line.

PQ is perpendicular to *AB* and bisects *AB*.

Draw a line from *P* to *Q*.

Don't rub out any of your construction lines – they show your working!

Exercise 12c

1 Draw these angles using a protractor.
Using compasses, construct the angle
bisectors.
Use a protractor to check your answers.
   a 80°   **b** 110°   **c** 96°   **d** 56°

2 **a** Draw a line *AB*, so that *AB* = 8 cm.
   b Using compasses, construct the
   perpendicular bisector of *AB*.
   c Check that this line
      i is perpendicular to *AB*
      ii bisects *AB*.

3 **a** Use a protractor and ruler to draw a
   5 cm by 8 cm rectangle.
   b Construct the perpendicular bisector of
   each side.
   c Draw the lines of symmetry for the
   rectangle.

4 **a** Draw a large triangle.
   b Using compasses, construct the
   angle bisector for each of the
   three angles.
   c Draw a circle inside the triangle
   using the point of intersection as
   the centre.
   The circle should just touch the sides
   of the triangle.

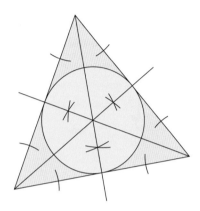

Problem solving

5 The diagram shows the construction of the angle bisector of
the angle *AOB*.
   a State the mathematical names of the shapes *OACB*, *OAC*
   and *OBC*.
   b Explain why the construction gives the angle bisector.

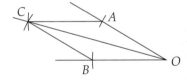

6 Draw a horizontal line *AB* = 10 cm.
Using compasses, construct the
perpendicular bisector of *AB*.
O is the point of intersection.
Draw *CD* = 10 cm, so that
CO = *OD* = 5 cm.
Find the centres and draw the five circles.

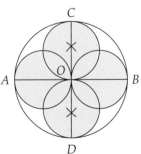

7 Using only compasses and a ruler construct a 45° angle.

Did you know?

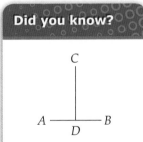

You can create
optical illusions using
perpendicular lines.
Which line is longer,
AB or *CD*?

You can construct perpendiculars between points and lines.

The shortest distance from a point to a line is the perpendicular distance.

The shortest distance is the red line.

Example

You can construct two types of perpendicular using compasses.

Draw a straight line *AB* and mark a point *P* above it. Using compasses construct the perpendicular from the point to the line.

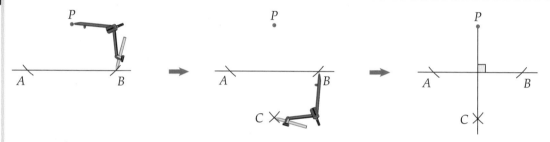

Use compasses to draw equal **arcs** from *P* on the line.

Draw equal arcs from *A* and *B* that **intersect** at *C*.

Draw a line from *P* through *C*.

Example

Draw a straight line *AB* and mark a point *P* on the line. Using compasses construct the perpendicular from the point on the line.

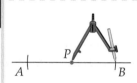

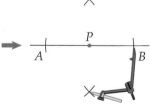

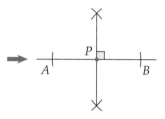

Use compasses to draw equal arcs from *P* on the line.

Draw equal arcs from *A* and *B* above and below the line.

Draw a line through the points of **intersection** of the arcs.

Exercise 12d

1 Draw a line *AB*, with a point *P* above the line.

P
•

A ——————————— B

  a Using compasses, construct the perpendicular to *AB* that passes through the point *P* and meets *AB* at *X*.

  b Measure the angle *PXB*.

2 Draw a line *AB* so that *AB* = 10 cm.
Mark the point *P* so that *AP* = 6 cm.

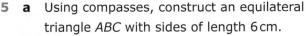

A ——————•——— B
  6 cm   4 cm

Construct the perpendicular to *AB* that passes through the point *P*.

3 A straight line passes through the points (0, 0), (2, 1) and (4, 2).

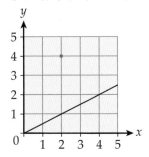

  a Draw the diagram on square grid paper.

  b Construct the perpendicular from the point (2, 4) to the line.

  c Measure the shortest distance from (2, 4) to the line.

Problem solving

4 Draw a line *AB* so that *AB* = 9 cm.
Mark the point *P* on *AB* so that *AP* = 3 cm.
Construct the perpendicular to *AB* passing through *P*.
Mark the points *C* and *D* on the perpendicular so that *PC* = *PD* = 3 cm.
Join the points *A*, *C*, *B* and *D* to form a quadrilateral.

  a State the mathematical name of the shape *ACBD*.

  b Use a protractor to measure the angles *A*, *B*, *C* and *D*.

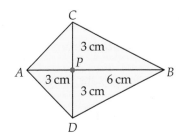

5 **a** Using compasses, construct an equilateral triangle *ABC* with sides of length 6 cm.

  b Construct the perpendiculars from

    i *A* to *BC*

    ii *B* to *AC*

    iii *C* to *AB*.

  c Draw the lines of symmetry for the equilateral triangle.

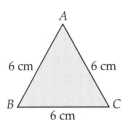

6 Draw a triangle ABC and construct the perpendiculars from
A to BC B to CA and C to AB.
Comment on what you find.

A point which moves according to a rule forms a **locus**.

▶ The **path** followed by an object is an example of a locus.

The plural of locus is loci.

Imagine the tip of a sail as it moves around.

▲ The locus is a circle.

Imagine the path of a cricket ball flying through the air.

▲ The locus is a curve.

Imagine the stone as it falls.

▲ The locus is a straight line.

Example

Construct the locus of the point that is **equidistant** from the points *A* and *B*.

$A\bullet$ $\bullet B$

The locus is the **perpendicular bisector** of the line *AB*.

Use compasses to construct the perpendicular bisector.

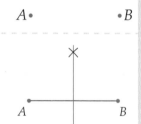

Equidistant means the same distance.

Example

Draw the locus of the point that is 2 cm from a fixed point *O*.

The locus is a circle of radius 2 cm centre *O*.
Use compasses to construct the circle.

Exercise 12e

1 Draw and describe in words the locus of
  a a ball thrown straight up in the air
  b the tip of the minute hand on a clock
  c a conker dropping from a tree
  d a competitor on a ski jump
  e the foot of a person doing a
    somersault on a snowboard.

2 a Draw an angle *AOB* of 130°.
  b Draw the locus of the point that is
    equidistant from *OA* and *OB*.

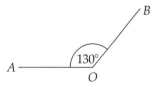

3 Draw the locus of a point that is 3 cm from
  a fixed point.

4 a Draw a line *AB* = 8 cm.
  b Using ruler and compasses, construct
    the locus of the point that is
    equidistant from *A* and *B*.

$$A \underset{8\text{ cm}}{\rule{3cm}{0.4pt}} B$$

Problem solving

5 Draw the locus of the point that is equidistant from
  parallel lines that are 4 cm apart.

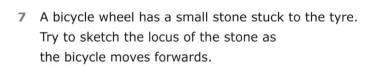

6 Kyle climbs halfway up a 5 metre ladder.
  The ladder starts to slide down the wall and along the ground.
  Kyle remains fixed to the midpoint of the ladder.
  Using a scale of 1 cm to represent 1 metre, draw different positions of
  the ladder as it slides.
  Draw the locus of Kyle.

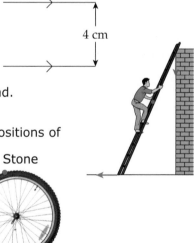

7 A bicycle wheel has a small stone stuck to the tyre.
  Try to sketch the locus of the stone as
  the bicycle moves forwards.

Stone

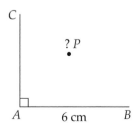

8 The lines AB and AC are at right angles.
  AB is 6 cm long. The point P is
  equidistant from the points A and B.
  The point P is also equidistant from the lines AB and AC.
  Copy the diagram and find the point P.

You can use **scale drawings** to **represent** real life objects.

100 cm

450 cm

Real life lengths are reduced or enlarged in proportion using a **scale**.

The scale allows you to interpret the scale drawing.

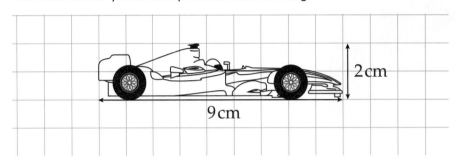

2 cm

9 cm

Scale: 1 cm represents 50 cm

Distances in real life are 50 times larger than on the scale drawing. So 450 = 9 × 50 and 100 = 2 × 50

Example

A mini snooker table measures 180 cm by 100 cm.

a Draw a scale drawing of the table using a scale of 1 cm represents 40 cm.

b Calculate the distance across the diagonal of the table.

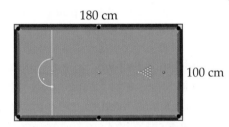

180 cm

100 cm

a

4.5 cm

2.5 cm

180 ÷ 40 = 4.5
100 ÷ 40 = 2.5

b Measuring the diagonal gives 5.1 cm on the scale drawing.

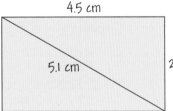

4.5 cm

5.1 cm

2.5 cm

Real life distance = 5.1 × 40
= 204 cm

You could give the final answer as 2.04 m.

Exercise 12f

1 A penny-farthing is an old type of bicycle.

Parminda wants to draw a scale drawing of the bicycle using a
scale of 1 cm to represent 20 cm.

Copy and complete the table.

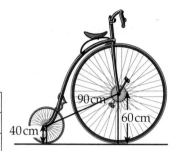

		Real life	Scale drawing
a	Radius of the small wheel		
b	Diameter of the small wheel		
c	Radius of the large wheel		
d	Diameter of the large wheel		
e	Distance between the centres of the wheels		

2 A pentagram is made from five straight lines with angles of 36°.
This scale drawing is used to construct a large pentagram using a
scale of 1 cm represents 100 cm.

a Measure the length of one line in the scale drawing.

b Calculate the length of this line and the size of one of the
marked angles in the large pentagram.

Scale: 1 cm represents
100 cm

Problem solving

3 Grace lives on the next street to Faith.

Grace has to walk 80 metres, turn a corner, then walk
another 50 metres if she wants to visit Faith.

a Draw a scale drawing of this journey using a scale
of 1 cm to represent 10 m.

b Calculate the direct distance between Grace and Faith.

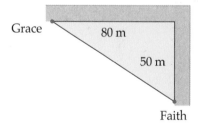

4 Using a scale of 1 cm represents 50 m, draw scale drawings
to represent the heights of these buildings.

Blackpool Tower is done for you.

Building	Approximate height
Blackpool Tower	150 m
The Shard, London	300 m
Chamberlain Clock Tower, Birmingham	100 m
Sutton Coldfield Mast, West Midlands	250 m
Rotunda, Birmingham	80 m

Draw scale drawings for other buildings around the world.

Scale: 1 cm represents 50 m

This mountain is called Snowdon.

It is the highest peak in Wales at 1085 metres.

The view is from a mountain ridge called Crib Goch.

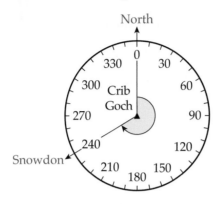

The **direction** of Snowdon from Crib Goch is 240°.

This angle is called a **three-figure bearing**.

> When you use **bearings**
> ▶ measure from North
> ▶ measure in a clockwise direction
> ▶ use three figures.

Example

Find the bearings from Crib Goch of the following places.

a Pen-y-pass Youth Hostel   **b** Snowdon   **c** Clogwyn Station

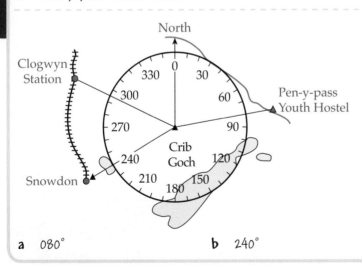

a 080°   **b** 240°   **c** 295°

Exercise 12g

1 The map shows the position of places relative to Middle School.

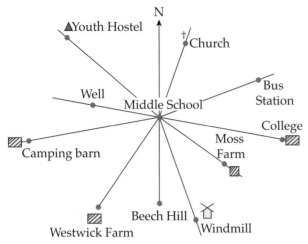

Name the places that are on these bearings from Middle School.

a 100°		**b** 160°
c 215°		**d** 125°
e 280°		**f** 020°
g 260°		**h** 070°
i 180°		**j** 310°

2 Copy and complete the table.

Direction	N	NE	E	SE	S	SW	W	NW
Bearing								

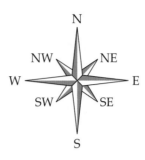

3 Use a protractor to draw accurate diagrams to show bearings at

a 050°	**b** 120°
c 200°	**d** 240°
e 300°	**f** 340°

N Remember to start with a North line.

Problem solving

4 The bearing of Baslow from Bakewell is 045°.
The distance from Bakewell to Baslow is 5 km.

   a Draw a **scale drawing** using a scale of 1 cm represents 1 km.

   b Measure the bearing of Bakewell from Baslow.

   c Explain why adding 180° to 045° gives your answer to part **b**.

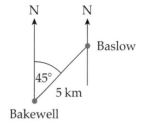

5 A speedboat travels

   ▶ on a bearing of 130° for 14 km

   ▶ then on a bearing of 220° for 10 km

   a Draw a scale drawing using a scale of 1 cm to 1 km.

   b Estimate

     i the speedboat's final distance from the starting point

     ii the speedboat's final bearing from the starting point.

Check out

You should now be able to ...

Test it ➡

Questions

✓ Construct triangles and quadrilaterals accurately.	6	1
✓ Construct angle bisectors, perpendicular bisectors and perpendicular lines.	6	2–5
✓ Describe the locus of a point and draw it accurately.	7	6, 7
✓ Use scale drawings to represent real life objects.	6	8
✓ Use bearings to specify direction.	6	9

Language	Meaning	Example
Construct	To draw a shape accurately using a ruler, protractor and pair of compasses	Drawing an SAS triangle is a construction
Perpendicular	At right angles	Horizontal and vertical lines are perpendicular
Bisect	To divide into two equally	The midpoint of a straight line bisects it
Locus (plural loci)	The locus of an object is its path.	A circle is the locus of points equidistant from a fixed point
Equidistant	The same distance from a given point	
Bearing	An angle, measured clockwise from north and quoted using three figures, used to describe a direction	East has a bearing 090° West has a bearing 270°
Scale drawing	A diagram which is used to accurately represent real life objects	Architects' plans are scale drawings of buildings

1 Construct these triangles.

a

b   7.1 cm
     81°
     62°
     143°   39°
     3.8 cm

c   d   35 mm
   4.7 cm   63 mm   52 mm
   58°
   5.2 cm

2   a   Use your protractor to draw an angle
        of 130°.
    b   Use a pair of compasses to construct
        the angle bisector.

3   a   Draw a line AB, so that AB = 9 cm.
    b   Using a pair of compasses, construct
        the perpendicular bisector of AB.

4   a   Draw a line AB so that AB = 11 cm.
    b   Mark the point P on AB so that
        AP = 4 cm.
    c   Construct the perpendicular to AB
        passing through P.

5   Copy the diagram on
    square grid paper.
    Construct the
    perpendicular from
    the point (4, 2) to
    the line.

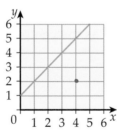

6   a   Draw a line AB where AB = 5 cm.
    b   Construct the locus of a point that is
        2 cm from the line AB.

7   a   Use your protractor to draw an angle
        AOB of 70°.

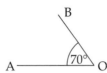

    b   Construct the locus of a point that is
        equidistant from OA and OB.

8   A

    25 m

    C   40 m   B

    a   Construct a scale drawing of this
        triangle using a scale of 1 cm to
        represent 5 m.
    b   Calculate the real life length of AB to
        the nearest metre.

9   Draw bearings at
    a   042°   b   304°

What next?

Score	0 – 3		Your knowledge of this topic is still developing. To improve look at Formative test: 2B-12; MyMaths: 1086, 1089, 1090, 1117 and 1147
	4 – 7		You are gaining a secure knowledge of this topic. To improve look at InvisiPen: 371, 372, 373, 374 and 375
	8 – 9		You have mastered this topic. Well done, you are ready to progress!

12a

1 Construct these triangles.
Measure the lengths of the sides and calculate the perimeter of each triangle.

a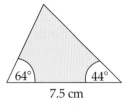

b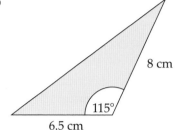

c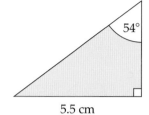

12b

2 Construct these triangles, using ruler and compasses.
State the mathematical name of each triangle.

a

25 mm   35 mm
30 mm

b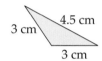

3 cm   4.5 cm
3 cm

c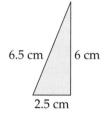

6.5 cm   6 cm
2.5 cm

12c

3 a Draw a large triangle.
b Construct the perpendicular bisector for each of the three sides.
c Draw a circle passing through the vertices of the triangle, using the point of intersection as the centre.

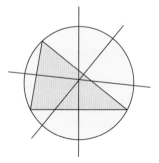

12d

4 Copy this diagram.
Using compasses, construct a vertical wall through the dot to separate the giraffe from the person.

5 Copy the diagrams on square grid paper.
Draw the locus of the point that is equidistant from P and Q.

a

b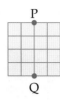

c

Equidistant means 'equal length'.

6 A sales brochure shows a scale drawing of a door.
The scale is 1 cm represents 50 cm.
Calculate

a the height

b the width

c the area of the real door.

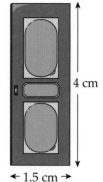

4 cm

← 1.5 cm →

Scale: 1 cm represents 50 cm

7 Measure the three-figure bearings of these places from Manchester.

a Leeds	**b** Liverpool	**c** Sheffield
d Preston	**e** Bradford	**f** Chester

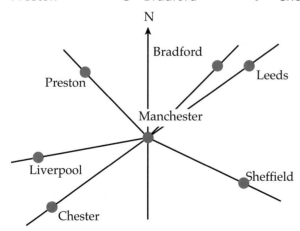

MyMathsLife 4: Paper folding

You can explore shapes and angles by simply folding paper.
Origami is an ancient Japanese art using folded paper to create beautiful shapes and figures.

Task 1

Take a square sheet of plain paper and fold it in half diagonally.

a If you open it out you should have two triangles. What type of triangles are they?

Now fold it in half again.

b If you open it out, how many triangles do you have now?

Keep folding it in half – see if you can fold it five times.

c When you open it out again, how many triangles are there now?

d Look at one of the triangles. Write down its three angles.

e Construct an accurate drawing of the whole triangle pattern.

Check that:

▸ Your triangles are congruent
▸ Your angles are accurate

Task 2

Take a square sheet of plain paper. Fold in half vertically, then unfold it again.

Being A down to F and make a crease. Open it out again.

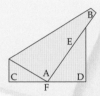

Now do the same with B and F.

▸ **Now do the same with C and E, then D and E.**
▸ **Open out the square and look at the creases.**

a How many triangles are there? What type of triangle are they?

b How many quadrilaterals are there? What type of quadrilateral are they?

c Construct an accurate drawing of the whole pattern.

How many times can you fold a piece of paper in half?

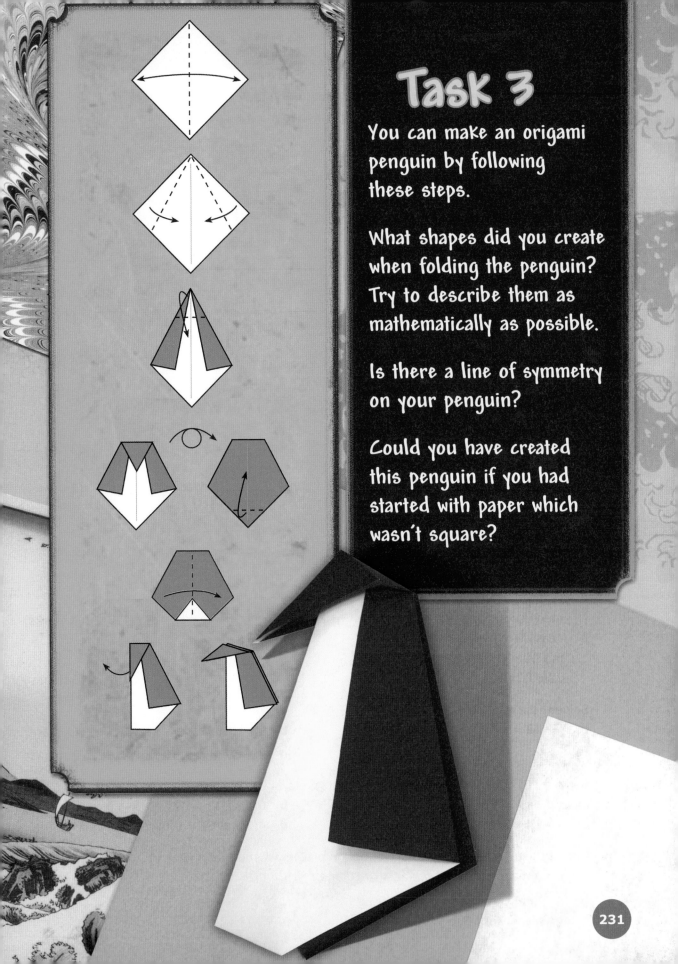

Task 3

You can make an origami penguin by following these steps.

What shapes did you create when folding the penguin? Try to describe them as mathematically as possible.

Is there a line of symmetry on your penguin?

Could you have created this penguin if you had started with paper which wasn't square?

These questions will test you on your knowledge of the topics in chapters 9 to 12.
They give you practice in the types of questions that you may eventually be given in your
GCSE exams. There are 80 marks in total.

1 Copy this diagram onto square grid paper.
  a Draw the image of shape A after reflecting
    it in the x-axis. Label the image B. (2 marks)
  b Draw the image of shape B after
    rotating it through 180° clockwise
    about the point X. Label the image C. (2 marks)
  c Draw the image of the shape C after
    translating it 4 units up.
    Label the image D. (1 mark)
  d What is the connection between
    shape A and shape D? (2 marks)

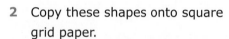

2 Copy these shapes onto square
  grid paper.
  a Draw any lines of symmetry
    on each of the shapes. (3 marks)
  b State the order of rotational
    symmetry of each shape. (3 marks)

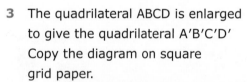

3 The quadrilateral ABCD is enlarged
  to give the quadrilateral A'B'C'D'
  Copy the diagram on square
  grid paper.
  a By drawing lines find the point of
    intersection and mark this point O. (4 marks)
  b Measure the lines OA and OA'
    and OB, OB' to determine the
    scale factor. (3 marks)

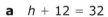
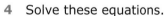

4 Solve these equations.
  a $h + 12 = 32$ (1 mark)   b $12 = j + 11$ (1 mark)
  c $\dfrac{g}{6} = 4$ (1 mark)   d $2x + 7 = x + 10$ (2 marks)

5 Solve these equations by expanding the brackets.
  a $3(d + 2) = 18$ (2 marks)   b $6(4t - 1) = 42$ (2 marks)
  c $5(r - 1) = 2r + 4$ (3 marks)   d $4(2w + 6) = 5(6w - 4)$ (4 marks)

6 One of the equations used to solve motion problems is $2s = t \times (u + v)$
  Work out the value of s if $u = 4$, $v = 10$ and $t = 5$. (4 marks)

7 Calculate these using a written method.
  a 9.34 + 3.6   **b** 86.4 − 64.9
  c 62.76 + 12.09 + 49.3   **d** 985.2 − 104.6   (4 marks)

8 Use the standard method to calculate these. Give an estimate first.
  a 8 × 4.65   **b** 16 × 2.73   (4 marks)

9 Calculate these using an appropriate method. Where appropriate,
   give your answer to 1 decimal place. Give an estimate first.
  a 76.3 ÷ 9   **b** 251 ÷ 15
  c 34.6 ÷ 4   **d** 234.3 ÷ 21   (8 marks)

10 Use a calculator to work out these.
    Where appropriate, give your answer to 2 dp.
  a $84 - 5.2^2 \times 2$ **b** $\dfrac{5 + 2^3}{64 - 7^2}$ (4 marks)

11 A scale drawing of the Nepalese flag
    is being made.
  a Construct an accurate copy
      using a ruler and a protractor.   (4 marks)
  b Measure the length of the
      perimeter.   (1 mark)

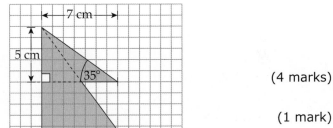

12 a Draw a line PQ so that
      PQ = 10 cm
      Mark the point O on PQ so that PO = 4 cm.   (2 marks)
  b Construct the perpendicular bisector of PQ passing through O.
      Label this line RS and make OR = OS = 5 cm.   (3 marks)
  c Join the points P, R, Q, S to form a quadrilateral.
      What is the mathematical name given to this shape PRQS?   (1 mark)
  d Measure the angles at P, Q, R and S.   (4 marks)

13 A helicopter landing area (H) is being constructed 100 m away
    from the entrance to the depot (D) and at a bearing of
    160° from the depot. There is an exclusion zone around the
    helicopter landing point of 20 m.
  a Draw an accurate diagram to show the positions of H and D.
      Use a scale of 1 cm = 10 m.   (2 marks)
  b Draw the locus of points that represents the helicopter
      exclusion zone.   (2 marks)
  c A wall extends south from the depot for over 200 m.
      What is the closest distance between this wall and the
      helicopter exclusion zone?   (1 mark)

13 Sequences

Introduction

There are lots of different types of sequences, even ones inside you! Every living cell of your body contains genetic information in a molecule called DNA. These DNA molecules contain four different bases (labelled A, T, C and G) which occur many times over. The sequences in which these bases occur determines the physical characteristics of each cell.

What's the point?

Being able to identify and describe a genetic sequence is useful for solving crimes and in the development of new ways to screen for and treat diseases.

Objectives

By the end of this chapter, you will have learned how to ...

- Find and use the term-to-term rule in a sequence.
- Find and use the position-to-term rule in a sequence.
- Use sequences in context and in real life.
- Recognise and describe geometric sequences.

Check in

1   Write the values of 2^2, 3^2 and 10^2.

2   **a**   Here is a sequence: 3   7   11   15

Write the next two numbers in the sequence.

b   Describe a rule for this sequence.

Starter problem

A mad scientist has invented a machine that 'evolves' any creature that enters it.

Here is a drawing of a dog and its first two evolutions.

Describe what has happened to the dog, and draw the next evolution.

Investigate

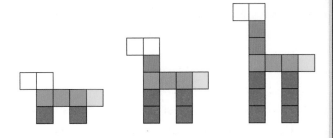

13a Term-to-term rules

Sam is laying a path using paving slabs in two colours.
She starts with one slab and then adds more slabs, three at a time, in alternating colours.

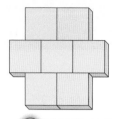

A sequence is a set of numbers, or terms.

After laying the first slab, it takes Sam 15 minutes to lay 3 new slabs.
Sam's path will contain 109 slabs.
How long will it take her to complete?

The sequence begins   1   4   7   ...   ...
The rule is *'start with 1 and add 3 each time'*.
The next two terms are 10 and 13.

> 🔘 **A term-to-term rule** gives the first term of a sequence and an instruction telling you how to get any term from the previous term.

Example

Here are two sequences
a   50   44   38   32   ☐   20
b   3   7   15   31   ☐   127
i   Find the term-to-term rule for each sequence.
ii   Find the two missing numbers.

- -

a   **i**   Each term is 6 less than the previous term.
Start with 50 and then subtract 6.
ii   32 – 6 = 26.
b   **i**   Each term is double the previous term
with 1 more added.
Start with 3 and then double and add 1.
ii   31 × 2 + 1 = 62 + 1 = 63.

Check your answers
work for the next term:
26 – 6 = 20 and
63 × 2 + 1 = 127.

Exercise 13a

1 These sequences are made using straws.
   For each sequence
   i   draw the next diagram in the sequence
   ii   write the first four terms
   iii find the term-to-term rule
   iv   write the next three terms.

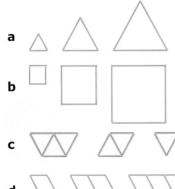

a

b

c

d

e

f

2 For each of these sequences
   i   find the term-to-term rule
   ii   write the next three terms of
        the sequence.
   a 2 5 8 11 ...
   b 4 9 14 19 ...
   c 8 12 16 20 ...

2 d 50 46 42 38 ...
   e 30 27 24 21 ...
   f 20 31 42 53 ...
   g 2 4 8 16 ...
   h 2 5 11 23 ...
   i 3 7 15 31 ...
   j 3 8 23 68 ...

3 Write the first six terms of the sequences
   with these rules.
   a *Start with 6 and add 4*
   b *Start with 8 and add 2*
   c *Start with 60 and subtract 5*
   d *Start with 5, double and add 1*
   e *Start with 2, double and add 4*
   f *Start with 100 and subtract 11*
   g *Start with 1, treble and add 1*
   h *Start with 0, treble and add 2*

4 Find the missing terms of these
   sequences.
   a 5 10 20 ☐ 80
   b 6 11 16 ☐ 26
   c 7 11 ☐ 19 23
   d 30 24 18 ☐ 6
   e 10 21 43 87 ☐
   f 6 11 21 41 ☐
   g ☐ 80 60 40
   h 3 8 18 ☐ 78
   i -15 -18 ☐ -24 -27
   j -1 -2 -4 ☐ -16

Problem solving

5 Find the 50th term of this sequence.
   8   12   16   20   ....
   Is using the term-to-term rule an efficient method?
   Can you find a more efficient method?
   Look again at the slab problem in the box on the page opposite.
   How many hours will it take Sam to complete her task?

This sequence of tiles grows by adding four extra tiles each time but I want to know how many tiles there will be in a particular **position**.

Position in sequence	1	2	3	4
Number of tiles	1	5	9	13

+4   +4   +4

Since the terms go up by 4, Sam looks at the 4 times table. Her sequence is 3 less.

Position	1	2	3	4	
4 × table	4	8	12	16	×4
No. of tiles (Term)	1	5	9	13	-3

Sam's rule is '*multiply the position by 4 and then subtract 3*'.

She can now find the number of tiles in any position.

For example, the 50th position has 50 × 4 − 3 = 200 − 3 = 197 tiles

🔴 A **position-to-term rule** works out the value of any term from its position in the sequence.

Example

The first four terms of a sequence are   5 8 11 14

a Find the position-to-term rule.   **b** Find the 5th term and the 100th term.

- - - - - - - -

a The sequence grows by adding 3 to the previous term.   5   8   11   14
Draw a table of values using the 3 times table.

+3   +3   +3

Position	1	2	3	4	
3 × table	3	6	9	12	×3
Term	5	8	11	14	+2

The position-to-term rule is '*multiply the position by 3 and then add 2*'.

b Use the 4th term.

The 5th term is 14 + 3 = 17.

Use the position-to-term rule.

The 100th term is 100 × 3 + 2 = 300 + 2 = 302.

You can write the nth term as $3n + 2$.

Exercise 13b

1 Look at this sequence of diagrams.

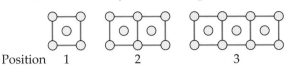

Position   1   2   3

   a How many extra circles are added to a position to make the next position?

   b Draw the diagram for position 4.

   c Copy and complete this table.
Use the correct 'times table' for the middle row.

Position	1	2	3	4
Times table				
Term (Number of circles)				

   d Find the position-to-term rule.

   e How many circles are there in the 4th diagram of the sequence?

   f How many circles are there in the 20th diagram of the sequence?

2 Use the method of question **1** for these sequences of circles. In each case,

   i draw the diagram for the next position

   ii make a table of values

   iii find the position-to-term rule for the number of circles

   iv find how many circles are in the 50th term of the sequence.

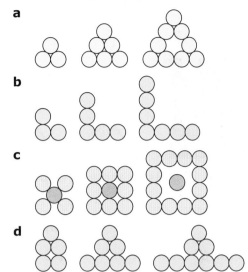

3 Find the position-to-term rule for each of these sequences.
Also find the next term in the sequence and the 50th term in the sequence.

   a 4 7 10 13 16   **b** 1 3 5 7 9

   c 1 5 9 13 17   **d** 6 10 14 18 22

   e 1 4 7 10 13   **f** 8 15 22 29 36

   g 5 13 21 29 37   **h** 4 5 6 7 8

Problem solving

4 **a** A sequence has first term 3 and ninth term 39. What is its twentieth term?

   b A sequence has tenth term 105 and twentieth term 205. What is the sequence?

5 Leonardo of Pisa, known as Fibonacci, was an Italian mathematician who lived about 800 years ago.
He learned about the 'new Arabic numerals' from his father and later travelled in the Middle East to learn more about mathematics.
Find all you can about his life and work, and about the **Fibonacci sequence.**

My friend Daniel, the farmer, is building a fence. He starts with two posts and then every hour he adds two more vertical posts and two more support posts. He wants to know how many posts he can put up in 40 hours.

1   2   3

The number of posts for these three **positions** is given by

2   6   10   The first three **terms** of the
  +4   +4   **sequence** are 2, 6, 10.

The **term-to-term** rule for the sequence is '*add 4*'.
So, the next term is 10 + 4 = 14. Daniel needs 14 posts for
position 4.
From this table the **position-to-term** rule is
'*multiply the position by 4 and then subtract 2*'.
The 40th term is 40 × 4 − 2 = 160 − 2
                                = 158
Daniel can put up 158 posts in 40 hours.

Position	1	2	3	4
4 × table	4	8	12	16
Term (Number of posts)	2	6	10	14

×4
-2

Example

Here are the first four terms of a sequence.   4   7   10   13   ....
a   Find the next term of this sequence.
b   Find the 100th term of the sequence.

a   The sequence increases in steps of 3.
    The term-to-term rule is 'add 3'.
    The next term is 13 + 3 = 16.
b   Draw a table of values.

Position	1	2	3	4
3 × table	3	6	9	12
Term	4	7	10	13

×3
+1

The position-to-term rule is 'multiply the position by 3 and then add 1'.
The 100th term is 100 × 3 + 1 = 301.

Exercise 13c

1 Melissa buys a plant with three leaves on it. Each week, it grows another two leaves.

Week 1   2   3

a Use a term-to-term rule to find the number of leaves on Melissa's plant in week 4 and week 5.

b Copy and complete this table of values to find the position-to-term rule.

Position (week)	1	2	3	4	5
Times table					
Term (leaves)					

c How many leaves will be on Melissa's plant after twelve weeks?

2 Wasim has £20 already saved. He takes a Saturday job earning £8 a week. This sequence gives the total amount that he has saved after each week.

20 28 36 44 ... ...

a Write the term-to-term rule.

b Write the next two terms in the sequence.

c Copy and complete this table of values and find the position-to-term rule.

Position (week)	1	2	3	4
Times table				
Term (£)				

d Find the 40th term of the sequence.

e How much will Wasim have saved after 40 weeks?

Problem solving

3 Migrating geese visit a local pond every winter. On Day 1, 50 geese are living there and then an average of 20 more geese arrive every day for a month.

a Use the term-to-term rule to write the next two terms of the sequence

50 70 90 110 ... ...

b Find the position-to-term rule.

c Find the 20th term of the sequence.

d How many geese are on the pond on Day 30?

4 Everyone in a group shakes hands with everyone else. If there are just two people in the group, there is just one handshake.

a If there are three people in the group, how many handshakes will there be?

b How many handshakes will there be for a group of 4, 5, 6, ... people?

c Find a sequence for the numbers of handshakes.

d Can you use a term-to-term rule to find the next term?

e Can you find a position-to-term rule? If not, why not?

13d Geometric sequences

Jack is exploring sequences involving **indices**.
He starts with 2, and raises it to increasing powers:

$$2^1, 2^2, 2^3, 2^4, 2^5, ...$$
$$= 2, 4, 8, 16, 32, ...$$

Jack now tries with 3:

$$3^1, 3^2, 3^3, 3^4, 3^5, ...$$
$$= 3, 9, 27, 81, 243, ...$$

> This sequence is **doubling** each time. You times by 2 to get the next term.

⦿ In a **geometric sequence**, you multiply each term by a fixed amount to get the next term.

8, 24, 72, 216, 648, ... is a geometric sequence.
   $24 = 3 \times 8$, $72 = 3 \times 24$, $216 = 3 \times 72$, etc.

Example

a Generate the first five terms of the sequence following this rule.
   Start with 6, and multiply each term by 4 to get the next one.

b Describe a term-to-term rule for this geometric sequence
   5, 15, 45, 135, 405, ...

c **i** Write the next two terms of this sequence
   200, 100, 50, 25, 12.5, ...

   ii Describe a term-to-term rule for the sequence.

> Sequences can go down as well as up.

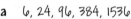

a 6, 24, 96, 384, 1536

b Start at 5 and multiply by 3

c **i** 6.25, 3.125

   ii Start at 200 and multiply by 0.5

Example

Geometric sequences occur in real life.
50 birds of prey are introduced to a region of the country.
The population doubles each year for five years, and then increases at a steady rate of 100 birds per year for the next five years.
How many birds are there after 10 years have elapsed?

1ˢᵗ 5 years: 50, 100, 200, 400, 800, 1600
Next 5 years: 1700, 1800, 1900, 2000, 2100
There are 2100 birds after 10 years.

Here's a quicker method.
$(50 \times 2^5) + (100 \times 5)$
$= 1600 + 500$
$= 2100$

Exercise 13d

1 Write the next two terms of each sequence.
  a 3, 6, 12, 24, 48, …
  b 4, 12, 36, 108, 324, …
  c 1, 6, 36, 216, 648, …
  d 1, 10, 100, 1000, 10 000, …
  e 1000, 500, 250, 125, 62.5, …
  f -32, -16, -8, -4, -2, …

2 Generate the first five terms of the sequence described by each rule.
  a Start at 3, multiply by 2
  b Start at 4, multiply by 5
  c Start at 2, multiply by 8
  d Start at -5, multiply by 3
  e Start at 8, multiply by -2
  f Start at 32, multiply by $2\frac{1}{2}$

3 Describe a term-to-term rule for each of these geometric sequences.
  a 2, 10, 50, 250, 1250, …
  b 3, 18, 108, 648, 3888, …
  c 0.5, 1.5, 4.5, 13.5, 40.5, …
  d -4, -16, -64, -256, -1024, …
  e 2, 3, $4\frac{1}{2}$, $6\frac{3}{4}$, $20\frac{1}{4}$, …
  f -2, 10, -50, 250, -1250, 6250, …

4 Find the 10th term of each of these geometric sequences.
  a 5, 10, 20, 40, …
  b 4, 20, 100, 500, …
  c Start at -2 and multiply by 4
  d Start at 8 and multiply by -1
  e 6, -12, 24, -48, …
  f 20, 10, 5, $2\frac{1}{2}$, …

Problem solving

5 Cassie is offered a summer holiday job for six weeks.
She is given a choice of payment.
Which option should Cassie choose?
Give your reasons.

Option A	Option B
£5 for week 1	£50 per week
£10 for week 2	Continuing until
£20 for week 3	week 6
And continuing to double until week 6	

6 Here are two geometric sequences:
Sequence A: 1,   6,   36,   216,   1296, …
Sequence B: 50,   150,   450,   1350,   4050, …
After how many terms does sequence A overtake sequence B?

7 Doctor Sequence is exploring some other sequences involving indices!
He starts with the power 2: $1^2, 2^2, 3^2, 4^2, 5^2,$ …
  a Write this sequence as numbers. What is this sequence commonly known as?
  b He now tries the power 3: $1^3, 2^3, 3^3, 4^3, 5^3,$ …
     Write out this sequence as numbers. What is this sequence commonly known as?
     Doctor Sequence is going power-crazy! He writes this sequence.
     1, 128, 2187, 16 384, 78 125, …
  c **i** Write this sequence as powers.
     ii Use a calculator to work out the 8th term in this sequence.

Check out

You should now be able to ...

Test it ➡

Questions

✓ Find and use the term-to-term rule in a sequence.	⬤	1–2
✓ Find and use the position-to-term rule in a sequence.	⬤	3–5
✓ Use sequences in context and in real life.	⬤	6
✓ Recognise and describe geometric sequences.	⬤	7

Language	Meaning	Example
Sequence	An ordered list of numbers, called *terms*, which often follow a pattern	2, 5, 8, 11, … is a sequence
Position	A number that counts the terms, in order, starting from 1	The first term has position 1, the second term has position 2 etc.
Term-to-term rule	An instruction how to get from one term in a sequence to the next term	For the sequence above the rule is +3
Position-to-term rule	A rule which works out the value of any term from its position in the sequence	For the sequence above, the term in the nth position is given by $3n - 1$
Geometric sequence	A sequence in which the term-to-term rule is multiplied by a fixed number	2, 6, 18, 54, 162, … each term is 3× the previous term

1 For each sequence

  i find the term-to-term rule

  ii write the next two terms.

  a 8 14 20 26   **b** 60 56 52 48

  c 2 4 8 16

2 Write the first 5 terms of these sequences.

  a Start with 9 and add 5

  b Start with 30 and subtract 3

  c Start with 1 and treble

  d Start with 5, double and subtract 2

3 This sequence of diagrams is formed by adding squares.

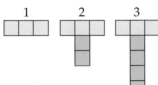

  a Draw the diagram for position 4.

  b Copy and complete this table, use the correct 'times table' for the middle row.

Position	1	2	3	4	5	6
Times table						
Term (squares)						

  c Find the position-to-term rule for the number of squares.

  d Find how many squares are in the 20th term of the sequence.

4 Find the position-to-term-rule for each of these sequences.

  a 9 12 15 18 21

  b 2 9 16 23 30

5 Find the 12th term of the sequences with these position-to-term rules.

  a Multiply the position by 3 then subtract 8

  b $5n + 6$

6 Debbie bought 2 raffle tickets on Monday, 5 on Tuesday, 8 on Wednesday and so on for the whole week.

  a Write a term-to-term rule for the number of raffle tickets bought each day.

  b How many tickets did she buy on Saturday?

  c How many tickets did she buy altogether over the 7 days?

  d Copy and complete the table.

Position (day)	1	2	3	4	5	6	7
Times table							
Term (squares)							

  e Find the position-to-term rule.

7 For each geometric sequence

  i find the term-to-term rule

  ii write the next two terms.

  a 3 6 12 36

  b 128 64 32 16

  c 1 -3 9 -27

What next?

Score	0 – 3		Your knowledge of this topic is still developing. To improve look at Formative test: 2B-13; MyMaths: 1165 and 1173
	4 – 6		You are gaining a secure knowledge of this topic. To improve look at InvisiPen: 282, 283 and 285
	7		You have mastered this topic. Well done, you are ready to progress!

13a

1 This sequence is made using straws.
   a Draw the next diagram in the sequence.
   b Write the first four terms.
   c Find the term-to-term rule.
   d Write the next three terms.

2 For each of these sequences, find the term-to-term rule and
   write the next three terms of the sequence.
   a 2 6 10 14 ...   b 3 8 13 18 ...
   c 2 5 11 23 ...   d 30 27 24 21 ...

3 Write the first six terms of each of the sequences with these rules.
   a *Start with 5. Add 4.*   b *Start with 12. Add 6.*
   c *Start with 40. Subtract 6.*   d *Start with 2. Double and add 1.*
   e *Start with 3. Double and subtract 2.*   f *Start with 100 and subtract 21.*

13b

4 This sequence of diagrams is made
   from triangles.
   a How many extra triangles
      are added to each position to
      make the next position?
   b Draw the diagram for position 5.
   c Copy and complete this table.
      Use the correct 'times table' for the
      middle row.
   d Find the position-to-term rule.
   e How many triangles are there in the 10th
      diagram of the sequence?

Position   1   2   3   4

Position	1	2	3	4
Times table				
Term (No. of triangles)				

5 a Find the position-to-term rule for
      this sequence.
      Find the next two terms of the
      sequence.

Sequence	4	7	10	13	16
Position →	1	2	3	4	5

   b Find the position-to-term rule for each of these sequences.
      Also find the next term and the 20th term in the sequence.
      i   1 3 5 7 9   ii 3 6 9 12 15
      iii 7 12 17 22 27   iv 19 18 17 16 15

6 Jamie bought three tins of cat food on the day he first owned some cats.

He then bought two tins every day after that.

The sequence for the total number of tins bought is 3 5 7 9 …

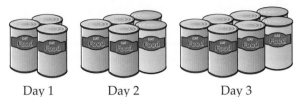

Day 1   Day 2   Day 3

a Find the term-to-term rule and the next two terms of this sequence.

b Copy and complete this table and find the position-to-term rule.

c Find the 20th term of the sequence.

d How many tins had he bought altogether by the 100th day?

Position (day)	1	2	3	4	5
Times table					
Term (tins)					

7 Abbi and Gail both decide to start saving for a new car in January.

Abbi's parents give her £500 at the start of the year and at the end of the month she adds £60.

Gail is given no money but can save £100 at the end of each month.

a Write out how much money each person has at the end of the first five months.

b Find the position-to-term rule for each person.

c Write out how much money each person has at the end of the first two years.

d When will each person have saved £3000?

8 Generate the first five terms of each sequence.

a Start at 3, multiply by 3

b Start at 2, multiply by 4

c Start at 4, multiply by 5

d Start at 16, multiply by $\frac{1}{2}$

9 Describe a term-to-term rule for each sequence.

a 2, 6, 18, 54, 162, …

b 3, 6, 12, 24, 48, …

c 4, 16, 64, 256, 1024, …

d 3, -9, 27, -81, 243, …

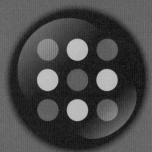

14 3D shapes

Introduction

The food you eat comes in many different forms of packaging. Cartons, boxes, bottles and cans dominate the supermarket shelves. Packaging protects and preserves the things you eat, but it adds to the price of the food and has implications for the environment.

Companies design their packaging to cut costs and reduce waste materials.

What's the point?

By understanding surface area and volume, companies can choose the optimum dimensions for packaging to cut costs and help reduce the impact on the environment.

Objectives

By the end of this chapter, you will have learned how to ...
- Recognise and name 3D solids and recognise their nets.
- Use isometric paper and draw plans and elevations of 3D shapes.
- Calculate the surface area and volume of cuboids.
- Calculate the volume of prisms.

Check in

1 Sketch a cube. State how many faces, edges and vertices it has.

2 Calculate

a $4 \times 5 \times 6$ **b** 3.5×4^2 **c** $7 \times 8 + 4 \times 6$ **d** 11^3

3 Calculate the areas of the following shapes.

a
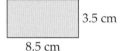
3.5 cm
8.5 cm

b
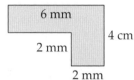
6 mm
2 mm
4 cm
2 mm

c
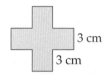
3 cm
3 cm

Starter problem

A drinks company needs to design a container to hold exactly 360 ml. They are aware of environmental issues and want to minimise the surface area of the container. The current container they use is 12 cm by 6 cm by 5 cm.

Design a container, in the shape of a cuboid, to hold exactly 360 ml, which has a smaller surface area than the original container.

Write a report and explain any practical considerations you might need to consider with your design.

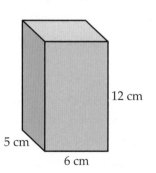

12 cm

5 cm

6 cm

A **solid** is a shape formed in three dimensions - it has **faces**, **edges** and **vertices**.

Vertex

Face

Edge

You should know the names of some common solids.

Cube	**Cuboid**
All the faces are square.	All the faces are rectangles.
Prism	**Pyramid**
The **cross section** is the same throughout the length.	The base tapers to a point.
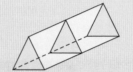	
The cross section decides the name of the prism – this is a triangular prism.	The base decides the name of the pyramid – this is a pentagonal pyramid.

A **net** is a 2D shape that can be folded to form a solid.

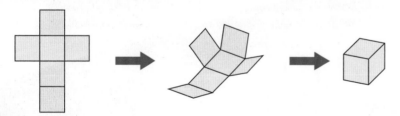

Example

The dimensions of a cuboid are 4 cm by 3 cm by 1 cm.

a Draw the cuboid on **isometric paper**.

b Draw the net of the cuboid.

Isometric paper is really good for drawing 3D shapes. Try it!

a

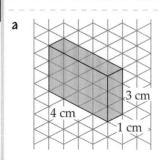

3 cm

4 cm

1 cm

b

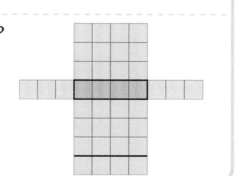

Exercise 14a

1 For each solid, state
   i the mathematical name
   ii the number of faces, vertices and edges.

   a   **b**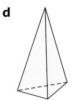

   c   **d**

   e 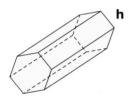 **f**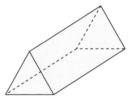

   g 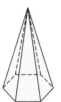 **h**

2 The dimensions of a cuboid are 4 cm by 4 cm by 3 cm.
   a Draw the cuboid on isometric paper.
   b Draw the net of the cuboid.
   c Calculate the area of the net.

3 Copy this net of a cube.
   a On your diagram, mark the edge that meets the red line when the net is folded.
   b On your diagram, mark the vertices that meet the red dot when the net is folded.

4 A cuboid is made from four blue rectangles and two green rectangles.
   The opposite faces are the same colour.
   Find the number of edges where
   a a blue face meets a blue face
   b a blue face meets a green face
   c a green face meets a green face.

5 **a** Draw a 3D shape with five faces.
   b State the number of vertices and edges on your shape.

Did you know?

The Azrieli centre in Tel Aviv, Israel is a commercial complex that includes square, triangular and circular based towers.

Problem solving

6 Here are three views of the same cube.
   a Draw a net of a cube.
   b Construct the cube using your net.
   c Which symbols are opposite each other?

These are different views of a Police Box.

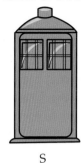

F
This is the front elevation (F).

S
This is the side elevation (S).

P
This is the plan view (P).

⬤ A **front elevation** (F) is the view from the front.

⬤ A **side elevation** (S) is the view from the side.

⬤ A **plan** (P) shows the view from above.

Example

This **solid** is made from four cubes.
On square grid paper, draw
a the front elevation (F)
b the side elevation (S)
c the plan view (P).

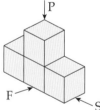

a

b

c

Front elevation

Side elevation

Plan view

The bold lines show where the level of cubes changes.

Example

Draw a solid on **isometric paper** that has these elevation and plan views.

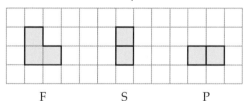

F
Front elevation

S
Side elevation

P
Plan view

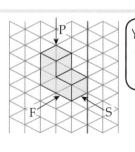

You must make sure to turn the isometric paper so that you have vertical lines.

Exercise 14b

1 On square grid paper, draw the front elevation (F), the side elevation (S) and the plan view (P) of these solids.

a

b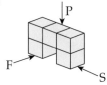

c

d

2 **i** On isometric paper, draw these solids after the shaded cube is removed.
   ii On square grid paper, draw the elevations and the plan views of the new solids.

a

b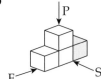

c

d

3 A 3D shape is made from some cubes. The elevations and the plan view are shown.

   a Draw the solid on isometric paper.
   b How many cubes are needed to make the shape?

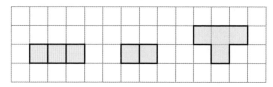

Front elevation   Side elevation   Plan view

4 **a** Match each solid (A–D) with its plan view (E–H).
   b Give the mathematical name of each solid.

A 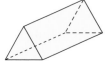   B

C   D

E   F

G   H

Problem solving

5 The front and side elevations and the plan view of this 3D shape are identical.
   a Make this shape using multilink cubes.
   b Draw the shape on isometric paper.
   c Can you find another solid that has identical elevations and plan view?

F   Front elevation
S   Side elevation
P   Plan view

⬤ The **surface area** of the cuboid is the total area of its faces.

If you unfold a cuboid, the six rectangles form a net and the area of this net is the surface area of the cuboid.

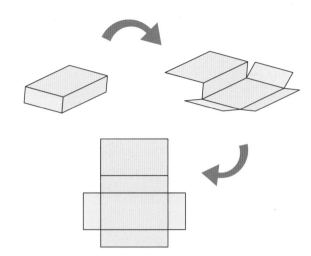

Example

A cuboid measures 4 cm by 3 cm by 2 cm.
Calculate the surface area of the cuboid.

Area of the green rectangle = 4 × 3 = 12 cm²
Area of the pink rectangle = 2 × 4 = 8 cm²
Area of the blue rectangle = 3 × 2 = 6 cm²
                                    26 cm²

Surface area = 26 × 2
             = 52 cm²

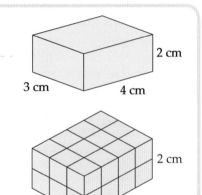

2 cm

3 cm   4 cm

2 cm

3 cm   4 cm

Example

The surface area of a cube is 96 cm².
Calculate   **a**   the area of one face
               b   the length of one side of the cube.

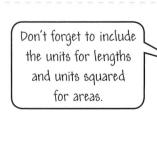

a   A cube has six square faces.
        The area of one face = 96 ÷ 6
                             = 16 cm²
b   Length of one side = √16
                           = 4 cm

Don't forget to include the units for lengths and units squared for areas.

Exercise 14c

1 These nets make cuboids.
Each square represents a 1 centimetre square.
Calculate the surface area of each cuboid.

a   **b**

c 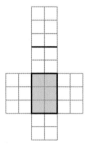 **d**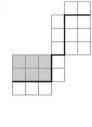

2 A 5 cm by 6 cm by 8 cm cuboid is shown.
Calculate

  a the area of the green rectangle
  b the area of the pink rectangle
  c the area of the blue rectangle
  d the surface area of the cuboid.

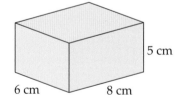

3 Calculate the surface area of these cuboids.
State the units of your answers.

a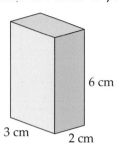

6 cm

3 cm   2 cm

b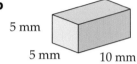

5 mm

5 mm   10 mm

c

1 m

5 m   4 m

4 Calculate the surface area of each cube.
State the units of your answers.
  a length = 5 mm
  b length = 9 m
  c length = 15 cm

length

5 Calculate the length of one side of a cube,
if the surface area of the cube is
  a 600 cm²
  b 384 cm²
  c 13.5 cm²

length

Problem solving

6 The areas of three of the faces of this cuboid are
15 cm², 24 cm² and 40 cm².
Find the length, width and height of the cuboid.

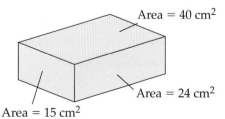

Area = 40 cm²

Area = 24 cm²

Area = 15 cm²

⬤ **Volume** is the amount of space inside a 3D shape.
  ▶ You measure volume in cubic units.

Always use a suitable unit to measure the volume of objects, depending on their size.

To measure the volume of …
you should use …

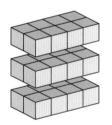

a room
cubic metres (m³)

a cereal box
cubic centimetres (cm³)

a pin head
cubic millimetres (mm³)

You can find the volume of a **cuboid** by counting layers of cubes.

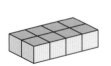

In one layer there are
2 × 4 = 8 cubes

In three layers there are
3 × 8 = 24 cubes

The volume of this cuboid is 24 cubes

This is the same as multiplying the length, width and height.

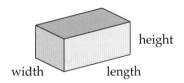

height
width length

⬤ **Volume of a cuboid = length × width × height**

Example

Calculate the volume of this cuboid.

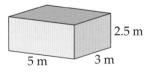

2.5 m
5 m 3 m

Volume = length × width × height
     = 5 × 3 × 2.5
     = 37.5 m³ ⟵ Don't forget the units.

256 **Geometry** 3D shapes

Exercise 14d

1 Choose the most appropriate unit to measure the volume of
   a a chocolate box b a seed
   c a fish tank   d a container on a lorry
   e a snooker ball   f a pea.

2 Calculate the volume of each cuboid. State the units of your answers.

   a
   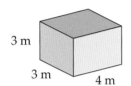
   3 m
   3 m
   4 m

   b
   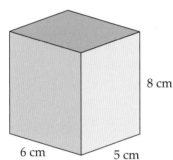
   8 cm
   6 cm
   5 cm

   c

   1.5 m
   5 m
   4 m

3 Calculate the volume of a cube of side 2.5 cm.

4 Calculate the missing lengths.

   a
   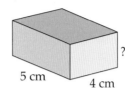
   5 cm
   4 cm
   ?
   Volume = 40 cm³

   b
   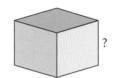
   ?
   A cube
   Volume = 216 cm³

   c

   5 m
   8 m
   ?
   Volume = 20 m³

   d
   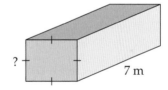
   ?
   7 m
   Volume = 54 cm³

Problem solving

5 A box measures 25 cm by 15 cm by 16 cm.
   a Calculate the volume of the cuboid.
   The box is filled $\frac{3}{4}$ full with sand.
   b Calculate the volume of sand.
   c Calculate the height of the sand.

   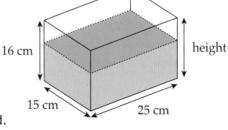
   16 cm
   height
   15 cm
   25 cm

6 Twenty cubes are arranged to form a cuboid. List the four possible cuboids that can be made using all 20 cubes.
   Calculate the surface area of each cuboid. Which cuboid has the smallest surface area?

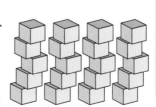
MyMaths.co.uk   Q 1137   SEARCH

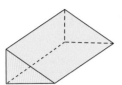

A **prism** is a 3D solid that has a constant cross section.

Examples of prisms include:

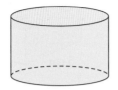

▲ Triangular prism   ▲ Cylinder   ▲ Hexagonal prism

A cuboid is a rectangular prism

To calculate the volume of a prism, you multiply the area of the cross section by the length of the prism.
Volume = Area of cross section × Length

Example

Find the volume of these prisms.

a

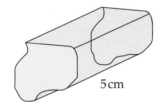

5 cm

Area = 72 cm²

b

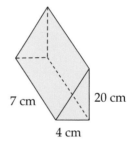

7 cm   20 cm

4 cm

a   Volume = Area of cross section × Length
= 72 × 5
= 360 cm³

b   Volume = Area of cross section × Length
= 10 × 4 × 7
= 280 cm³

Example

The volume of a prism is given as 1200 cm³ and the length of the prism is 24 cm.
Find the area of the cross section.

Volume = Area of cross section × Length
Area of cross section = Volume ÷ Length
= 1200 ÷ 24
= 50 cm²

Exercise 14e

1 Name the following prisms.

a
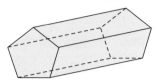

b
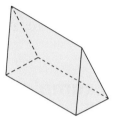

c
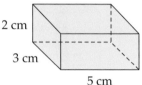

2 Find the volumes of the following prisms.

a

2 cm
3 cm
5 cm

b
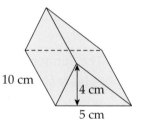

10 cm
4 cm
5 cm

c
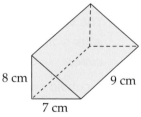

8 cm
9 cm
7 cm

3 A prism has a triangular cross section. The base of the triangle is 4 cm and the perpendicular height is 5 cm. The length of the prism is 18 cm. Find the volume.

4 Find the lengths of the following prisms.

a
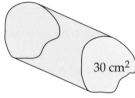

30 cm²

Volume = 240 cm³

b
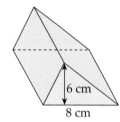

6 cm
8 cm

Volume = 360 cm³

c
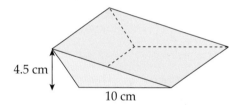

4.5 cm
10 cm

Volume = 78.75 cm³

5 A triangular prism has a volume of 24 cm³ and a length of 8 cm. If the base of the triangular cross section is 4 cm, find the height of the triangle.

Problem solving

6 A chocolate company is designing the packaging for a new product. They decide to make the package in the shape of a triangular prism. If the area of the cross section is 6 cm² and the length is 8 cm

a find the volume of chocolate that can be contained

b find the amount of cardboard required to make each package.

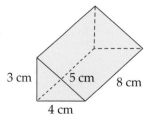

3 cm
5 cm
8 cm
4 cm

Check out

You should now be able to ...

Test it ➡

Questions

✓ Recognise and name 3D solids and recognise their nets.	6	1–3
✓ Use isometric paper and draw plans and elevations of 3D shapes.	6	4–5
✓ Calculate the surface area and volume of cuboids.	6	6–9
✓ Calculate the volume of a prism.	6	10, 11

Language	Meaning	Example
Solid	A shape formed in three dimensions.	Cubes, spheres and cones are solids
Face	A flat surface of a solid	Vertex — Edge — Face
Edge	The line where two faces meet	
Vertex	The point where three or more edges meet	
Net	A 2D shape that can be folded to form a solid	An opened out cardboard box forms a net
Surface area	The total area of all the faces of a solid shape	The surface area of a cube is six times the area of one square face
Volume	The amount of space inside a 3D shape	The volume of a cube is its side length cubed
Prism	A 3D shape with a constant cross-section	A cuboid could be called a rectangular prism, and a cylinder is a circular prism
Cross-section	The 2D shape made when a 3D solid is cut along its length	Cross-sections of a cylinder include circles and rectangles

1 **a** What is the mathematical name for this solid?
   b State the number of
      i faces **ii** vertices
      iii edges.

2 **a** What is the mathematical name for this solid?
   b State the number of
      i faces **ii** vertices
      iii edges.

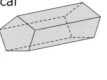

3 Draw the net of a cuboid with dimensions 3cm by 2cm by 4cm.

4 On square grid paper draw
   a the front elevation (F)
   b the side elevation (S)
   c the plan view (P) of this solid.

5 A 3D solid is made from some cubes. The elevations and plan view are shown.

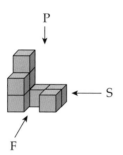

front elevation   side elevation   plan view

   a Draw the solid on isometric paper.
   b How many cubes are needed to make the shape?

6 Calculate the surface area of this cuboid. Give the units of your answer.

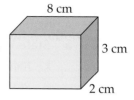

8 cm
3 cm
2 cm

7 A cube has a surface area of 294cm². Calculate the length of one side of the cube.

8 Calculate the volume of the cuboid. Give the units of your answer.

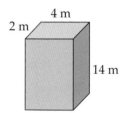

4 m
2 m
14 m

9 A cube has a volume of 729cm³. What is the length of one side of the cube?

10 Calculate the volume of this prism.

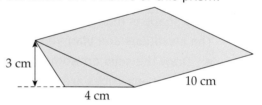

3 cm
4 cm
10 cm

11 A prism has volume 72m³ and length 1.2m. What is the cross sectional area of the prism?

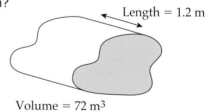

Length = 1.2 m

Volume = 72 m³

What next?

Score		
	0–4	Your knowledge of this topic is still developing. To improve look at Formative test: 2B-14; MyMaths: 1078, 1098, 1106, 1107, 1137, and 1139
	5–9	You are gaining a secure knowledge of this topic. To improve look at InvisiPen: 321, 322, 323, 325, 326 and 327
	10–11	You have mastered this topic. Well done, you are ready to progress!

14a

1 A prism is shown.
   a State the number of
      i faces
      ii vertices
      iii edges.
   b Draw the solid on isometric paper.

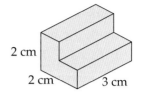

2 cm
2 cm 3 cm

2 **a** Draw a shape with six faces and ten edges.
      How many vertices does the shape have?
   b Draw a shape with nine edges and six vertices.
      How many faces does the shape have?

14b

3 Sketch the front elevation (F), the side elevation
   (S) and the plan view (P) of this dice.

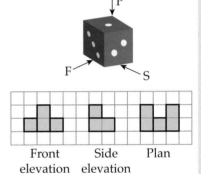

P

F   S

4 A 3D shape is made from cubes.
   The elevations and plan view are shown.
   a Draw the solid on isometric paper.
   b How many cubes are needed to make the solid?

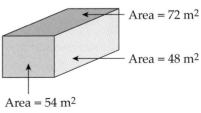

Front   Side   Plan
elevation elevation

14c

5 Calculate the surface area of these cuboids.
   a   **b**   **c**

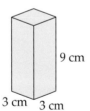

3 cm
7 cm 6 cm

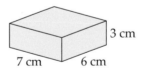

4 cm
10 cm 8 cm

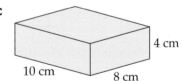

9 cm

3 cm 3 cm

6 Calculate the length of one side of the cube, if the surface
   area of the cube is
   a 294 cm²   **b** 1536 cm²   **c** 235.5 cm²

length

7 A cuboid has three faces with areas 54 m², 48 m²
   and 72 m². What are the dimensions of the cuboid?

Area = 72 m²

Area = 48 m²

Area = 54 m²

8 Copy and complete the table for the cuboids.

	Length	Width	Height	Volume
a	9 m	8 m	8 m	
b	15 mm	10 mm	20 mm	
c	2.5 cm	2 cm	8 cm	
d	5 m	3.5 m	3.2 m	
e	6 cm	2 cm		42 cm³
f	4 m	4 m		48 m³
g	7 cm		20 cm	280 cm³
h	9 cm		32 cm	288 cm³

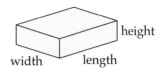

height

width   length

9 A cube has volume 91.125 mm³.

What is the length of the cube's edge?

10 Find the volumes of these prisms.

a

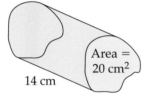

Area = 20 cm²

14 cm

b

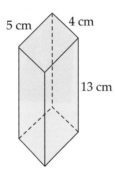

5 cm   4 cm

13 cm

c

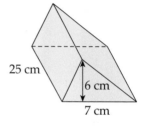

25 cm

6 cm

7 cm

11 Find the area of the cross section of these prisms.

a

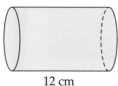

Volume = 360 cm³

12 cm

b

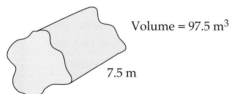

Volume = 97.5 m³

7.5 m

MyMaths.co.uk

For thousands of years, artists have tackled the problem of representing the 3D world in a 2D picture. During the Renaissance, the principles behind perspective were developed and these ideas are still used by artists, architects and graphic designers today.

Task 1

Here are two paintings. The one on the left is from the 14th century, and the one on the right is from the 15th century. Which painting do you think looks most realistic and why?

Task 2

Renaissance artists used the idea that the further away objects are, the smaller they look. This is called foreshortening, and we still use this today.

Look at the two pictures on the right. Picture 1 shows

an avenue with seven trees on each side.
Piture 2 shows how a computer graphic designer might portray this.

a Describe what is happening to the "trees" as they get further away.
b Draw a similar picture to Picture 2, but with 8 trees on each side.

Compare your picture with a friend's. Whose picture looks most accurate and why?

Task 3

Renaissance artists began to use a single **vanishing point** to add realism. The vanishing point is clearly seen in this photograph.

Check the perspective in the two paintings on the left hand page. Do either of them have a vanishing point?

Task 4

Many Renaissance artists placed the vanishing point near the main subject of their painting. A famous example of this is The Last Supper by Leonardo da Vinci.

The vanishing point is set at the height of the eye-line. In this drawing, the green cuboid appears to be above the viewer and the blue cuboids below.

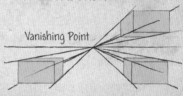

Vanishing Point

- Make your own drawing of cubes using single point perspective. Describe your findings.
- What do you notice about cubes that are a long way to the left or right of the vanishing point?

Task 5

When an object is edge on, **two point perspective** gives a more realistic impression, using two vanishing points, both on the same horizontal eye line, as in the picture.

vanishing point   eye-line   vanishing point

a Use two point perspective to draw a cube edge on, as if looking at it from above.

b Now draw a second cube edge on, this time as if looking at it from below.

Reasearch the meaning of three point perspective.

Try to draw a cube using this perspective.

> **Hint**: Keep your uprights vertical, and place your vanishing points first.

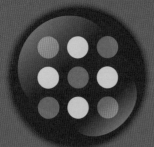

15 Ratio and proportion

Introduction

The idea of creating things which are in proportion is vital to art and architecture. However there is one number, called the 'Golden Proportion', which is supposed to be the most pleasing to the eye.

The Golden Proportion relates to a rectangle whose ratio of length to width is 1.6180339887 : 1. There is evidence that the ancient Greeks and Egyptians used this proportion in the design of many of their buildings, and Renaissance artists used it commonly in their paintings.

What's the point?

The Golden Proportion occurs widely in nature, so it is unsurprising that artists and architects throughout history have chosen to integrate this mathematical dimension into their work.

Objectives

By the end of this chapter, you will have learned how to …

- Simplify and use ratios.
- Solve problems involving direct proportion.
- Calculate a percentage of an amount.
- Calculate a percentage increase or decrease.
- Use fractions, decimals and percentages to compare simple proportions and solve problems.

Check in

1 Calculate these percentages using a mental or informal written method.

   a 15% of 80   **b** 20% of £60   **c** 40% of 180g

2 Copy and complete this table using a calculator where appropriate.

Fraction	Decimal	Percentage
$\frac{17}{20}$		
	0.78	
		96%

Starter problem

Leonardo da Vinci thought that your head (measured from your forehead to your chin) was exactly one tenth of your height.

Is this true?

15a Ratio

You can compare the size of quantities by writing them as a **ratio**.

| Bruno has 75p, and Esme has £1.25. | $\Rightarrow$ | First convert to the same units (pence). | $\Rightarrow$ | Now **simplify** the ratio. |

$$75p : £1.25 \Rightarrow 75p : 125p \Rightarrow$$

$$\div 5 \left(\begin{array}{c} 75 : 125 \\ 15 : 25 \\ 3 : 5 \end{array} \right) \div 5$$
$$\div 5 \qquad\qquad \div 5$$

The ratio of Bruno's money to Esme's money is $3:5$.

To **simplify** a ratio, you divide both parts by the same number.

You can solve ratio problems by multiplying both parts by the same number.

The ratio of men to women in a sports club is $7:11$. There are 175 men.
How many women are there?

For every 7 men there are 11 women.
For 175 men, there are 275 women in the sports club.

men : women

$$\times 25 \left(\begin{array}{c} 7 : 11 \\ 175 : 275 \end{array} \right) \times 25$$

Multiply both parts of the ratio by $175 \div 7 = 25$

A map has a scale of $1:200$.

a What distance does 8 cm on the map represent in real life?

b In real life the distance between the Post Office and church is 30 m.
What is the distance on the map?

a   map : real life

$$\times 8 \left(\begin{array}{c} 1 : 200 \\ 8\,cm : 1600\,cm \end{array} \right) \times 8$$

Multiply both parts of the ratio by 8 cm

The real life distance $= 200 \times 8\,cm = 1600\,cm = 16\,m$

b 30 m = 3000 cm

map : real life

$$\times 15 \left(\begin{array}{c} 1 : 200 \\ 15 : 3000 \end{array} \right) \times 15$$

Multiply both parts of the ratio by $3000 \div 200 = 15$

The distance on the map is 15 cm

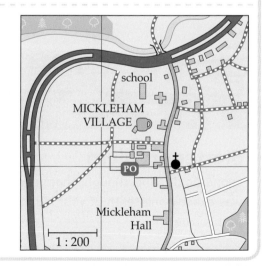

1 : 200

Exercise 15a

1 Write each of these ratios in its simplest form.

a	4 : 14	**b**	12 : 18
c	15 : 25	**d**	14 : 21
e	40 : 25	**f**	35 : 56
g	64 : 40	**h**	72 : 63
i	121 : 77	**j**	72 : 144
k	27 : 81	**l**	74 : 222
m	1024 : 64	**n**	56 000 : 16 000

2 Write each of these ratios in its simplest form.

a	40 cm : 1 m	**b**	90p : £2
c	25 mm : 4 cm	**d**	300 ml : 1 litre
e	4 km : 2500 m	**f**	1500 g : 2 kg
g	3 hrs : 40 mins	**h**	80p : £1.80
i	3 hrs : 1 day	**j**	40 mins : 1 day
k	4 ft : 6 yds	**l**	8 inches : 5 ft
m	9 miles : 30 km	**n**	15 kg : 11 lbs

Problem solving

3 Write these as ratios in their simplest form.

a A cake recipe requires 150 g of sugar for every 100 g of butter. What is the ratio of sugar to butter?

b At Wellbeing 11–18 Comprehensive School there are 1100 students in Years 7 to 11 and 250 students in the sixth form. What is the ratio of sixth form students to Y7 to Y11 students?

c A model of a car is 15 cm long. The real car is 3.75 m long. What is the ratio of the model to the real car?

3.75 m · · · · · 15 cm

4 Solve each of these problems.

a At a dance club the ratio of boys to girls is 3 : 7. There are 91 girls at the club. How many boys are there?

b The main ingredients in a recipe are cauliflower and cheese in the ratio 4 : 3 by weight. How many grams of cheese are needed if the cauliflower weighs 640 g?

c A map has a scale of 1 : 250.

   i What is the distance in real life of a measurement of 12 cm on the map?

   ii What is the distance on the map of a measurement of 50 m in real life?

d A model of a space shuttle is built to a scale of 1 : 24. The length of the real shuttle is 36 m. How long is the model of the shuttle?

5 Rukshana is 12 years old and her sister Rowshanara is 4.

a What is the ratio of their ages?

b What will be the ratio of their ages in 10 years' time?

c Investigate what happens to the ratio of their ages as Rukshana and Rowshanara get older.

⦿ You can divide a quantity in a given ratio using **a unitary method**.
You find the value of one equal share of the quantity.

Example

Stefan and Naomi share a 200g bar of chocolate in the ratio 2 : 3.
How much chocolate do they each receive?

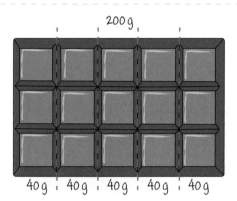

200 g

40 g · 40 g · 40 g · 40 g · 40 g

Number of equal parts   2 + 3 = 5

Each of the parts weighs   200 ÷ 5 = 40 g
Stefan gets 2 parts   2 × 40 g = 80 g
Naomi gets 3 parts   3 × 40 g = 120 g

Here are two ways to check that Stefan's and Naomi's amounts are correct.

By simplifying,

Stefan : Naomi

80 g : 120 g

80 : 120

÷40 ( ) ÷40

2 : 3 ✔

By adding,

80 g + 120 g
= 200 g
✔

Both checks are correct, so the answer is correct.

Exercise 15b

1 Divide these quantities in the ratios given.
   a £50 in the ratio 2 : 3
   b 60 cm in the ratio 5 : 7
   c 72 MB in the ratio 4 : 5
   d 90 p in the ratio 1 : 5
   e 120 seconds in the ratio 3 : 5
   f £240 in the ratio 5 : 3

2 Sian picks some apples.

2 She shares out 15 apples between herself and her mum in the ratio 2 : 3.
   a Draw a diagram to show how Sian divides the apples.
   b Write the number of apples she gives to her mum.

3 Morgan wins £40.
   He shares the £40 between himself and his dad in the ratio 3 : 5.
   a Draw a diagram to show how Morgan divides the money.
   b Write the amount of money he gives to his dad.

Problem solving

4 Solve each of these problems.
   a At a gym club the ratio of boys to girls is 3 : 4. There are 63 children in total at the club. How many girls are there?
   b Jack and Mona share £84 in the ratio 2 : 5. How much money does Jack receive?

5 For each of these questions, check that the answer is correct. Explain your reasoning in each question.
   a In a chemistry lab, the ratio of funnels to beakers is 2 : 3. There are 25 pieces of equipment in total. How many funnels and how many beakers are there?

   Answer There are 10 funnels and 15 beakers.

   b Javed and Oprah share £65 in the ratio 4 : 9. How much money do they each receive?

   Answer Javed receives £12 and Oprah receives £30.

6 Meredith wants to design a flag using two colours – blue and green.
   The flag must be coloured blue to green in the ratio 3 : 5.
   a Draw a rectangle 5 cm by 16 cm.
      Colour the flag blue and green in the ratio 3 : 5.
   b Draw a different rectangle 12 cm by 8 cm.
      Colour the flag blue and green in the ratio 3 : 5.
   c How can you tell which sizes of rectangular flags, drawn on square grid paper, can easily be coloured in blue and green in the ratio 3 : 5?

15c Direct proportion

Here is an approximate **conversion** table for miles and kilometres.

Miles	Kilometres
10	16
20	32
5	8

÷2 (×2 ( ) ×2) ÷2

- If you double the number of miles, you double the number of kilometres.
- If you halve the number of miles, you halve the number of kilometres.

The number of miles is **directly proportional** to the number of kilometres.

> ● When two quantities are in **direct proportion**, if one of them increases the other one increases by the same proportion.

You can use direct proportion to solve simple problems.

Example

Three litres of water costs £2.09.
What is the cost of six litres of water?

×2 (3 litres   £2.09) ×2
    (6 litres   £4.18)

Six litres of water costs £4.18

> ● You can use the **unitary method** to solve problems involving direct proportion.

It is called the unitary method because you start by finding the value for one unit.

Example

a 20 text messages cost 48p. What is the cost of 15 text messages?
b There are 140 calories in a 40g piece of cheese. How many calories are there in a 70g piece of the same cheese?

a
÷20 (20 texts   48p) ÷20
     (1 text   2.4p)
×15 (15 texts   36p) ×15

15 text messages cost 36p.

b
÷40 (40g   140 calories) ÷40
     (1g   3.5 calories)
×70 (70g   245 calories) ×70

70g of cheese contains 245 calories.

272   **Number** Ratio and proportion

Exercise 15c

1 48 bags of crisps cost £11.04. Work out the cost of
   a 24 bags of crisps   **b** 12 bags of crisps   **c** 1 bag of crisps
   d 5 bags of crisps   **e** 50 bags of crisps   **f** 6 bags of crisps.

2 Here are three offers for text messages on a mobile phone.
   In which of these offers are the numbers in direct proportion?
   In each case explain and justify your answers.

D-Mobile

Text messages	Cost
10	£0.40
20	£0.80
40	£1.60

Yellow

Text messages	Cost
5	£0.19
20	£0.72
45	£1.56

Codaphone

Text messages	Cost
20	£0.68
50	£1.70
120	£4.08

Problem solving

3 Use direct proportion to solve each of these problems.
   a Four apples cost 92p. What is the cost of 12 apples?
   b 28 g of cashew nuts contain 14 g of fat.
       How many grams of fat are there in 42 g of cashew nuts?
   c 200 g of chips contain 500 calories.
       How many calories are there in 40 g of chips?
   d A soup recipe for four people uses 500 g of mushrooms.
       i What weight of mushrooms is needed for seven people?
       ii How many grams of mushrooms are needed for 13 people?

4 Solve each of these problems.
   a Three litres of lemonade costs £1.11.
       What is the cost of   **i** 9 litres of lemonade   **ii** 8 litres of lemonade?
   b Four identical pans have a total capacity of 14 litres. What is the
       capacity of seven of these pans?
   c 16 pencils cost £1.92. What is the cost of seven pencils?
   d £3 is worth 27 Chinese Yuan. How much is £25 worth in Chinese Yuan?
   e 35 litres of petrol costs £38.15. What is the cost of 40 litres of petrol?
   f A recipe for four people needs 300 g of pasta. How much pasta is
       needed to make the recipe for seven people?

5 Use direct proportion to copy and complete
   this approximate conversion table for converting
   between kilograms and pounds.

   How many pounds make 1 kg?
   How many kilograms make 1 lb?

Kilograms (kg)	Pounds (lb)
1	
	4
5	11
10	
23	
	110

15d Ratio and proportion

○ **Ratio** compares the size of the parts.

○ **Proportion** compares the size of a part with the whole.

This is the national flag of Nigeria.

The ratio green : white = 2 : 1

The proportion of green = $\frac{2}{3}$

The proportion of white = $\frac{1}{3}$

Example

Wendy is trying to eat more fruit.
In the last seven days Wendy ate nine apples and six oranges.

a What proportion of the fruit eaten is apples and what proportion is oranges?

b What is the ratio of apples to oranges?

a There were 9 + 6 = 15 pieces of fruit

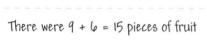

Proportion of apples = $\frac{9}{15}$ = $\frac{3}{5}$ (÷3)   Proportion of oranges = $\frac{6}{15}$ = $\frac{2}{5}$ (÷3)

$\frac{3}{5}$ of Wendy's fruit were apples and $\frac{2}{5}$ of her fruit were oranges.

b The ratio compares how many apples she ate to how many oranges she ate.
The ratio apples : oranges = 3 : 2

apples : oranges

÷3 $\left(\begin{array}{c} 9 : 6 \\ 3 : 2 \end{array}\right)$ ÷3

Example

Jermaine and Gina share £150 in the ratio 3 : 2.
How much money do they each receive?

Use the ratio to tell you what proportion of the money each person receives.

Jermaine receives $\frac{3}{5}$ of £150 = £90

Gina receives $\frac{2}{5}$ of £150 = £60

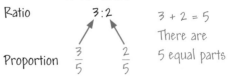

Jermaine : Gina

Ratio   3 : 2

Proportion $\frac{3}{5}$ $\frac{2}{5}$

3 + 2 = 5
There are
5 equal parts

Exercise 15d

1 For each of these diagrams

   i find the ratio of red sections to yellow sections (in its simplest form)

   ii find the proportion of the shape shaded red (as a fraction in its simplest form)

   iii copy and complete these two sentences for each shape:

   red section $= \dfrac{\square}{\square} \times$ yellow section

   yellow section $= \dfrac{\square}{\square} \times$ red section

a 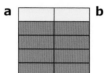   **b**   **c**

2 In a class of 32 students, there are 20 girls.

   a Write the ratio of boys to girls in the class.

   b Write the proportion of the class that are girls.

   c Write the proportion of the class that are boys.

3 In a fish tank, there are 20 goldfish and 25 angelfish.

   a Write the ratio of goldfish to angelfish in the tank.

   b Write the proportion of the fish that are goldfish.

4 Use a suitable method to work out these.

   a Divide 40 kg in the ratio 3 : 2

   b Divide £120 in the ratio 1 : 5

   c Divide 360 degrees in the ratio 4 : 5

   d Divide 180 cats in the ratio 5 : 7

   e Divide £4 in the ratio 3 : 5

   f Divide 6 m in the ratio 7 : 5

5 Bill and Ben mix blue and yellow paint to each make three shades of green. Bill uses these ratios of blue : yellow

   a 2 : 8   **b** 3 : 6   **c** 4 : 12

   Ben uses these proportions of blue

   A $\dfrac{1}{4}$ **B** $\dfrac{1}{5}$ **C** $\dfrac{1}{3}$

   Match the ratios with the correct proportions.

Problem solving

6 a Amy has 28 plates in her cupboard. The ratio of large plates to small plates is 3 : 4. How many small plates does Amy have in her cupboard?

   b Keiley has 54 files stored on her phone. The ratio of music to video files is 7 : 2.

     i How many music files does Keiley have on her phone?

     ii What proportion of the files on her phone are video files?

7 a $\dfrac{3}{5}$ of the people at a pop concert are women. What is the ratio of men to women at the pop concert?

   b Harry and Posy shared some money in the ratio 3 : 4. Harry received £36. How much money did Harry and Posy share?

8 A sponge cake is made from flour, sugar and margarine in the ratio 4 : 5 : 3 by weight. How many grams of margarine and sugar are needed to mix with 280 g of flour?

Did you know?

All the colours of the rainbow can be made by combining red, green and blue in the right proportions.

A **percentage of an amount** can be calculated using an equivalent fraction or decimal.

To find 23% of £75, you can use an equivalent fraction ...

... or an equivalent decimal.

▲ Shops often use special offers to try to persuade you to buy.

$$23\% \text{ of } 75 = \frac{23}{100} \text{ of } 75$$
$$= \frac{23 \times 75}{100}$$
$$= \frac{1725}{100}$$
$$= £17.25$$

$$23\% \text{ of } 75 = \frac{23}{100} \text{ of } 75$$
$$= 0.23 \times 75$$
$$= £17.25$$

Percentage increases and decreases occur often in real life.

Example

A packet of crisps normally weighs 125 g. The packet is increased in weight by 20%. What is the new weight of the packet of crisps?

First find the size of the increase:
20% of 125 g

$$10\% \text{ of } 125\,g = \frac{1}{10} \text{ of } 125 \qquad \text{Find } 10\%$$
$$= 12.5$$

$$20\% \text{ of } 125\,g = 2 \times 12.5 \qquad \text{Double it}$$
$$= 25\,g$$

Then add the increase to the original weight.
New weight = 125 + 25 = 150 g

Example

Harry weighs 80 kg. After a diet he reduced his weight by 12%. What is Harry's new weight?

$$12\% \text{ of } 80\,kg = 0.12 \times 80 \qquad \text{First find the weight}$$
$$= 9.6\,kg \qquad \text{reduction.}$$

$$80 - 9.6 = 70.4\,kg \qquad \text{Subtract from original weight.}$$

Exercise 15e

1 Match the equivalent quantities.

a 0.33   **A** $\dfrac{16}{100}$

b 12.5%   **B** 50%

c $\dfrac{1}{2}$ **C** $\dfrac{1}{8}$

d 16%   **D** 33%

2 Calculate these percentages using a mental or informal written method.

   a 10% of 80   **b** 20% of £60

   c 5% of 180 g   **d** 15% of £300

   e 40% of 320 N   **f** 25% of 160 mm

   g 55% of £2800   **h** 65% of £88

   i 17% of £36   **j** 72% of 9 kg

3 Calculate these using a suitable method.

   a 13% of £50   **b** 42% of 67

   c 50% of 86 kg   **d** 16% of $24

   e 37% of £45   **f** 17.5% of 80 km

   g 65% of £230   **h** 95% of 19.2 kg

4   **a** Increase £50 by 15%.

   b Decrease £50 by 15%.

   c Increase 160 m by 25%.

   d Decrease 360° by 10%.

   e Increase 60 kg by 5%.

   f Decrease £1700 by 13%.

   g Increase £240 by 45%.

   h Decrease 240 J by 36%.

Problem solving

5   **a** Archenal football stadium has 43 400 seats.
It is rebuilt with an increased seating of 45%.
How many seats are there at the new stadium?

   b A top secret file of size 208 kB is saved on a computer. After some information is stolen and deleted from the file, it is decreased in size by 5%. What is the new size of the file?

   c A bottle of olive oil holds 560 ml.
It is increased in capacity by 15%.
What is the new capacity of the new bottle?

6 Here are five items for sale in Cheapos shop with their original prices.
In a 21-day sale, Cheapos reduce all their prices by 21%.

   a Calculate the sale price of each of the items.

   b How could the sales assistants work out the sale price of an item after a 21% reduction using just a single multiplication?

   c Investigate increasing and decreasing the prices by other percentages. Find a single multiplication which works out the increase or decrease for each of your percentages.

7 Increase £400 by 10% and then decrease the result by 10%. Explain your answer.

> **Proportions** can be described using fractions, decimals or percentages.

What proportion of this shape is shaded yellow?

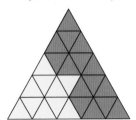

You can give the answer as a fraction ...

... or as a percentage.

Proportion shaded yellow

$$= \frac{10}{25} \underset{\div 5}{\overset{\div 5}{=}} \frac{2}{5}$$

Proportion shaded yellow

$$= \frac{10}{25} \underset{\times 4}{\overset{\times 4}{=}} \frac{40}{100} = 40\%$$

Example

Leroy asked some students in Year 8 which subject they liked best.

a i What proportion of the boys chose Maths?

ii What proportion of the boys chose Science?

b Compare the proportions of boys and girls that chose Maths or Science.

Subject	Boys	Girls
Maths	8	2
English	2	10
Science	7	9
French	1	1
Geography	2	2
History	1	3
Total	21	27

a Proportion of boys

i who chose Maths

$= \dfrac{8}{21}$

$= 0.380\ 95$

$= 38.1\%$ (1 dp)

ii who chose Science

$= \dfrac{7}{21}$

$= 0.333\ 33$

$= 33.3\%$ (1 dp)

b Proportion of girls

who chose Maths

$= \dfrac{2}{27}$

$= 0.074\ 074$

$= 7.4\%$ (1 dp)

who chose Science

$= \dfrac{9}{27}$

$= 0.333\ 33$

$= 33.3\%$ (1 dp)

A greater proportion of boys than girls chose Maths as their favourite subject.

The same proportion of boys and girls chose Science.

Exercise 15f

1 Convert these fractions into percentages using a calculator where appropriate.

    a $\dfrac{7}{10}$ **b** $\dfrac{23}{50}$ **c** $\dfrac{14}{25}$

    d $\dfrac{5}{4}$ **e** $\dfrac{17}{40}$ **f** $\dfrac{5}{12}$

    g $\dfrac{33}{35}$ **h** $\dfrac{5}{7}$ **i** $\dfrac{4}{5}$

    j $\dfrac{13}{20}$ **k** $\dfrac{1}{8}$ **l** $\dfrac{1}{6}$

2 Write the proportion of each of these shapes that is shaded red.

2 Write each of your answers as

    i a fraction in its simplest form

    ii a percentage (to 1 dp where appropriate).

    a 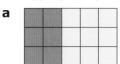   **b**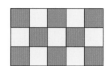

    c   **d**

Problem solving

3 Express each of your answers to these problems

    i as a fraction in its simplest form

    ii as a percentage (to 1 dp where appropriate).

    a Morton scores 49 out of 70 in his English test. What proportion of the test did he answer correctly?

    b Class 8X has 33 students. 21 of these students are boys. What proportion of the class are girls?

4 a Hilary McGoalmachine has scored 23 goals in 35 games for her club.
Jodie Goalpoacher has scored 20 goals in 29 games for the same club. Who is the better goal scorer? Explain and justify your answer.

    b Tina put £120 into a savings account. After one year the interest was £8. Harriet put £90 into a savings account. After one year the interest was £7. Who had the better deal?

Did you know?

As of 2014, the top goalscorer in the men's football Premier League since it started in 1992 is Alan Shearer with 260 goals in 441 appearances. However that doesn't give him the top scoring rate!

5 Here are the Summer exam results of some students in History, Geography and Religious Studies. For each student, show clearly in which subject they did the best. Explain and justify your answers.

Name	History (60 marks)	Geography (70 marks)	Religious Studies (80 marks)
Zak	24	30	33
Wilson	20	14	16
Yvonne	45	50	52
Ulf	55	64	73
Veronica	30	38	33

Check out
You should now be able to ...

Test it ➡
Questions

✓ Simplify and use ratios including dividing a quantity in a given ratio.	5	1–4
✓ Solve problems involving direct proportion.	6	5, 6
✓ Understand and use the relationship between ratio and proportion.	6	7, 8
✓ Calculate a percentage of an amount.	6	9
✓ Calculate a percentage increase or decrease.	6	10, 11
✓ Use fractions, decimals and percentages to compare simple proportions and solve problems.	6	12, 13

Language	Meaning	Example
Ratio	The relationship between parts of a whole	red : yellow = 1 : 2 is the ratio of colours used to make light orange
Proportion	The relationship between one part and the whole	The proportion of red in light orange is $\frac{1}{3}$
Unitary Method	The method for dividing into a given ratio or proportion using the value of one equal share	To divide £20 in the ratio 2 : 3 1 share is 20 ÷ (2 + 3) = £4 2 shares are 2 × 4 = £8 and 3 shares are 3 × 4 = £12
Direct proportion	Quantities are in direct proportion if when you increase one the other increases in the same proportion	The perimeter of a square is directly proportional to the length of one side: doubling the length of a side doubles the perimeter

1 Write each of these ratios in its simplest form.

   a 15:45   **b** 30:24

   c 95cm:2m   **d** £3:84p

2 A scale drawing is made with a scale of 1:50.

   a What is the distance in real life of a measurement of 9cm on the drawing?

   b What length on the drawing would be needed to represent a distance of 8m?

3 Divide

   a £90 in the ratio 2:3

   b 117g in the ratio 8:1

4 In a choir, the ratio of men to women is 4:7. If there are 12 men, how many women are there?

5 A recipe for four people requires 360g of pasta. How much pasta will be needed for six people?

6 100g of brioche contains 345 calories. A slice of brioche is about 30g. Approximately how many calories does it contain?

7 A farm has 28 cows and 42 sheep.

   a What is the ratio of cows to sheep?

   b What proportion of the animals are cows?

8

   a What proportion of the pentagon is yellow?

   b What is the ratio of yellow to blue?

9 Calculate these percentages using a suitable method.

   a 35% of 120

   b 78% of 59

10 Increase 88kg by 12.5%

11 Decrease £6500 by 65%

12 Convert these fractions into percentages.

   a $\frac{18}{25}$ **b** $\frac{28}{35}$ **c** $\frac{14}{17}$

13 Medication A cured 78 out of 94 patients and medication B cured 86 out of 109. Which is the most effective medicine?

What next?

Score	0 – 5	Your knowledge of this topic is still developing. To improve look at Formative test: 2B–15; MyMaths: 1032, 1036, 1038 and 1039
	6 – 10	You are gaining a secure knowledge of this topic. To improve look at InvisiPen: 152, 192, 193 and 194
	11 – 13	You have mastered this topic. Well done, you are ready to progress!

1   Write each of these ratios in its simplest form.

   a   6 : 18   b   5 : 15   c   8 : 12   d   6 : 15
   e   35 : 28   f   32 : 56   g   63 : 90   h   70 : 60
   i   24 : 100   j   24 : 104   k   128 : 256   l   64 : 176

2   Write each of these ratios in its simplest form.

   a   20 cm : 3 m   b   50 p : £4   c   65 mm : 8 cm
   d   70 cl : 2 litres   e   7 km : 700 m   f   1900 g : 4 kg
   g   1 hr 20 mins : 80 mins   h   70 p : £1.70   i   18 inches : 2 feet

3   Solve these problems.

   a   In a fishing club, the ratio of men to women is 7 : 2. There are 84 men
       in the club. How many women are there?

   b   In a school, the ratio of boys to girls is 8 : 9. If there are 624 boys at the
       school, how many girls are there?

   c   A map has a scale of 1 : 10 000.

       i   What is the distance in real life of a measurement of 3 cm on the map?
       ii   What is the distance on the map of a measurement of 5 km in real life?

4   Divide these quantities in the ratios given.

   a   Divide 65 km in the ratio 6 : 7   b   Divide £225 in the ratio 8 : 7
   c   Divide 256 MB in the ratio 3 : 5   d   Divide 4500 N in the ratio 4 : 5
   e   Divide 3 minutes in the ratio 4 : 5   f   Divide £2 in the ratio 7 : 13

5   Solve these problems.

   a   In a running club, the ratio of boys to girls is 5 : 3. There are 96 children
       in total at the club. How many girls are there?

   b   Sam and Siobhan share £2400 in the ratio 7 : 5. How much money does
       Sam receive?

   c   A pizza is made with dough and toppings in the ratio 3 : 5. The total weight
       of the pizza is 320 g. What weight of dough has been used to make the pizza?

6   Here are three offers for different types of bread. In which of these offers are the
    numbers in direct proportion? In each case explain and justify your answers.

   a   **Wholemeal loaves**

Weight of bread	Cost
300 g	£0.45
400 g	£0.60
800 g	£1.20

   b   **Croissants**

Weight of bread	Cost
50 g	£0.32
125 g	£0.75
200 g	£1.25

   c   **Currant teacakes**

Weight of bread	Cost
40 g	£0.24
100 g	£0.60
240 g	£1.44

7 Use direct proportion to solve each of these problems.

a Five pears cost 82p. What is the cost of 15 pears?

b 150 g of crisps contain 240 calories. How many calories are there in 50 g of crisps?

c A recipe for six people uses 420 g of flour.
  i What weight of flour is needed for seven people?
  ii How much flour is needed for three people?

d Five litres of water costs £1.45.
  i What is the cost of seven litres of water?
  ii What is the cost of 17 litres of water?

8 a Steve and Jenny break a 120 g chocolate bar into two pieces. Steve has $\frac{3}{8}$ of the bar and Jenny has the rest. What is the ratio of Jenny's piece of the bar to Steve's piece of the bar?

b $\frac{8}{9}$ of the people who attended a cricket match were men. What was the ratio of men to women at the cricket match?

c Shirley and Hanif share some money. Shirley receives $\frac{2}{5}$ of the money and Hanif receives £66. How much money did Shirley and Hanif share?

9 a Increase £30 by 10%
b Decrease 700 euros by 5%
c Increase 8 miles by 20%
d Decrease 180° by 15%
e Increase 280 kg by 25%
f Decrease £100 000 by 3%
g Increase 250 rabbits by 30%
h Decrease 2500 kJ by 22%
i Increase 70 g by 9%
j Decrease £1.80 by 35%

10 a Chelski football stadium has 71 440 seats. It is rebuilt with an increased seating of 15%. How many seats are there at the new stadium?

b A jar of jam holds 370 g. It is increased in capacity by 23%. What is the new capacity of the jar? (Give your answer to the nearest gram.)

c A memory stick normally costs £36. It is reduced in price in a sale by 17.5%. What is the sale price of the memory stick?

11 a Dan scores 62% in his Maths exam, $\frac{37}{60}$ in his Science exam and $\frac{29}{50}$ in his English exam. In which subject did Dan do the best?

b Megan and Jane play tennis. Last week Megan played seven matches and won five of them. Last month Jane played 20 matches and won 14 of them. Who is the better tennis player? Explain and justify your answer.

16 Probability

Introduction

In medicine, clinical trials are performed on large groups of people to test the safety and performance of new drugs. Statisticians have to make sure that the tests are fair, to tell if the new drug has worked. They do this by only giving the new drug to half of the people who are in the test. The rest of the people get a fake drug, called a placebo. The statisticians then compare the results of the two groups of people.

What's the point?

Probability is used widely to determine whether or not the findings of a clinical trial are the result of a genuine difference made by the new drug or whether it is just due to chance.

Objectives

By the end of this chapter, you will have learned how to …

- Use diagrams and tables to record mutually exclusive outcomes.
- Find probabilities based on equally likely outcomes.
- Calculate the probability that an event does not occur from the probability that it does occur.
- Estimate probabilities by collecting data from an experiment.
- Compare experimental probabilities with theoretical probabilities.
- Use the language of sets and use sets to calculate probabilities.

Check in

1. Think about what the weather is likely to be where you live tomorrow.
   Describe in words the likelihood of each of these types of weather.
   a Rain   **b** Temperatures over 50 °C   **c** Snow   **d** Cloud

2. Convert each of these fractions to decimals.
   a $\frac{1}{2}$ **b** $\frac{2}{5}$ **c** $\frac{3}{8}$

3. Convert these percentages to decimals.
   a 35%   **b** 63.5%   **c** 0.7%

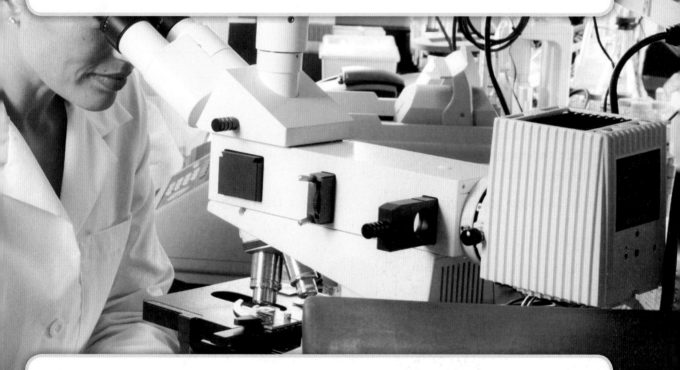

Starter problem

If you roll a dice what is the probability of a five?

If you roll two dice what is the probability of a five?

Does the probability of getting a five change if you roll more dice?

Investigate.

16a Listing outcomes

Probability is the study of chance.

Here are some words that you need to know:

> A **trial** is a statistical experiment, like throwing a dice.

> An **outcome** is a possible result of a trial, like throwing a five.

> An **event** is a collection of outcomes, like throwing an odd number (1, 3 or 5).

▲ Dice have been used for thousands of years. This one is from ancient Egypt.

This **tree diagram** show possible outcomes when a normal dice is rolled.

You label the end of each branch with the outcome

You can record the outcomes for two events using either a **tree diagram** or a **sample space diagram**. Both of these diagrams show the possible outcomes when you spin two coins.

Here is a **sample space diagram**:

		Second coin	
		Heads	**Tails**
First coin	**Heads**	(H, H)	(H, T)
	Tails	(T, H)	(T, T)

Here is a **tree diagram**:

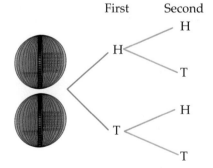

First   Second

H
H
T

H
T
T

You can choose to use a tree diagram or a sample space diagram depending on the problem you are solving.

Exercise 16a

1 Draw tree diagrams to show the results of these experiments.

   a Carole shuffles a set of cards marked 1 to 5, and then picks one at random and records the number on it.

   b Lee rolls an ordinary dice once, and records whether the score is odd or even.

2 The list on the right shows the possible outcomes when Danni chooses a flavour of food to feed her cat.
Draw a tree diagram to show the possible outcomes.

Flavours available
Chicken
Tuna
Beef
Cod

3 For each of the following situations, draw
   i a two-stage tree diagram, and
   ii a sample space diagram to show the possible outcomes.

   a John throws two darts at a dartboard, aiming at the bull's-eye (centre). Each throw is either a hit or a miss.

   b Karen takes two Spanish tests. For each test, she can either pass or fail.

   c A hockey team plays two matches. Each match results in a win, a draw or a loss.

4 This sample space diagram shows the possible setting of two sets of traffic lights on a road.

		Second set		
		Red	**Amber**	**Green**
First set	**Red**	(R, R)	(R, A)	(R, G)
	Amber	(A, R)	(A, A)	(A, G)
	Green	(G, R)	(G, A)	(G, G)

Draw a tree diagram to represent the same set of information.

5 This tree diagram shows the possible marks a student can be given in the school register for two days.

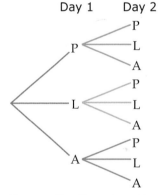

Day 1   Day 2

P = Present, L = Late, A = Absent

Draw a sample space diagram to represent the same set of information.

Problem solving

6 You have used tree diagrams and sample space diagrams to show the possible outcomes of single events, and of two successive events.
What sort of diagram would you use if you wanted to show the outcomes of three successive events?

Did you know?

The sequence of numbers on a standard dart board was chosen in order to penalise inaccurate throws.

● Probability describes how likely an event is.
  ▶ It can be shown on a scale of 0 to 1.

Can you think of some examples that lie at various points on the probability scale?

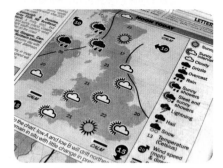

▲ Weather forecasters often quote the probability that it will rain tomorrow.

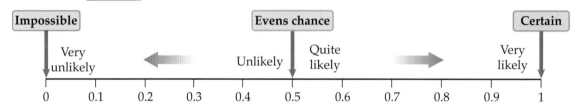

You can work out the probability of a simple event using a **formula**.

● Probability of an event
$$= \frac{\text{Number of \textbf{outcomes} that belong to the event}}{\text{Total number of possible outcomes}}$$

The formula only works if all the possible outcomes are equally likely.

Example

Six students in a class of thirty wear glasses. What is the probability that a student chosen at random

a wears glasses **b** does not wear glasses?

a There are 30 possible outcomes.
There are 6 outcomes of 'the student wears glasses'.
Using the formula
probability $= \frac{6}{30} = \frac{1}{5}$

b Probability of wearing glasses = 0.2
Probability of not wearing glasses = 1 − 0.2 = 0.8

● If the probability of an event occurring is p, then the probability of it not occurring is $1 - p$.

Exercise 16b

1 Copy this probability scale.

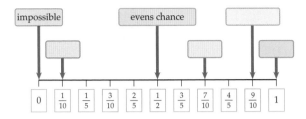

Write each of these words into the appropriate box. The first two are done for you.

| impossible | evens chance | very unlikely |
| likely | almost certain | certain |

2 Explain in words how likely each of these events is.
Suggest a possible value for the probability in each case.

   a It will snow at your school tomorrow.

   b A person chosen at random from your class is twelve years old.

   c You will have a maths lesson next week.

   d You get an even score when you roll an ordinary dice.

3 An ordinary dice is rolled once. Use the formula to work out the probability of the number rolled being

   a exactly 6   **b** a multiple of 3

   c less than 4   **d** 7

4 **a** The probability of a football team winning a game is 0.3.
   What is the probability that they will not win the game?

   b There is a 45% chance of snow tonight. What is the probability that it will not snow?

   c A teacher chooses a student at random from class 8X. If the probability of the chosen student being female is $\frac{7}{16}$, what is the probability that they are male?

5 A box contains 10 number cards, marked with the numbers 1 to 10. A card is chosen at random. Find the probability that it is

   a 7   **b** an even number

   c greater than 8   **d** 13

   e less than 3 or greater than 8

Problem solving

6 Sarah carried out a survey asking teenagers on which days they preferred to go shopping. Before starting the survey she said, 'There are two days in the weekend, so the probability that people pick a Saturday or Sunday should be $\frac{2}{7}$.' Is Sarah correct?

7 Doctor Dice makes his decisions on the roll of a dice!
If he rolls a prime number, he will have eggs for breakfast.

   a Find the probability that Doctor Dice will not have eggs for breakfast.

   b In one month Doctor Dice has eggs for breakfast 23 times. Do you think his dice is fair?

Did you know?

In the British national lottery there are 49 balls and six are chosen at random. You have a 1 in 13 983 816 chance of winning the big prize!

Ravi the technician is testing computers. He wants to know the likelihood of a computer passing a quality test. He tests 100 computers and finds that 78 pass the test.

Ravi **estimates** the probability of passing as $78 \div 100 = 0.78$

⬤ An **experiment** is a series of **trials**.

In an experiment, you can estimate the probability of an event using this formula.

⬤ Experimental probability $= \dfrac{\text{Number of successful trials}}{\text{Total number of trials}}$

Example

Ravi carries out safety checks on 46 projectors. Two of the projectors fail the test.
a Estimate the probability of a projector failing the test.
b How could Ravi get a better estimate?

- -

a This is an experiment with 46 trials, and two 'successes'.
Using the formula

$$\text{Experimental probability} = \dfrac{\text{Number of projectors that fail}}{\text{Total number tested}}$$

$$= \dfrac{2}{46} = \dfrac{1}{23}$$

> You could convert the probability to a decimal. Use a calculator to work out $1 \div 23 = 0.043$ (3 dp)

b Ravi could test more projectors.

Example

The table shows the preferred subject of a **sample** of students, from these four subjects.

Subject	Science	English	Maths	Art
Number of students	6	10	9	5

Estimate the probability that a randomly chosen student from the whole school will prefer English.

Total number of students = $6 + 10 + 9 + 5 = 30$

Probability of preferring English $= \dfrac{10}{30} = \dfrac{1}{3}$

Exercise 16c

1   A scientist checks some trees to see whether they are infected with a disease. She checks 28 trees, and 5 of them are infected. Estimate the probability that a tree chosen at random has the disease.

2   The table shows the results of a survey about Year 8 students' journeys to school.

Transport	Cycle	Walk	Bus	Car
Number	18	29	14	8

Estimate the probability that a student chosen at random from Year 8 would have
   a   cycled to school
   b   walked to school
   c   not taken the bus to school.

3   This table shows the number of points scored by 20 competitors in an athletics competition.

15   14   11   8   11   17   7   16   16   8
18   10   4   17   13   6   15   3   9   12

Use the data in the table to estimate the probability that a competitor chosen at random would have scored more than ten points.

4   Andy and Ben both carry out experiments to estimate the probability of a particular kind of seed germinating. The table shows their results.

	Andy	Ben
Germinated	32	58
Failed	18	42

   a   Estimate the probability of a seed germinating, using Andy's results.
   b   Now estimate the probability using Ben's results.
   c   Whose results do you think should be more reliable – Andy's or Ben's?

Problem solving

5   Tara wants to estimate the probability of it snowing in London next Christmas Day. Explain how she could do this.

6   Three friends carried out an experiment to see if they could balance a coin on their nose for ten seconds. They each had 12 attempts. The table shows how often they were successful.

Lily	Poppy	Rose
4	6	5

If you picked a friend at random how likely is it that they could balance a coin on their nose for ten seconds?

Did you know?

Most of the UK was covered in snow at Christmas in 2010. However it is much more likely to snow between January and March than in December.

16d Theoretical and experimental probability

⬤ You can use an experiment to estimate a probability.

If you repeat an experiment you will usually get different results. Increasing the number of trials should give more reliable estimates.

Example

Karl and Jenny both tested this spinner.
The table shows their results.
Estimate the probability of the spinner landing on green using

a   Karl's data   b   Jenny's data.

	Red	Blue	Green	Yellow
Karl	8	14	16	22
Jenny	12	24	28	36

a   16 green
   8 + 14 + 16 + 22 = 60 outcomes altogether
   Estimated probability = $\frac{16}{60}$ = 0.266...

b   28 green
   12 + 24 + 28 + 36 = 100 outcomes altogether
   Estimated probability = $\frac{28}{100}$ = 0.28

   Jenny's results should be more reliable because her experiment had more trials.

Example

Jim tests a coin by spinning it 20 times.
The coin lands on Heads 14 times.
Is the coin fair?
How can Jim be sure that his results are reliable?

The theoretical probability of getting Heads with a fair coin is 0.5
Estimated probability = $\frac{14}{20}$ = 0.7
The difference between the probabilities suggests that the coin might be **biased** towards Heads.
However the number of trials in the experiment is low (only 20).
Jim could be more convinced if he spun the coin more times.

⬤ An experiment is **biased** if not all outcomes are equally likely.

Exercise 16d

1   Sam tested a coin to see if it was fair. The table shows his results.

Heads	Tails
31	49

   a How many trials did Sam carry out?
   b Estimate the probabilities of getting heads and tails with this coin, using the results of Sam's experiment.
   c Explain whether you think the coin was fair or not.
   d Explain what Sam could do to make his results more reliable.

2   Sally repeated Sam's test with a second coin. She obtained 23 heads and 27 tails. Explain whether you think Sally's coin was fair or not.

3   A technician tested all of the computers on a network. Each machine either passed or failed the test. The table shows the results of the tests.

Pass	Fail
62	15

   a Use these results to estimate the probability that a computer chosen at random would pass the test.
   b The technician then tested the machines on another network. 28 machines were tested and five of them failed the test. Were the machines on this second network more or less likely to pass the test than those on the first network? Explain your answer.

Problem solving

4   Kelly put these cards into a bag. She then picked one card out of the bag, noted the colour, and put the card back.

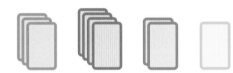

   a Work out the theoretical probability of Kelly picking each colour.

   Kelly carried out an experiment to estimate the probability of picking each colour. The table shows her results.

Colour	Green	Red	Blue	Yellow
Frequency	48	51	19	12

   b Use the results in the table to estimate the experimental probability for each result.
   c Why are the experimental and theoretical probabilities different?

5   Jenny tested a dice by rolling it 50 times. Ben tested the same dice, with the same number of trials in his experiment.
   a Would you expect Ben and Jenny to get the same results?
   b Ben suggests that they will get more reliable results if they combine their data. Suggest why this might be a good idea.

● A **set** is a collection of **elements**.

▶ To identify a set, use curly brackets.

● The **universal set**, which has the symbol Ω, is the set containing all the elements.

Example

Ω = {2, 3, 6, 7, 11, 15}, P = {prime numbers} and E = {even numbers}

a List the elements in set P.   **b** List the elements in set E.

c Which element is in P and E?   **d** Which element is not in set P or set E?

- - -

a $P = \{2, 3, 7, 11\}$ **b** $E = \{2, 6\}$

c 2   **d** 15

A ∩ B means 'the **intersection** of A and B'.

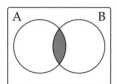

A ∪ B means 'the **union** of A or B'

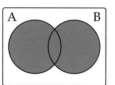

A' means 'the **complement** of A'.

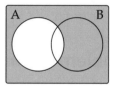

● You can use **Venn diagrams** to work out probabilities.

$$\text{Probability of A} = \frac{\text{number of elements in set A}}{\text{total number of elements}}$$

$P(A) = 1 - P(A')$

Example

Abi asked the 24 students in her form group if they study French or German.

She sorted the students into F = {studies French} and

G = {studies German}

She showed her results on a Venn diagram.

a Shade the region F'.

b How many students are in F ∩ G?

c Abi chooses a student at random. Find

i P(F')   **ii** P(F ∩ G)   **iii** P(G)

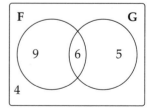

- - -

a
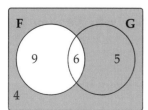

b 6 students

c i $P(F') = \frac{5 + 4}{24} = \frac{9}{24} = \frac{3}{8}$

ii $P(F \cap G) = \frac{6}{24} = \frac{1}{4}$

iii 6 + 5 = 11 students study German. $P(G) = \frac{11}{24}$

Exercise 16e

1 For these sets

  a Ω = {whole numbers from 1–12},
     A = {multiples of 3} and
     B = {3, 7, 9, 10, 11}

  b Ω = {1, 2, 3, 5, 8, 13, 21, 34, 55},
     A = {number less than 20} and
     B = {factors of 24}

  c Ω = {whole numbers from 1–16},
     A = {odd numbers} and
     B = {prime numbers}

  list the elements in

  i A   **ii** A′   **iii** B′
  iv A ∩ B   **v** A ∪ B   **vi** A ∩ B′

2 Malik investigated how the 25 students in his class keep in touch with their friends after school.

He sorted his results in to
S = {social media} and T = {texting}.

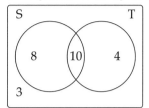

Find

  a P(T)   **b** P(S′)
  c P(S ∩ T)   **d** P(S ∪ T)

Problem solving

3 Miss Perry is organising a school trip to France. Her students can sign for two activities, a trip to a waterpark or going to the beach.

She shows the results on a Venn diagram.

The trip to the waterpark costs £11 and the trip to the beach costs £7.

Miss Perry collects £393 to pay for the activities.

  a How many students signed up for both activities?

  b Two students change their minds when they get to France. Clara, who didn't sign up to any activities, goes to the beach and the waterpark. Joel goes to the waterpark instead of the beach.

    Draw a new Venn diagram to show the activities that the students took part in.

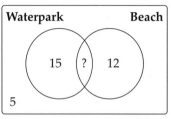

4 Ella sorts 20 elements into the sets A and B.
She writes four fact cards.

  (P(A ∩ B) = 0.3)   (P(A) = 0.5)

  (P(B) = 0.7)   (P(A ∪ B) = 0.9)

Complete Ella's Venn diagram showing the number of elements in each region.

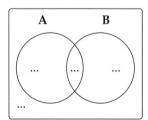

Check out

You should now be able to ...

Test it ➡

Questions

✓ Use diagrams and tables to record mutually exclusive outcomes.	6	1, 2
✓ Find probabilities based on equally likely outcomes.	6	3
✓ Calculate the probability that an event does not occur from the probability that it does occur.	6	4
✓ Estimate probabilities by collecting data from an experiment.	6	5
✓ Compare experimental probabilities with theoretical probabilities.	6	6
✓ Use the language of sets and use sets to calculate probabilities.	6	7

Language   Meaning   Example

Language	Meaning	Example
Trial	An experiment with an uncertain outcome	Throwing a dice to see which number is on top
Outcome	A possible result of a trial	For a dice the possible outcomes are 1, 2, 3, 4, 5 and 6
Event	A collection of outcomes	The event an even number consists of the outcomes 2, 4 and 6
Tree diagram	A diagram which uses branches to record possible outcomes	See page 286
Sample space diagram	A diagram which uses a table to record possible outcomes	See page 286
Experiment	A series of trials which can be used to estimate a probability	Rolling a dice 600 times to see if it is biased is an experiment
Biased	A trial in which all the individual outcomes are *not* equally likely	A coin which shows heads twice as often as tails is biased

1 Dave picks a card from a pack of red and black cards, and records if it is black or red. He replaces it then selects another and again records the colour.

  a Draw a tree diagram to show the possible outcomes.

  b Draw a sample space diagram to show the possible outcomes.

2 This sample space diagram shows the possible lunch choices of a student.

		Food		
		Chicken	**Fish**	**Veg**
Drink	**Water**	(W,C)	(W,F)	(W,V)
	Squash	(S,C)	(S,F)	(S,V)

Draw a tree diagram to represent the same set of information.

3 A bag contains three white and five red counters. What is the probability that a randomly chosen counter will be

  a white

  b blue?

4 The probability that a person chosen at random from a doctor's waiting room will be a child is 0.3. What is the probability of choosing an adult?

5 The test results of 20 students are

14	12	15	12	18
20	17	15	11	9
12	14	16	17	19
8	10	13	17	16

A mark of 14 or more is needed to pass. Estimate the probability that a student chosen at random has passed the test.

6 Jen rolled a dice and recorded whether or not it showed a six. The results are in the table.

Six	**Not a six**
150	450

  a How many trials did Jen carry out?

  b Estimate the probability of getting a six with this dice.

  c Explain whether you think the dice was fair.

7 Ω = {whole numbers from 1 to 16}, A = {multiples of 3} and B = {prime numbers}

For the following sets

  i list the elements in the set

  ii give the probability that a randomly selected number is in the set.

  a A   **b** A′   **c** B′

  d A ∩ B   **e** A ∪ B   **f** A ∩ B′

What next?

Score		
	0 – 3	Your knowledge of this topic is still developing. To improve look at Formative test: 2B-16; MyMaths: 1199, 1209 and 1211
	4 – 6	You are gaining a secure knowledge of this topic. To improve look at InvisiPen: 452, 453, 461 and 462
	7	You have mastered this topic. Well done, you are ready to progress!

16a

1 Draw a tree diagram for each of these situations.

   a An ordinary dice is rolled, and the score is noted; then a coin is spun, and the result is recorded.

   b An experimenter rolls an ordinary dice, and notes whether the score is odd or even; then a coin is spun, and the result is recorded.

   c A coin is spun, and the result is written down; then the experimenter rolls a dice and records whether or not the result is a multiple of 3.

2 Draw a sample space diagram for each of these situations.

   a A player turns up two cards from a pack of playing cards, and notes the suits.

   b A player picks two letters from a bag of letter tiles. Each tile has a vowel or a consonant.

   c A shopper picks two cans of cat food from a shelf. The flavours available are chicken, beef and fish.

Hearts   Diamonds   Clubs   Spades

16b

3 A computer is used to choose a random whole number between 1 and 100 (inclusive). Find the probability that the chosen number is

   a exactly 13   b even
   c a multiple of 10   d a multiple of 7
   e less than 25 or greater than 85   f not a multiple of 7

16c

4 Here are the scores obtained by a sample of people who carried out a safety test.

15	17	13	18	19	20	19	13	14	19
20	11	12	16	18	17	20	14	18	13

   a A score of 15 or more is needed to pass the test.
     Estimate the experimental probability of passing the test.

   b If 500 people took the test, how many would you expect to pass?
     Explain your answer.

5 Alexa and Bella each carried out an experiment to see how likely a seed was to germinate if it wasn't watered. The table shows their results.

	Alexa	Bella
Germinated	18	50
Failed	32	70

   a Estimate the probability of germination for Alexa and Bella.
   b Explain whose results are more reliable and why.
   c What is the best estimate of the probability of germination based on these results?

6 In an experiment a dice was rolled several times to see if it was fair.
The table shows the number of times an even or an odd number was obtained.

Even	Odd
36	54

a Calculate the theoretical probabilities of obtaining an even or an odd number for a fair dice.

b Estimate the probabilities of obtaining an even or an odd number using the experimental data.

c Explain whether you think the dice is biased or not.

7 Max put 25 blue counters, 50 red counters and 25 yellow counters into a bag.
He shook the bag, picked a counter without looking, recorded the colour and returned the counter to the bag. He did this 200 times altogether.

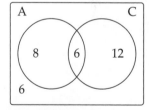

a Calculate the theoretical probability of choosing each colour.

b Max actually obtained 61 blues, 108 reds and 31 yellows.
Estimate the experimental probability of obtaining each colour.

c Max thought that the theoretical and experimental probabilities were different.
Give an example of a factor that could have caused this difference.

8 Sasha surveyed the students in his class to see who had participated in athletics or cricket in the previous week.
He put his results into a Venn diagram.
Find

a P(A) **b** P(C) **c** P(A′)

d P(C′) **e** P(A ∪ C) **f** P(A ∩ C)

A = {Athletics}
C = {Cricket}

9 Jenny sorts 24 elements into two sets X and Y.
She writes four fact cards.

$P(X \cap Y) = \frac{1}{4}$ $P(Y) = \frac{5}{12}$

$P(X') = \frac{1}{2}$ $P(X \cup Y) = \frac{2}{3}$

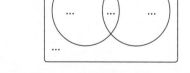

Complete Jenny's Venn diagram showing the number of elements in each region.

Free-range eggs are laid by free-range hens. Strict rules must be obeyed for hens to be called 'Free-range.'

Free-range rules

Outside: 1 hen to every 4 m²

Inside: 7 hens to every 1 m²

Task 1

The table shows the space allocated to hens in four farms.

a For each farm, work out whether it has free-range hens or not. Show your working.

b For any of the farms that are not free-range, describe what would need to change to make them free-range.

Farm	Number of hens	Outside area, m²	Inside area, m²
A	18	60	2
B	250	1000	36
C	120	500	16
D	24	100	4

Task 2

This hen enclosure contains eight hens.

Its total area is 34 m², including both outside and inside spaces.

The outside and inside spaces are both rectangular.

Sketch a possible layout for the enclosure, showing that these hens could be free-range. Label your sketch with dimensions.

FREE-RANGE EGGS £1.92 PER DOZEN

CAGED EGGS £1.20 PER DOZEN

Task 3

How much would you have to pay for

a 2 dozen free-range
c 4 dozen free-range
e 1 free-range

b 2 dozen caged
d 4 dozen caged
f 1 caged egg ?

Task 4

Here is a recipe for baked custard.

Copy and complete the table.

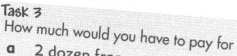

BAKED CUSTARD (Serves 8)

8 egg yolks
75 g castor sugar
500 ml whipping cream
freshly grated nutmeg

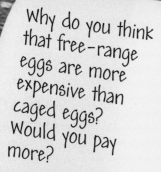

Why do you think that free-range eggs are more expensive than caged eggs? Would you pay more?

Cost of eggs by serving		
	Free-range	Caged
Serves 8	£ 1.28	
Serves 4		£ 0.80
Serves 16		
Serves 12		
Per serving		

301

These questions will test you on your knowledge of the topics in chapters 13 to 16.
They give you practice in the types of questions that you may eventually be given in your GCSE exams. There are 85 marks in total.

1   For these sequences
    i   find the term-to-term rules in the form 'start with …. and ….'   (3 marks)
    ii write the next three terms in the sequence.   (3 marks)
    a   3, 10, 17, 24, …   **b**   18, 13, 8, 3, ….   **c**   2, 4, 10, 22, ….

2   For these sequences
    i   find the term-to-term rules   (3 marks)
    ii   find the position-to-term rules in the form
             'multiply the position by … and then …'   (3 marks)
    iii write these position-to-term rules in terms of the nth term   (3 marks)
    iv   use the nth term to find the 50th term of each sequence.   (3 marks)
    a   1, 3, 5, 7, …   **b**   4, 8, 12, 16, ….   **c**   11, 18, 25, 32, ….

3   A farmer is building a fence around his field
    using pieces of wood as shown in the diagram.
    a   Construct a sequence to show for each
            fence the number of pieces of wood used.   (2 marks)
    b   What is the term-to-term rule?   (2 marks)
    c   Write the position-to-term rule in
            terms of n.   (2 marks)
    d   To complete the fence the farmer
            requires wood up to the 40th term.
            How many pieces does he need?   (1 mark)

4   A cuboid is 2 cm wide, 3 cm high and 5 cm long.
    a   Draw the net of the cuboid on square
            grid paper.   (2 marks)
    b   How many faces, vertices and edges
            does it have?   (3 marks)
    c   Calculate the area of the cuboid.   (3 marks)
    d   Calculate the volume of the cuboid.   (2 marks)

5   This solid is made from four cubes.
    a   On square grid paper, draw
            i   the front elevation (F)
            ii   the side elevation (S)
            iii the plan view (P).   (3 marks)
    b   Draw the solid using isometric paper.   F   (3 marks)

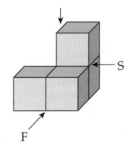

6 **a** What is the mathematical name for this solid?   (1 mark)
   b How many faces, vertices and edges does it have?   (2 marks)
   c On square grid paper draw the net of this solid.   (2 marks)
   d Calculate the surface area of this solid.   (2 marks)
   e Calculate the volume of this solid.   (2 marks)

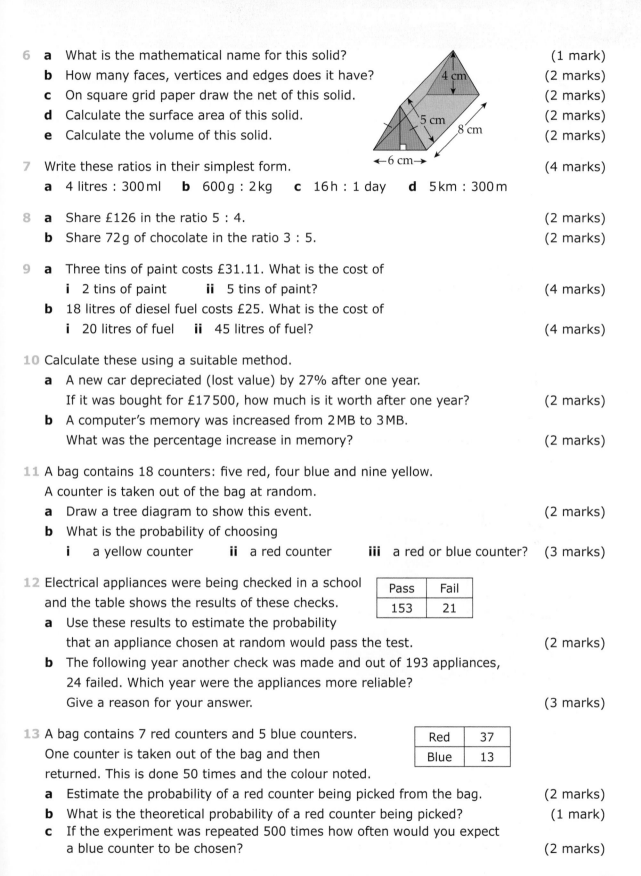

7 Write these ratios in their simplest form.   (4 marks)
   a 4 litres : 300 ml   **b** 600 g : 2 kg   **c** 16 h : 1 day   **d** 5 km : 300 m

8 **a** Share £126 in the ratio 5 : 4.   (2 marks)
   b Share 72 g of chocolate in the ratio 3 : 5.   (2 marks)

9 **a** Three tins of paint costs £31.11. What is the cost of
          i 2 tins of paint   **ii** 5 tins of paint?   (4 marks)
   b 18 litres of diesel fuel costs £25. What is the cost of
          i 20 litres of fuel   **ii** 45 litres of fuel?   (4 marks)

10 Calculate these using a suitable method.
    a A new car depreciated (lost value) by 27% after one year.
           If it was bought for £17 500, how much is it worth after one year?   (2 marks)
    b A computer's memory was increased from 2 MB to 3 MB.
           What was the percentage increase in memory?   (2 marks)

11 A bag contains 18 counters: five red, four blue and nine yellow.
    A counter is taken out of the bag at random.
    a Draw a tree diagram to show this event.   (2 marks)
    b What is the probability of choosing
           i   a yellow counter   **ii** a red counter   **iii** a red or blue counter?   (3 marks)

12 Electrical appliances were being checked in a school
    and the table shows the results of these checks.

Pass	Fail
153	21

    a Use these results to estimate the probability
           that an appliance chosen at random would pass the test.   (2 marks)
    b The following year another check was made and out of 193 appliances,
           24 failed. Which year were the appliances more reliable?
           Give a reason for your answer.   (3 marks)

13 A bag contains 7 red counters and 5 blue counters.
    One counter is taken out of the bag and then
    returned. This is done 50 times and the colour noted.

Red	37
Blue	13

    a Estimate the probability of a red counter being picked from the bag.   (2 marks)
    b What is the theoretical probability of a red counter being picked?   (1 mark)
    c If the experiment was repeated 500 times how often would you expect
           a blue counter to be chosen?   (2 marks)

It is getting close to the end of the school year and the time for holidays. Soon you will meet Miss Perry. She is busy getting ready to take Year 8 on a camping trip to France. There is a lot happening and she would like you to help her to solve all the problems she has.

Solving real life problems often requires you to think for yourself and to use several pieces of mathematics at once. If you are going to be successfull you will need to practice your basic skills.

- **Fluency** – Do you know how to do arithmetic or algebra?

- **Reasoning** – Can you interpret results and test out your ideas?

- **Problem solving** – Can you cope if a problem involves several steps?

Fluency

If you run a small business you need to be able to do your accounts. Are you making a profit? Is the money you make from sales bigger than all your overheads – wages, rent, materials...

People often use spread sheet type programs to help them to do their accounts. However should you trust what they say? It helps if you have a 'feel' for what the right answer should be and if you can quickly do simpler versions of the calculations yourself as checks.

Reasoning

Sometimes finding the answer to a mathematical problem is the easy part. The hardest part can be convincing other people that your solution is the right one.

One way to help persuade other people is by choosing the best graph to show your results.

You also need to be able to back up your results with carefully reasoned explanations.

Problem solving

Controlling a robot is surprisingly complex. It requires breaking down into smaller tasks in order to be manageable.

Each of these smaller tasks might need skills from several different areas of mathematics. To control a robot's movements you will need to use geometry, coordinates and algebra to represent instructions.

Miss Perry is planning a trip for year 8.
They will travel from Birmingham to Sarlat in France by coach and ferry.

She has to work out the cost of the trip for 50 students.

Here are the costs for the whole journey.

Coach	£3460
Ferry berths	£875
Accommodation	£1475
Food	£1450
Insurance	£516
Activities	£1700

1   Miss Perry has to pay deposits to some of the companies.
Work out how much she will need to pay for these items.

   a   accommodation   10%   **b**   coach   15%

   c   activities   25%   **d**   ferry berths   20%

   e   insurance $12\frac{1}{2}\%$

2   In order to pay the deposits Miss Perry will need to obtain
money in advance.

There are 50 students.

   a   What is the total cost of the company deposits?

   b   What is the deposit that she will need to collect from each student?

   Miss Perry does not want exact amounts if they involve
   pence, so work out a sensible deposit that covers the costs
   but is not too large. Explain your thinking.

3   It is decided to round up, to the nearest £10, the full amount
each student must pay. The extra money will be used for
emergencies and returned if not used.

   a   What is the total cost to each student?

   b   After paying their deposits, how much does each student still owe?

   c   The school allows parents 10 weeks to pay the rest of the money.
   How much will they pay each week?

4   The parents would like to know how the money is going to
    be spent so the Cooper's School illustrates the costs in a letter.

    Miss Perry works out the percentages using a calculator.

$$875 \div 9476 \times 100$$
$$9.233853947$$

She rounds the percentage to the nearest whole
number and shows that the ferry bill is 9% of
the total.

> Divide the ferry costs by
> the total cost and multiply
> by 100 to convert the
> decimal to a percentage.

a   Finish the calculations for Miss Perry.

b   What should the total percentage be?

5   Some of the bills have to be paid in euros (€).
    The school pays its bills with cheques.

> To convert £ p to € e use
> $$e = \frac{6 \times p}{5}$$

Coach bill

Ferry bill

MyMaths Bank   Date: 9ᵗʰ May 2009

Pay: *The Coach Company the sum*
     of four thousand, one hundred   € 4152.00
     and fifty-two Euros

                              Signed: *J. Medina*
                              Headteacher of Cooper's School

MyMaths Bank   Date: 10ᵗʰ May 2009

Pay: *The Ferry Company the sum*
     of one thousand and five hundred   € 1500.00
     Euros

                              Signed: *J. Medina*
                              Headteacher of Cooper's School

Accommodation bill

Activities bill

MyMaths Bank   Date: 19ᵗʰ May 2009

Pay: *The Camp Company the sum*
     of two thousand and forty Euros   € 2040.00

                              Signed: *J. Medina*
                              Headteacher of Cooper's School

MyMaths Bank   Date: 8ᵗʰ June 2009

Pay: *The Active Company the sum of*
     one thousand, seven hundred and   € 1770.00
     seventy Euros

                              Signed: *J. Medina*
                              Headteacher of Cooper's School

a   Which cheques have been converted properly into euros?

b   Which two companies' payments have been mixed up?

> To convert € e to £ p use
> $$p = \frac{5 \times e}{6}$$

6   Use the formula to convert these euro prices into GB pounds.

€3.00

€2.40

€45

€119.99

17b Camp Sarlat

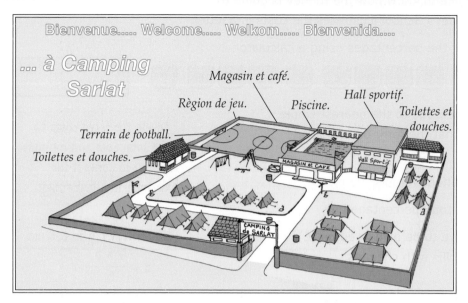

Bienvenue...... Welcome...... Welkom...... Bienvenida....

... à Camping Sarlat

Magasin et café.

Règion de jeu.

Piscine.

Hall sportif.

Toilettes et douches.

Terrain de football.

Toilettes et douches.

The students are staying in tents. There are three sizes of tent: 2 person, 3 person and 4 person.

1 Working with a partner use the information given to calculate the missing quantity for each tent.

a

2.2 m

Area = x

←1.5 m→

b

3 m

Area = y

←1.75 m→

c

3.5 m

Area 8.75 m²

← z m →

2 The students are shown to their tents. Here are the first five tents – A to E.

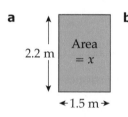

A

sleeps 4

B

sleeps 2

C

sleeps 2

D

sleeps 4

E

sleeps 3

Boys and girls are in separate tents.

Again with a partner, use these clues to work out which tents Carl, Cherry, John, Kadeja and Magnus are in.

- 15 students are put in these tents: seven girls and eight boys.
- John's tent is at the end of the row.
- Cherry shares a tent with three other girls.
- The four boys in the tent beside Carl's tent make a lot of noise.
- Kadeja likes her tent because it is far away from the noisy boys' tent!
- Carl, Cherry, John, Kadeja and Magnus are in different tents.

The students are given a map of the camp.

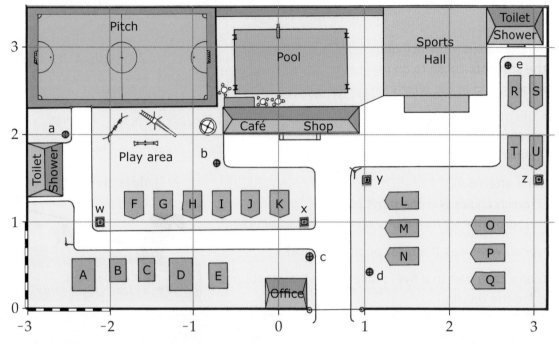

3 a What would you find at these coordinates?

　i (0.5, 2.7)　**ii** (2.2, 3.3)　**iii** (-2.5, 2.8)　**iv** (-0.4, 2.1)　**v** (-1.5, 2.0)

b Which tent is at each of these coordinates?

　i (1.4, 0.6)　**ii** (3.0, 1.8)　**iii** (-2.3, 0.4)　**iv** (-1.0, 1.2)　**v** (-1.6, 0.5)

c Which building would you be standing beside at the coordinates (0.0, 0.0)?

4 Kelly is standing in the middle of the centre circle of the football pitch.
Give the coordinates for her position.

5 There are 5 bins around the site, marked 🔲. and 4 water taps marked ⊕.
Give the coordinates for the bins labeled a to e, and the taps labeled w to z.

6 a Which grid squares are shown here?

i

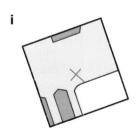

ii

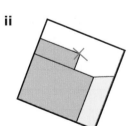

iii

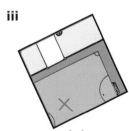

b In each case give the approximate grid reference of the spot marked ✕.

17c The sports day

On the first day at Camp Sarlat there is a sports day.

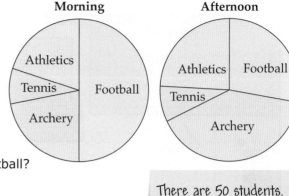

1 The pie charts show the activities that the students chose to do in the morning and in the afternoon.

a In the morning,

   i which choice was the least popular?

   ii what fraction of students played football?

b In the afternoon,

   i which choice was the most popular?

   ii approximately how many students did athletics?

c Overall, what was the most popular choice?

> There are 50 students.

2 Five teams take part in a five-a-side football competition. These are the results.

Round 1				
High 5	2	v	Superstars	4
Champions	3	v	Cheetahs	1
High 5	2	v	All Stars	2
Cheetahs	0	v	Superstars	2
Champions	2	v	All Stars	1

Round 2				
High 5	3	v	Cheetahs	2
All Stars	1	v	Superstars	1
High 5	0	v	Champions	0
All Stars	2	v	Cheetahs	5
Champions	2	v	Superstars	2

a How many goals were scored in total in the competition?

b What is the modal average number of goals scored in all the matches?

c Copy this table of results and complete it.
You can work with a partner.

	Games				Goals		Points
	played	won	drawn	lost	for	against	
All Stars	4						
Champions	4						
Cheetahs	4						
High 5	4						
Superstars	4						

> **Points scoring system**
> win = 3 pt
> draw = 1 pt
> lose = 0 pt

d Calculate the mean average for the number of goals scored in all matches.

e There is a tie for first place. Without playing another match, explain how you would decide who was the winning team.

3 Four students take part in an archery competition.

Each competitor fires four arrows. Their scores are shown below the targets.

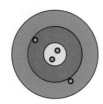   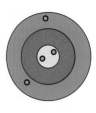

23 points   17 points   20 points   20 points

a Using this information, how many points do you get for a hit in the

  i red circle   **ii** blue circle   **iii** gold bull's eye?

b What is the mean average of the students' scores?

4 Five people raced in a 100 m sprint.

a Round their times to the nearest $\frac{1}{10}$th of a second.

  i 16.35 s   **ii** 14.37 s   **iii** 17.33 s   **iv** 15.08 s   **v** 14.62 s

b Write the rounded times in order, from fastest to slowest.

5 In the shot put, each competitor has three puts. These are the results in metres.

a The sum of the best two throws are used to decide the winner. List the competitors in order from first to fifth.

b If, instead, the mean average of all three puts is used to decide the winner, work out the new positions.

Name	Put 1	Put 2	Put 3
Darren	6.8	7.1	6.3
Hamed	5.9	6.9	6.6
Reece	5.8	6.8	6.8
Hussain	6.2	7.2	6.5
Carl	7.0	6.8	7.4

6 Roger has three practice puts
- the first put is 6.3 m
- the second put is 8.7 m
- the mean average of the three puts is 7.5 m

How long was the third put?

17d The expedition

The group is going on an expedition and must pack their own rucksacks. To be safe and comfortable a rucksack should weigh no more than one fifth ($\frac{1}{5}$) of your body weight.

1 **a** Calculate the maximum weight of each student's rucksack using the above proportion.

Delica 45 kg   Lau It 35 kg   Dan 70 kg

Think how to deal with answers that are not whole numbers.

b Ian has 4.2 kg in his rucksack.
What is the least that he should weigh?

c Who is closest to the mean weight of the six students?

This is the route the students will take from Camp Sarlat.

Eddy 40 kg   Ahmed 61 kg   Maggie 50 kg

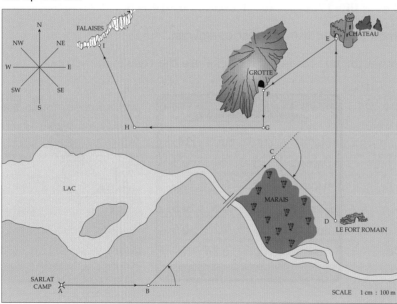

2 **a** What is the distance and direction of travel between these points?
    i B to C   **ii** C to D   **iii** D to E   **iv** E to F   **v** F to G

The distance and direction of travel from points A to B is approximately 250 m, East.

b At point B the students turn towards the bridge.
Is this turn clockwise or anticlockwise?

c How many degrees is the turn at point C; is it clockwise or anticlockwise?

3 **a** The Roman fort was occupied from 35 BC to 65 AD. How many years is this?

b In the cave are drawings that were made in 2010 BC. How long ago is this?

At the end of the journey the students learn to rock climb.

On The Rocks!

4 Measure these angles to the nearest degree.

  a i $\widehat{ABC}$ **ii** $\widehat{BCD}$ **iii** $\widehat{CDE}$ **iv** $\widehat{DEF}$

  b i $\widehat{KLM}$ **ii** $\widehat{LMN}$ **iii** $\widehat{MNO}$

  c Use your knowledge of angles around a point to find these reflex angles.

  i $\widehat{GHI}$ **ii** $\widehat{HIJ}$ **iii** $\widehat{MNO}$

5 The scene is drawn to a scale of 1 cm : 1 m (1 : 100)

  a To the nearest half metre give these distances in real life.

  i HI   **ii** MN   **iii** ED   **iv** LM

  b One climber has finished. Approximately how high above the ground is she?

17e Camp-life

The day started badly for Miss Perry — her tent leaked in the night and she is not pleased.

Mr Powell thinks that with the help of some students he can make a new tent for her.

1   Here are the measurements for the tent.

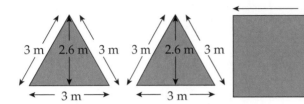

a   What is the total area of the material
    Mr Powell used for the tent?
    Give your answer to the nearest 1 m².

b   The tent was cut from a 6 m by 7 m piece
    of material. How much material was wasted?

Things become worse still. Miss Perry refuses to use
the showers — they are just too dirty for her!
She has a private shower.

The students have to carry the water to her
shower in containers.

2   Tariq and Emma argue about who has carried the most water.
    Tariq carries five full jerrycans and one litre bottle of water.
    Emma carries three full jerrycans and 11 litre bottles of water.

a   They both carried an equal amount of water.
    How much water does one full jerrycan hold?

b   How much water is in a full can if, instead
    i   4 cans + 11 bottles = 6 cans + 5 bottles
    ii 3 cans +   3 bottles = 1 can + 12 bottles?

While waiting to board the coach to go home, the students gather in the play area.

Sam has placed his sandwich on the roundabout which is rotating slowly in a clockwise direction.

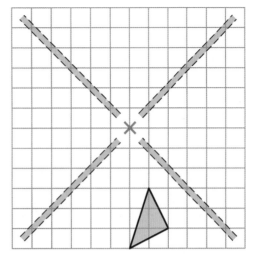

3 On graph paper draw the centre of rotation and the position of the sandwich. Beginning from the start position, rotate the shape through

   a 90° in a clockwise direction and draw the image.

   b 270° in a clockwise direction and draw the image.

4 Claire sits on the see-saw. She weighs 37 kg. Which of the weights shown can be used to balance her?

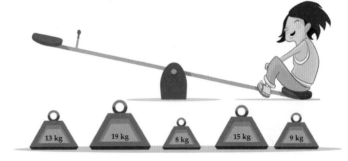

Miss Perry calls to the students from a plane. She explains that her best friend Rupert happened to be flying by and offered her a lift home. She decided to hurry back and complete all her unfinished marking.

5 The distance from Camp Sarlat to Birmingham is 550 miles. Rupert can fly at an average speed of 100 mph. How long will it take them to fly home?

Check in 1

1 **a** 0.47, 0.5, 0.512, 0.52, 0.55
  b -10, -6, -4, 3, 5, 9
2 **a** -5 **b** -3 **c** -9
3 **a** 35 **b** 3 **c** 54 **d** 9
4 **a** 7, 14, 21 **b** 1, 2, 3, 4, 6, 12
  c 2, 3, 5, 7, 11
5 **a** 42.875 **b** 216 **c** 256

MyReview 1

1 **a** $-16 > -16.5$ **b** $0.457 < 0.52$
  c $0.043 < 0.34$ **d** $-0.56 < -0.055$
2 **a** -5, -3, 0, 6 **b** -2.6, -2.4, -0.9, 1.3
3 **a** -15 **b** -14 **c** 9 **d** 8
4 **a** -15 **b** 28 **c** -5 **d** 10
5 **a** 1, 3, 6 **b** 6, 12, 18
6 **a** No **b** Yes
  c No **d** No (11×13)
7 2, 3, 5
8 **a** $3 \times 3 \times 7$ **b** $5 \times 7 \times 11$
9 **a** 25 **b** 1
10 **a** 84 **b** 48
11 1, 4
12 **a** 8 **b** 5 **c** 11 **d** 1
13 **a** 8 **b** 4 **c** 64 **d** 6

Check in 2

1 **a** 3000 **b** 56 **c** 46 **d** 8.5
2 **a** 132 **b** 36 **c** 8 **d** 9
3 **a** 20 **b** 8 **c** 100 **d** 4
4 **a** Area = $6\,cm^2$ Perimeter = $12\,cm$
  b Area = $5\,cm^2$ Perimeter = $12\,cm$
  c Area = $8\,cm^2$ Perimeter = $12\,cm$

MyReview 2

1 **a** m **b** km **c** mm **d** kg
2 **a** $2\,700\,000\,cm$ **b** $1.25\,kg$
  c 0.55 litres **d** $0.005\,km$
3 **a** $12.5\,cm$ **b** 6 litres
4 **a** $3\,kg$ **b** $20\,kg$ **c** $24\,kg$
  d $36\,kg$ **e** $48\,kg$
5 $77\,cm^2$
6 $28\,m$
7 $34\,cm^2$
8 **a** $12\,cm^2$ **b** $30\,mm^2$
9 $6\,cm$
10 **a** (Right) trapezium **b** $50\,cm^2$

Check in 3

1 $(4 \times 12) + (3 \times 6) = 66$
2 **a** 16 **b** 100 **c** 180

MyReview 3

1 **a** $5b$ **b** $3t$ **c** $\dfrac{k}{2}$ **d** $3f$
2 **a** 12 **b** -4 **c** 4 **d** 40
3 **a** 3^9 **b** 5^7

4 **a** $2n + 6m$ **b** $-2g + 3h$ **c** $8y + 5y^2$
5 **a** $9p + 9q$ **b** $6v - 12$ **c** $x^2 + x$
  d $3x^2 - 4x$
6 **a** $7u + 10$ **b** $-4v - 61$
7 22
8 75
9 **a** $P = 26 + 2n$ **b** $P = 3s + 4$
  c $P = 4x + 4$
10 **a** $C = 250 + 50x$ **b** 600p or £6

Check in 4

1 **a** 0.3 **b** 7.4 **c** 0.05
2 0.23, 0.3, 0.35, 0.39, 0.4
3 **a** £30 **b** $3.5\,kg$ **c** $18\,m$

MyReview 4

1 **a** 2.45, 2.5, 2.56, 2.57
  b 0.0078, 0.008, 0.07, 0.077
2 **a** 0.3 **b** 0.8 **c** 0.15 **d** 0.28
3 **a** $\dfrac{7}{10}$ **b** $\dfrac{1}{50}$ **c** $\dfrac{2}{250}$ **d** $\dfrac{7}{4}$
4 $\dfrac{1}{4}, \dfrac{3}{10}, \dfrac{3}{8}, \dfrac{2}{5}$
5 **a** $\dfrac{1}{6}$ **b** $\dfrac{2}{3}$ **c** $\dfrac{13}{18}$ **d** $\dfrac{83}{42}$
6 **a** £4 **b** 12 students
7 **a** 9 **b** $\dfrac{9}{2}$ or $4\dfrac{1}{2}$
8 **a** $\dfrac{2}{3}$ **b** $\dfrac{1}{6}$
9 **a** 2.5 **b** 56 **c** 99 **d** 792
10 **a** 16.28 **b** 358.40
11 **a** 60% **b** 20% **c** 4% **d** 120%
12 **a** 0.73 **b** 0.165
13 **a** $\dfrac{13}{65}$ **b** $\dfrac{2}{25}$
14 **a** 40% **b** 32%

Check in 5

1 **a** Acute **b** Obtuse **c** Straight
  d Reflex **e** Right
2 **a** 90 **b** 50 **c** 72

MyReview 5

1 $a = 97°$ $b = 113°$ $c = 128°$ $d = 68°$
  $e = 68°$ $f = 112°$ $g = 96°$ $h = 44°$
  $i = 96°$ $j = 40°$ $k = 147°$ $l = 270°$
2 $a = 51°$ $b = 76°$ $c = 70°$ $d = 85°$
3 $a = 125°$ Alternate angles
  $b = 85°$ Corresponding angles
4 **a** Rhombus **b** Kite **c** Trapezium
5 Check interior angles are all 135° (allow ±2°)
  and all sides are the same length.
6 $a = 75°$ $b = 75°$ $c = 15°$
7 **a** 7 cm **b** 15 cm **c** 25°

Check in 6

1

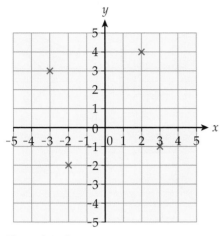

The points form a square.

2 a i 1 **ii** -4 **iii** 7 **iv** 4

   b i 2 **ii** -1 **iii** 5 **iv** $2\frac{1}{2}$

   c i 3 **ii** 2 **iii** 3 **iv** 1

   d i 0 **ii** -7 **iii** 9 **iv** $5\frac{1}{2}$

3 Your own answers.

MyReview 6

1 a

x	0	1	2	3	4
y	1	4	7	10	13

   b

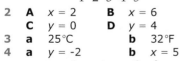

2 A $x = 2$ **B** $x = 6$
   C $y = 0$ **D** $y = 4$

3 a 25°C **b** 32°F

4 a $y = -2$ **b** $x = 5$
   c $y = 4x, y + x = 8$ **d** $y = 3x^2$

5 a i C **ii** A **iii** E
   b Home

6

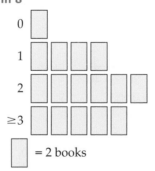

Check in 7

1 a i 3000 **ii** 3500 **iii** 3460
   b i 5000 **ii** 5300 **iii** 5280
   c i 1000 **ii** 800 **iii** 790
   d i 1000 **ii** 1100 **iii** 1080

2 a 95 **b** 56 **c** 12.1 **d** 6.3

3 a 86.1 **b** 67.8

4 a 390 **b** 480 **c** 0.58 **d** 48.5

5 a 153 **b** 195 **c** 228 **d** 198

6 a 480 **b** 16 **c** 4770 **d** 13

MyReview 7

1 a 30 **b** 29.5 **c** 29.51

2 a £10.13 **b** £16.67

3 a 32.9 **b** 20.9 **c** 17.9 **d** 13.16
   e 10.52 **f** 3.55 **g** 0.42 **h** 24.12

4 a 5.6 **b** 1.03 **c** 0.7 **d** 0.04
   e 0.025 **f** 40 **g** 99000 **h** 3.5
   i 870 **j** 0.009

5 a £6.50 **b** 0.29 kg

6 a 7 **b** 915 **c** 78 **d** 11.7

7 a 81 **b** 93.6 **c** 11 **d** 41

8 a 228 **b** 992 **c** 218.4 **d** 34.2

9 £4.23

10 a £14.82 **b** 95 cups **c** 15.6p

11 a 24 **b** £1.76

Check in 8

1 a

0

1

2

≥3

☐ = 2 books

b

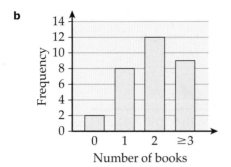

2

No.	Frequency	No.	Frequency
1	10	4	14
2	8	5	9
3	12	6	7

MyReview 8

1 **a i** Primary   **ii** Continuous
   b i Secondary   **ii** Discrete
   c i Secondary   **ii** Discrete

2

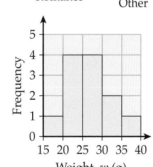

3

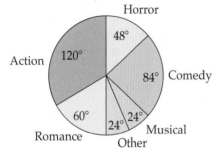

4 **a** 5 and 6   **b** 5.1
   c 5   **d** 4
5 **a** 3   **b** 2.65
6 **a** Check points correct: (65, 25), (40, 35),
         (50, 30), (30, 40), (20, 50), (15, 45),
         (60, 25)
   b Negative
7 **a** 56   **b** 27

Check in 9

1 **a** (3, 1) **b** (-3, -1) **c** (-1, -2)
2 **a** D   **b** C   **c** B   **d** A

MyReview 9

1 Rhombus with vertices at (8, 2), (7, 5), (8, 8), (9, 5)
2 **a i** 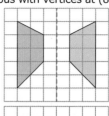   **ii**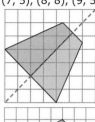

2 **b i** 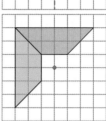   **ii**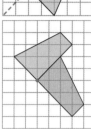

3 **a, b**

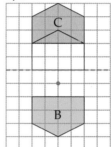

   c Translation of 2 units up
4 **a** 2 lines of symmetry   **b** Order 2
5 No
6

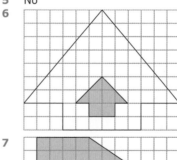

7

Check in 10

1 **a** 9   **b** 6   **c** 7   **d** 20
2 **a** 7   **b** 8
3 8

MyReview 10

1. a 33   b 21   c 29   d 8
   e 11   f 9   g 36   h 16
2. a 9   b 6   c 17   d 9
   e 6   f 9   g 12   h 5
3. a 4   b 8   c 1   d 13
4. a -3   b 2   c -1   d -4
   e 0   f -4
5. a $\frac{1}{2}$ b $\frac{3}{2}$ c $\frac{5}{4}$ d $\frac{1}{3}$
6. -10
7. a $y = 0.85x$
   b i £10.20   ii £19.13   iii £1275
   c i 5m   ii 7.5m   iii 1500m
8. a $y = 75 + 200x$ b 8
   c This would be the cost of $9\frac{1}{8}$ pallets.

Check in 11

1. a 21.1   b 6.47   c 4.81
   d 3.36   e 5.17
2. a 6.3   b 21   c 16.8
   d 22 r10 or $22\frac{2}{3}$ e 149.1
3. a 561.39   b 233.07
4. a 33.57   b 20.04   c 39.1
   d 43.2   e 22.78
5. a 7.9   b 4.4   c 28
   d 45   e 33.4

MyReview 11

1. a 71.2   b 249.945
   c 15.37   d 754.31
2. a 1872   b 31.2   c 183.3   d 274.32
3. a 27   b 23
4. 2
5. a 9.7   b 18.8   c 6.8   d 25.7
6. a 27   b 9   c 96   d 14
   e 40   f 4
7. a $(4 + 8) \div 4 - 1$ b $(4 + 8) \div (4 - 1)$
   c $(6 - 3) \times (12 - 8)$ d $6 - 3 \times (12 - 8)$
8. 186.47 kg
9. £137.32
10. £1.24
11. 165.69
12. 18 minutes

Check in 12

1. a Check all arcs pass through circle's centre.
   b 8.7 cm
2. a 40°   b 135°   c 235°

MyReview 12

1. a Check ASA 143°, 3.8 cm, 39°
   b Check ASA 81°, 7.1 cm, 37°
   c Check SAS 5.2 cm, 58°, 4.7 cm
   d Check SSS 63 mm, 52 mm, 35 mm
2. a Angle of 130°   b Angle of 65°
3. a Line of 9 cm, labeled AB
   b Check 90° angle and 4.5 cm length along AB

4. a Line of 11 cm, labeled AB
   b Point P on AB so that AP = 4 cm
   c Check 90° angle at P
5.
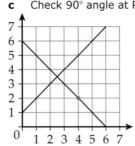
6. a, b

7. a Angle of 70°   b Bisected angle of 35°
8. a Right-angled triangle, height 5 cm, length 8 cm
   b 47 m
9. a   N   b   N

Check in 13

1. $2^2 = 4$, $3^2 = 9$, $10^2 = 100$
2. a 19, 23
   b Start at 3 and add 4

MyReview 13

1. a i Start with 8 and add 6   ii 32, 38
   b i Start with 60 and subtract 4   ii 44, 40
   c i Start with 2 and double   ii 32, 64
2. a 9, 14, 19, 24, 29   b 30, 27, 24, 21, 18
   c 1, 3, 9, 27, 81   d 5, 8, 14, 26, 50
3. a Shown rotated

   b
Position	1	2	3	4	5	6
2 × table	2	4	6	8	10	12
Term	3	5	7	9	11	13

   c Multiply the position by 2 and add 1 or $2n + 1$
   d 41
4. a Multiply the position by 3 and add 6 or $3n + 6$
   b Multiply the position by 7 and subtract 5 or $7n - 5$
5. a 28   b 66

6 a Start with 4 and add 3   **b** 17   **c** 77

d

Position (day)	1	2	3	4	5	6	7
3 × table	3	6	9	12	15	18	21
Term	2	5	8	11	14	17	20

   e Multiply the position by 3 and subtract 2 or $3n - 2$

7 a i Start with 3 and multiply by 2
     ii 72, 144
   b i Start with 128 and multiply by $\frac{1}{2}$
     ii 8, 4
   c i Start with 1 and multiply by -3
     ii 81, -243

Check in 14

1 Your own sketch
   6 faces, 12 edges, 8 vertices
2 a 120   **b** 56   **c** 80   **d** 1331
3 a 29.75 cm²   **b** 16 mm²   **c** 45 cm²

MyReview 14

1 a Square-based pyramid
   b i 5   **ii** 5   **iii** 8
2 a Pentagonal prism
   b i 7   **ii** 15   **iii** 10
3 For example

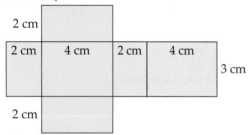

2 cm   2 cm   4 cm   2 cm   4 cm   3 cm   2 cm

Check two 3 × 2, two 2 × 4 and two 3 × 4 rectangles.

4 a 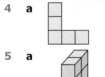   **b**   **c**

5 a   **b** 7

6 92 cm²
7 7 cm
8 112 m³
9 9 cm
10 60 cm³
11 60 m²

Check in 15

1 a 12   **b** £12   **c** 72 g

2

Fraction	Decimal	Percentage
$\frac{17}{20}$	0.85	85%
$\frac{39}{50}$	0.78	78%
$\frac{24}{25}$	0.96	96%

MyReview 15

1 a 1:3   **b** 5:4   **c** 19:40   **d** 25:7
2 a 4.5 m   **b** 16 cm
3 a £36, £54   **b** 104 g, 13 g
4 21
5 540 g
6 103.5 calories
7 a 2:3   **b** $\frac{2}{5}$ or 40%
8 a $\frac{3}{5}$ or 60%   **b** 3:2
9 a 42   **b** 46.02
10 99 kg
11 £2275
12 a 72%   **b** 80%   **c** 82.4%
13 A, $\frac{78}{94} = 0.83... > \frac{86}{109} = 0.79$

Check in 16

1 Suitable words include (very/not very) likely, unlikely, etc.
2 a 0.5   **b** 0.4   **c** 0.375
3 a 0.35   **b** 0.635   **c** 0.07

MyReview 16

1 a First card   Second card

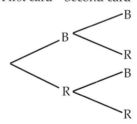

b

		Second Card	
		Black	**Red**
First Card	**Black**	(B, B)	(B, R)
	Red	(R, B)	(R, R)

2   Food   Drink

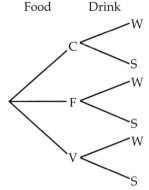

3 a $\dfrac{3}{8}$ **b** 0

4 0.7

5 0.6 or 60%

6 a 600   **b** 0.25 or 25%
  c Unfair, would expect probability near 0.17

7 a i A = {3, 6, 9, 12, 15}   **ii** P(A) = $\dfrac{15}{16}$

  b i A' = {1, 2, 4, 5, 7, 8, 10, 11, 13, 14, 16}
    ii P(A') = $\dfrac{11}{16}$

  c i B' = {1, 4, 6, 8, 9, 10, 12, 13, 14, 15, 16}
    ii P(B') = $\dfrac{11}{16}$

  d i A ∩ B = {3}   **ii** P(A ∩ B) = $\dfrac{1}{16}$

  e i A ∩ B = {2, 3, 5, 6, 7, 9, 11, 12, 13, 15, 16}
    ii P(A ∩ B) = $\dfrac{11}{16}$

  f i A ∩ B' = {6, 9, 12, 15}   **ii** P(A) = $\dfrac{1}{4}$

Index